CW00926427

CAMBRIDGE STUDIES IN RUSSIAN LITERATURE

Velimir Khlebnikov

A critical study

CAMBRIDGE STUDIES IN RUSSIAN LITERATURE

General editor MALCOLM JONES

In the same series

Novy Mir
EDITH ROGOVIN FRANKEL

The enigma of Gogol
RICHARD PEACE

Three Russian writers and the irrational
T. R. N. EDWARDS

Word and music in the novels of Andrey Bely
ADA STEINBERG

The Russian revolutionary novel
RICHARD FREEBORN

Poets of modern Russia
PETER FRANCE

Andrey Bely
J. D. ELSWORTH

Nikolay Novikov
W. GARETH JONES

Vladimir Nabokov
DAVID RAMPTON

Portraits of early Russian liberals
DEREK OFFORD

Marina Tsvetaeva
SIMON KARLINSKY

Velimir Khlebnikov

A critical study

RAYMOND COOKE

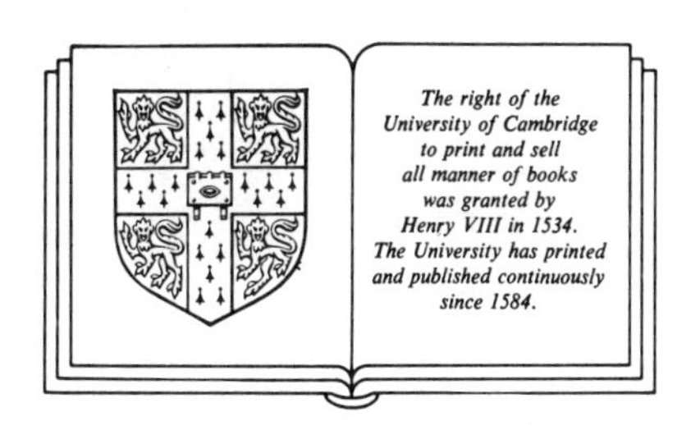

CAMBRIDGE UNIVERSITY PRESS

CAMBRIDGE
NEW YORK NEW ROCHELLE
MELBOURNE SYDNEY

Published by the Press Syndicate of the University of Cambridge
The Pitt Building, Trumpington Street, Cambridge CB2 1RP
32 East 57th Street, New York, NY 10022, USA
10 Stamford Road, Oakleigh, Melbourne 3166, Australia

First published 1987

Printed in Great Britain at
the University Press, Cambridge

British Library cataloguing in publication data

Cooke, Raymond
Velimir Khlebnikov: a critical study. –
(Cambridge studies in Russian literature)
1. Khlebnikov, Velimir – Criticism and interpretation
I. Title
891.71'3 PG3476.K485Z/

Library of Congress cataloguing in publication data

Cooke, Raymond.
Velimir Khlebnikov: a critical study.
(Cambridge studies in Russian literature)
Bibliography: p.
Includes index.
1. Khlebnikov, Velimir, 1885–1922 – Criticism and interpretation.
I. Title. II. Series.
PG3476.K485Z54 1987 891.78'309 87-303
ISBN 0 521 32670 2

CE

Contents

Preface

This book began life as a doctoral thesis. It has undergone considerable revision and I hope that the text which has emerged does not sit too uneasily between the world of the specialist in Russian literature and that of the interested layman, towards whom it is also directed. I have tried to cover a fairly broad spectrum in my approach, though, inevitably, while some of the points made will already be familiar to readers well-versed in Khlebnikov's work, there are also many omissions. This study was never intended to be a comprehensive 'life and works'.

It is, however, hoped that for those who know little of Khlebnikov's work this book will provide something of an overview and an introduction. For those who are already initiated in this complex poetic world, it is hoped that they too will find examined here at least some new areas which will complement and supplement the studies which have already been carried out.

I do not dwell on problems of poetics. The approach is mainly interpretative. I have, moreover, perhaps not always maintained that critical distance which some might feel suited for a study of this nature. Over my many years of involvement with Khlebnikov's work, I have come to recognize that despite all his complexities, he is a unique literary phenomenon, deserving of serious attention. To come close to this phenomenon, however, one has to enter his poetic world, to look at it from the inside, and to learn to make out some of its chief landmarks.

This is an interpretation of a poetic world which is still largely uncharted. It is an examination of ideas and themes, a search for meaning and coherence in the works of a poet, who, for many, is still a symbol of incomprehensibility.

There are many debts which I must acknowledge to people and to institutions for help in the preparation of this work. Robin Milner-Gulland, Reader in Russian Studies at the University of Sussex, was the first to direct me towards Khlebnikov's works. The British Library in London and the Taylor Institution in Oxford provided invaluable materials for my research, as did the Lenin Library in Moscow and the Saltykov-Shchedrin Library in Leningrad. I am grateful to all these libraries for their assistance. I am indebted to the British Council, which awarded me scholarships on three occasions to pursue my studies in the Soviet Union. I owe a particular debt to the facilities and staff of the Central State Archive for Literature and Art (TsGALI) and the manuscript department of the Gorky Institute of World Literature (IMLI) in Moscow, where I was able to examine the manuscripts of Khlebnikov and others. Conversations with Soviet scholars such as Aleksandr Parnis, Viktor Grigoryev, Nikolay Khardzhiev and Rudolf Duganov have contributed substantially to my endeavours. Amelia Cantelli of the University of Oxford assisted me with linguistic problems which arose (though I am, of course, responsible for errors which occur). I would also like to acknowledge a debt to Henry Gifford, who read the original thesis and gave me the encouragement and guidance to reshape it into a work more fit for publication. I am grateful to Ronald Vroon at the University of Pennsylvania for advice and assistance on specific points and for reading the biographical section in manuscript and making pertinent suggestions. Julian Graffy at the School of Slavonic and East European Studies at the University of London was kind enough to read the whole of the work in typescript and many of his invaluable suggestions have been incorporated in the final version. Finally, this work would never have been completed if it were not for the facilities and financial help provided by St Antony's College, Oxford, which for 1984–85 elected me its 'Max Hayward Fellow in Russian Literature'.

RAYMOND COOKE
Oxford, 1986

Note on transliteration, abbreviations and text

I have adopted the 'British' system of transliteration which renders proper names normally ending in -iy, -yy and -y simply as ending in -y (for example, Yur*y* Tynyanov, Vasil*y* Kamensk*y*). I have omitted, moreover, from proper names in the body of the text the soft sign (′) to facilitate reading. The soft sign has been reinstated in the notes and the bibliography. Certain names have been left throughout in their more accustomed variants (for example, Mandelstam, Burliuk, Khardzhiev, Jakobson).

To avoid an unwieldy number of notes I have given abbreviated references in the text to several editions of Khlebnikov's works:

SP *Sobraniye proizvedeniy*, 5 vols., ed. N. Stepanov (Leningrad, 1928–33)

IS *Izbrannyye stikhotvoreniya*, ed. N. Stepanov (Moscow, 1936)

NP *Neizdannyye proizvedeniya*, ed. N. Khardzhiev and T. Grits (Moscow, 1940)

SS *Sobraniye sochineniy*, 4 vols., ed. V. Markov (Munich, Wilhelm Fink Verlag, 1968–72). Vols. 1–3 of this edition contain a reprint of the SP followed (vol. 3) by some previously uncollected material; vol. 4 comprises a reprint of the NP.

The SP and SS references are followed by volume numbers (Roman small cap. numerals) and page numbers (Arabic numerals). The NP and IS references are simply followed by page numbers.

All references to archive material, unless stated otherwise, are to Khlebnikov's archive at the Central State Archive for Literature and Art (*Tsentral'nyy gosudarstvennyy arkhiv literatury i iskusstva*) (abbreviated to TsGALI), *fond* 527, *opis'* 1, *yedinitsy khraneniya* 1–351. I have abbreviated the term *yedinitsa khraneniya* (storage unit) to *yed. khr.* This is followed by the page (*list*) and reverse page (*list ob.*) numbers of the manuscripts cited.

The few angled brackets which occur in quotations from Khlebnikov indicate tentative readings.

Dates are given according to the custom of the time. There is thus no reference to new style or old style.

Translations are my own except where stated otherwise. I have provided prose translations of transliterated Khlebnikov verse quotations. These translations should not be judged as necessarily conveying the 'poetry' of the originals. I hope, however, that they convey the meaning.

1

Biography, discourse

I

Khlebnikov is 'impossible to read', the poet Vladimir Mayakovsky wrote in his obituary notice shortly after Khlebnikov's death in June 1922. And he also noted: Khlebnikov is not a 'poet for consumers', but a 'poet for producers'.[1] This much-quoted pronouncement set the seal on a reputation which Khlebnikov acquired in his lifetime and which was to last for many years to come.

Khlebnikov might have expected a more sympathetic appraisal from the fellow Futurist who had some years earlier proclaimed him the 'king of Russian poetry' (SP v 333). However, Mayakovsky was doing no more than echoing the opinion of his time. For most of his contemporaries Khlebnikov was in particular the author of the renowned neologistic poem 'Incantation by Laughter' ('Zaklyatiye smekhom') and in general the author of 'transrational' (*zaumnyy*) verse, and the purveyor of gibberish. It was generally considered, as Mayakovsky wrote in his obituary, that out of every 100 people who read Khlebnikov only 10 would be able to 'know and love' him and these would be Futurist poets and formalist philologists.[2] If Mayakovsky is voicing such opinions, then it is little surprise that a less sympathetic obituary writer could refer to Khlebnikov as an 'eternal failure and half-crazy versifier'.[3]

There was, however, some justification for the unhappy remarks of Mayakovsky and other writers and critics of his time. As another obituary writer, the poet Sergey Gorodetsky, noted, at the time of Khlebnikov's death in 1922 a large part of his work remained unpublished and thus unknown.[4] The early literary assessments of Khlebnikov were often unfounded because they were based on insufficient information.

When, for example, the first volume of Khlebnikov's *Collected Works* (*Sobraniye proizvedeniy*) appeared in 1928, about half of the long poems (*poemy*) it contained were being published for the first time, and these included Khlebnikov's masterpiece of the revolutionary period, 'Night Search' ('Nochnoy obysk'). Khlebnikov's flowering as a writer coincided with years which were not conducive to stable publication. They were years of world war, of revolution and of civil war. When Khlebnikov did succeed in publishing his works they appeared for the most part in small journals and miscellanies which circulated only erratically, if at all. These problems were compounded by Khlebnikov's own apparent neglect of his manuscripts and by the cavalier fashion in which his texts were edited by others. Small wonder then that he became the subject of ill-informed criticism.

The publication between 1928 and 1933 of the *Collected Works* certainly helped to eradicate some of the misconceptions which had prevailed. Printed here at last were not only previously unpublished works, but also works which appeared in publications which had subsequently become bibliographical rarities. Edited by Nikolay Stepanov, this edition has, however, proved somewhat unreliable and its effect, in any case, was muted by the change for the worse in the Soviet literary climate which was under way at the time of its publication. By the time the fifth volume appeared, the Soviet Communist Party had tightened its grip on literature and the arts. Khlebnikov's work now became the object of a more ideologically motivated brand of criticism. Khlebnikov had, in his own way, supported the Bolshevik revolution, but his works did not conform to the now official Soviet literary standards of socialist realism. Although in subsequent years (1936, 1940, 1960) individual editions were published, introductions by their editor Stepanov included statutory remarks on Khlebnikov's 'failure' to understand the revolution correctly.[5] Less sympathetic critics attacked his 'anti-Soviet sentiments' and branded him a 'poet for aesthetes' and a 'literary pygmy'.[6] Remarkably, Nikolay Khardzhiev and T. Grits managed to secure the publication in 1940 of some unpublished works by Khlebnikov in an excellent scholarly edition,[7] but no collected edition of several volumes has appeared since Stepanov's unsatisfactory *Collected Works*.

At present, however, both in the Soviet Union and in the west a reassessment of Khlebnikov's literary achievements is in progress and the early reputation which he acquired as a purveyor of 'transrational' gibberish and the notion that he left nothing that could survive as an accomplishment is being forcefully questioned. Since the 1960s not only have a number of important studies been published about him, but also anthologies and individual translations of his works have appeared in most major European languages, and even Japanese. A difficult poet he may be at times, but it has proved not only possible to read him, but also to translate him.

Khlebnikov's contemporary, the poet Aleksandr Blok, suspected that Khlebnikov was 'significant'; Osip Mandelstam saw in Khlebnikov 'a citizen of the whole of history, of the whole system of language and poetry'; and Mayakovsky, to give him his due, also regarded Khlebnikov as one of his 'teachers', as a 'Columbus of new poetic continents'.[8] Moreover, today, over a hundred years after his birth and despite a knowledge of his work which is sometimes only superficial, Khlebnikov is an acknowledged influence for many Russian writers.[9] His contribution to literature has been, and still is, a vital force.

II

In an article which prefaces the first volume of Khlebnikov's *Collected Works*, the critic Yury Tynyanov stressed the dangers of Khlebnikov's poetry being eclipsed by his biography (SP I 29). The problem, as Vladimir Markov notes, was that Khlebnikov was a natural eccentric.[10] Consequently, the memoirs of his life have produced a fascinating array of anecdotes, each one more bizarre than the next. In a sense, Tynyanov's warning has proved well-founded, since it is this anecdotal and 'legendary' image of Khlebnikov which has persisted in the public's literary imagination, along with the idea of Khlebnikov as an idiot poet, writing gibberish. However, despite Tynyanov's remarks, Khlebnikov's poetry has survived while his biography still remains to be written. And this 'real' biography (as opposed to the 'biography by anecdote') is not going to prove an easy task.

Khlebnikov himself did not leave any extensive autobiographical writings. Nothing, for example, to match the well-ordered diaries and notebooks of Blok. Some information can be gleaned from jottings which approximate to diary entries, but these often offer only tantalizing snippets of information which beg more questions than they answer. Khlebnikov replied briefly on occasion to some questionnaires about his life and works, but for more detailed information one has to turn to his correspondence and to the reminiscences of others.

Khlebnikov *did* leave a few works which contain descriptions of some autobiographical events. Such writings, however, reflect, to paraphrase Shklovsky, an 'aesthetic experience of facts'.[11] Khlebnikov did not dissociate his life from his literature. Indeed, if some memoirists are guilty of 'mythologizing' the poet's life, then Khlebnikov himself is guilty of some 'self-mythologizing'.

Viktor Vladimirovich Khlebnikov (who was to become known to the world as Velimir Khlebnikov) was born on 28 October 1885 in Astrakhan province not far from the estuary of the River Volga as it flows into the Caspian Sea. The place where he spent the first six years of his childhood was not so much a village as a winter settlement of the nomadic Kalmyk people, for whom his father was a district administrator.[12] This area, and in particular the nearby city of Astrakhan where his family eventually settled, was to provide for him an important staging post in his wanderings across Russia. For Khlebnikov this was frontier country, a meeting place of land and sea, of Europe and Asia, where, as he put it, the 'scales' of Russia's affairs were frequently grasped and tipped (NP 352). The region was, however, not only a source of past and potential conflict, it was also a source of possible harmony and was singled out by Khlebnikov as a location for his futuristic utopia. Moreover, he looked back upon this region as on a childhood idyll.

Almost as important as the geographical location for Khlebnikov was the ethnographical make-up of the region. As a child he was surrounded by the Kalmyk tribes – 'Mongol nomads of the Buddhist faith' (NP 352), whose lifestyle became for him an object of some reverence. Such people seemed at one with nature, and nature was one of Khlebnikov's chief loves. Undoubtedly a major influence on the poet in this regard was his father, Vladimir Alekseyevich Khlebnikov, who was a naturalist and an ornithologist of some standing. The young Khlebnikov soon developed his father's enthusiasms.

When in 1891 the family moved westwards into Volhynia province, Khlebnikov found an ideal place to continue his natural education. Hunting, fishing and catching butterflies are the childhood activities he recalls (SP IV 120–1). His youthful observations of the natural world also show evidence of an artistic response.

Khlebnikov's earliest known poem is a description of a bird in a cage.[13] This poem was written in 1897 when he was 11 years old, the same year the family moved back eastwards into Simbirsk province. It was here that Khlebnikov began his formal schooling which was continued in Kazan where the family moved the following year.

The family home at Kazan was to be Khlebnikov's last real 'fixed abode', and in a sense the ground had already been laid by this time for his future wanderings across Russia. The nomadic lifestyle of the Kalmyk people as well as the moves by his family before it settled in Kazan will have exerted some influence. Khlebnikov also believed that the wandering instinct was part of his heritage and that he had explorers' blood in his veins (SP v 279, NP 352). More importantly, his interest in the natural sciences meant that as a youth he had already begun to do some exploring himself. In the summer of 1903, for example, he is said to have taken part in a geological expedition to Dagestan (IS 9). The natural sciences were not, however, his only preoccupation. His final school report noted his 'great interest' (IS 9) in mathematics and it was the mathematics department at Kazan university which Khlebnikov joined as a student in the autumn of 1903.[14]

Apparently, Khlebnikov began university life with some enthusiasm, but this was soon disrupted. Only a few weeks after starting his first term, in November–December 1903, he spent a month in Kazan prison after being arrested during a student demonstration.[15] Like many of his generation Khlebnikov had become caught up in the tide of troubles which culminated in the revolutionary upheaval of 1905. Soon after his release, he left the university and travelled north on a visit to Moscow. However, by the summer he was back in Kazan where he rejoined the university, but this time in the department of natural sciences.

In May 1905 Khlebnikov embarked, together with his brother Aleksandr, on a major nature expedition to the Urals, which lasted some five months. Several years later (in 1911) they published a paper outlining the ornithological observations they had made on this trip. Nor was this to be Khlebnikov's first such publication. As early as 1907 he had published another paper on an ornithological topic.[16]

Some of the notes Khlebnikov made on the expedition to the Urals have been likened to the preparatory sketches for a story.[17]

Certainly, by this time Khlebnikov was beginning to take his literary endeavours quite seriously. By the end of 1904 he had already sent work to the writer Maxim Gorky who had duly returned the manuscript 'marked' in red. Memoirs from this period indicate that Khlebnikov was reading the Russian Symbolist literature of his day and was also becoming acquainted with the work of some major west European writers.[18]

In 1908 Khlebnikov left university without completing his course, but in September of that year he enrolled in the natural sciences department of the physics and maths faculty of the University of St Petersburg. Before moving north to the Russian capital, however, he had made his first significant literary contact. While visiting Sudak in the Crimea – in 1908 – Khlebnikov met one of the leading Symbolist poets, Vyacheslav Ivanov. Little is known about the encounter, but not long before the meeting, Khlebnikov had written to Ivanov from Kazan, sending him 14 poems and asking his opinion of them (NP 354). Clearly, even before he reached St Petersburg, Khlebnikov regarded Ivanov as something of a literary mentor.

Upon his arrival in Russia's capital, Khlebnikov's interest in academic pursuits and any desire he may have had to pursue a career as a naturalist suffered a rapid decline. He soon began to involve himself in literary affairs and by October 1908 had already come into contact with the poets Sologub and Gorodetsky (SP v 284). By the following year his contacts with leading literary figures were further established and he had renewed his acquaintance with Vyacheslav Ivanov. In May 1909 he wrote and told his father that Ivanov had a 'highly sympathetic attitude' to his literary beginnings (SP v 286).[19]

Other letters of the period reflect his literary enthusiasms and aspirations. He records meetings with, among others, Gumilyov, Aleksey Tolstoy and Mikhail Kuzmin, who he names as his 'teacher'. 'Some', he wrote, were forecasting 'great success' for him (SP v 287) and there had been talk of his 'lines of genius' (SP v 289).

Khlebnikov became a visitor to the gatherings at Ivanov's 'tower' (so called because of the external appearance of Ivanov's flat) where the literary elite assembled to read and discuss their work. He also read his work at Ivanov's 'Academy of Verse' and had hopes of publishing some works in the journal *Apollon* (*Apollo*) which was being planned by some of his new literary acquaintances.

However, Khlebnikov's work was obviously not to the liking of the *Apollon* editor Sergey Makovsky and his hopes of publication were frustrated.[20] Khlebnikov subsequently broke with the literary establishment which had seemed to promise him so much. The failure of *Apollon* to publish his work must have been a considerable disappointment and was undoubtedly a major factor in the rift which occurred.

Khlebnikov did not, however, break with establishment writers with the intention of joining or forming the Futurist movement. The Russian Futurists did not exist as a movement at this time and Khlebnikov's alienation from the *Apollon* writers was merely one of the links in the chain which led to its appearance. Another link was the fact that long before the first edition of *Apollon* even appeared, Khlebnikov had established contact with Vasily Kamensky, who was to become a leading figure in the Russian Futurist movement. Kamensky, who was then editor of the journal *Vesna* (*Spring*), published in October 1908, to Khlebnikov's delight, a highly neologistic piece of his prose. Khlebnikov recorded his happiness in a letter to his sister, and added: 'I shall have a smooth pathway in the fields of praisedom if there is a willingness to venture' (NP 420). Moreover, in the same month Khlebnikov published (anonymously) in the newspaper *Vecher* (*Evening*) his 'Proclamation of Slav Students' ('Vozzvaniye uchashchikhsya slavyan'), an angry outburst of pan-Slavism against the annexation by Austria of Bosnia and Hercegovina.[21]

At the beginning of 1910, at about the same time as Khlebnikov was noting his own absence from the 'Academy of Verse' (SP v 290), Kamensky introduced him to the painter-composer Mikhail Matyushin and his wife, the writer Yelena Guro. Through these Khlebnikov also met the radical artist and poet David Burliuk. Khlebnikov's initial contacts with this group coincided with the staging of one of the many art exhibitions which were being held during that period. This exhibition was to have an accompanying publication, and it was here that Khlebnikov found the further outlet for his work that *Apollon* had denied him. The publication, edited by Nikolay Kulbin, and entitled *Studio of Impressionists* (*Studiya impressionistov*), included two poems by Khlebnikov, one of which was his neologistic 'Incantation by Laughter'. This was subsequently 'ridiculed'[22] in numerous reviews and articles. Khlebnikov also participated in a further collection, *Trap for Judges*

(*Sadok sudey*), which appeared soon afterwards in April 1910 and also included works by David Burliuk, his two brothers Nikolay and Vladimir, Yelena Guro and Kamensky. There was a deliberately anti-establishment and anti-aesthetic flavour about this publication. It was printed on wall-paper and contained a satirical assault by Khlebnikov, 'Marquise Dezes' ('Markiza Dezes'), on the artists and writers connected with *Apollon*. It was this collection which Markov's history of Russian Futurism has described as 'the real appearance of the Russian Futurists as a group'.[23]

In spite of a lull in publishing activity between 1910 and 1912 Khlebnikov was by no means creatively idle. He spent the summer of 1910 in the Burliuk household at Chernyanka, near Kherson in the south of Russia, and towards the end of the year already had hopes of publishing a volume of collected works (SP v 292). By summer 1911 he had been sent down from university for non-payment of fees. This expulsion was merely a matter of form, since he had long since given up any serious academic pursuits and was already devoting his life entirely to his writing. However, it was not only 'literature' in the accepted sense of the word which was taking up his time. As he wrote to his brother Aleksandr in February 1911, he was 'assiduously busy with numbers' (SP v 292). This is one of the earliest references by Khlebnikov to the mathematical tables and calculations which were to preoccupy him for the rest of his life.

These calculations were connected with establishing 'laws' which Khlebnikov had come to believe governed the development of history and fate. He was later to testify that his interest in such matters had first been aroused by the need to understand the reasons for the destruction of the Russian fleet at Tsushima in the war with Japan (SP II 10). Whatever the initial impetus, by the beginning of 1911 Khlebnikov was imparting considerable energy to his work 'on numbers and the fates of peoples' (NP 360). Such concerns were at the centre of his first work in an individual edition, the pamphlet *Teacher and Pupil* (*Uchitel' i uchenik*), published in 1912, with the financial assistance of David Burliuk, in whose household Khlebnikov stayed for a second time in the spring and summer of that year.

The year of 1912 also proved eventful for Khlebnikov in another respect, for it was at the beginning of that year that he first met the poet and artist Aleksey Kruchonykh. The fruitful creative relationship they shared did not take long to mature and by the autumn of that year they had co-authored and published an edition of the long poem *Game in Hell* (*Igra v adu*). As in Burliuk, Khlebnikov found in Kruchonykh an able propagandist for his work and a fellow writer with an extraordinary talent for transforming manuscripts into innovative and striking published material. Another event made 1912 something of a milestone for Khlebnikov. In Moscow in December of that year he was co-signatory, together with Kruchonykh, Mayakovsky and David Burliuk, of the now infamous manifesto 'A Slap in the Face of Public Taste' ('Poshchochina obshchestvennomu vkusu').[24] This iconoclastic literary proclamation attacked both the literature of the past and the literature of the present. It called for Pushkin, Dostoyevsky, Tolstoy 'and so forth' to be 'thrown overboard from the ship of Modernity'; and it rounded on contemporary writers, Symbolist and others. Although this brief manifesto is recalled chiefly for its polemics and literary impudence, it also attempted to provide something of a literary programme, expressing hatred for the existing language, calling for word creation and announcing the arrival of the 'self valuing (self-sufficient) word' – 'samotsennoye (samovitoye) slovo'. The 'self-sufficient word' has since become seen as one of the keystones of Russian Futurist aesthetics.

Any attempt to define Russian Futurism will prove problematic. Although, as a movement, it was marked by specific aesthetic stances, it also had an amorphous quality which renders most definitions unsatisfactory, since they fail to convey adequately its dynamism and diversity. It was, as Victor Erlich has pointed out, 'the most influential, the most vocal and possibly the most seminal movement within the Russian modernistic ambience', but it would, as Erlich also argues, perhaps be misleading to equate it with the whole of the post-Symbolist Russian avant-garde movement.[25] Nevertheless, it encompassed within itself many divergent and contradictory trends and certainly the most significant of these was the one which became known as Hylaea or Russian Cubo-Futurism and which recognized in Khlebnikov one of its leading figures.

Hylaea was the name given by the ancient Greeks to the area around Chernyanka where the Burliuk family lived. It was a term which Khlebnikov accepted and used in his work (SP II 116), in spite of its European origins. Khlebnikov had a strong dislike of borrowings in Russian from western languages (particularly words reflecting Latin and Germanic influences) and as a rule he eliminated them from his writings. Although the term Hylaea does not seem to have caused offence to his Russian ear, the appellation Futurists (in Russian *futuristy*) certainly did. As a consequence, in line with the group's proclaimed literary tenets of word creation, he coined a Russian equivalent, *budetlyanin* (from the Russian *budet* – it will be – and meaning roughly 'a man of the future').[26] This word was also used by other members of the group, particularly since the name *futuristy* had already been adopted in 1911 by a different literary grouping, the Ego-Futurists.

The December 1912 'Slap' manifesto was published without any label being attached to the group of signatories. The name Hylaea first surfaced in March 1913 in the third issue of the journal *Union of Youth* (*Soyuz molodyozhi*). However, a few months later the Hylaea group also appeared under the label *Futuristy* when David Burliuk began producing a series of booklets with the imprint 'Literary Company' of Futurists 'Hylaea' (*'Literaturnaya kompaniya' futuristov 'Gileya'*). In accepting the Futurist appellation, David Burliuk was merely recognizing a *fait accompli*, since the press and the public had begun to use the term rather indiscriminately and the Hylaeans had become generally known along with other groups as 'Futurists'. In any case the boundaries between the different literary alliances to which the name was applied proved rather flexible, and by early 1914 David Burliuk and Mayakovsky had already toured and appeared in print with the Ego-Futurist Igor Severyanin.[27] Yet in spite of such shifting alliances and Russian Futurism's amorphous quality, it is certainly possible to point to some of the elements which provided a framework for the Hylaean or Cubo-Futurist grouping to which Khlebnikov was aligned. The names themselves offer us some guide in this aesthetic maze and both, in effect, indicate the importance for the movement of the visual arts.

The term Hylaea might at first sight seem an odd name for a group of painters and writers who were later to become known as Futurists. This ancient name, however, reflected the primitivist tendencies which were of considerable importance in their work. Hylaea evoked for them the ancient inhabitants and the mythology of the region whose name it was. This was the site of Scythian burial mounds and of the pagan effigies of stone women, later to figure so prominently in Khlebnikov's works. The leading exponents of the primitivist trend in the visual arts (David Burliuk, Natalya Goncharova and Mikhail Larionov) all contributed illustrations to the Russian Futurist collections. Primitivist traits can also be found in the literature of the Futurists, not least in Khlebnikov's work. He wrote, for example, a self-styled 'stone age tale' 'I and E' ('I i E'). These two apparently contradictory trends of primitivism and Futurism were able to run in tandem because in their primitivism the incipient Futurists were looking back in order to look forward. What they saw as the stale art of the present had to be reinvigorated by a return to the more genuine and unspoiled art of the past. They saw it as their task to restore what had been ruined and to revive what was dead.[28]

The term Cubo-Futurism clearly derives from the Cubist movement in art. This had its roots in France, but soon exerted an influence in Russia on the work of artists and thence on the progressive writing of the period.[29] This was particularly the case with the Hylaeans, since many of the writers associated with the group, including David Burliuk, Mayakovsky and Kruchonykh, came to poetry from painting. Khlebnikov too was a competent artist and techniques in the visual arts clearly exerted an effect upon his writing. 'We want the word boldly to follow painting', he once wrote (NP 334); and this desire is reflected in the *Word as Such* (*Slovo kak takovoye*) manifesto, of which he was a co-signatory with Kruchonykh. This compares the Futurist writers' (*budetlyane rechetvortsy*) dissection of words, use of half words and their 'transrational' combination with the sections and parts of bodies portrayed by the Futurist painters (*zhivopistsy budetlyane*).[30] Some of the terminology applied in the manifesto to literature is also taken from the language of painting. Khlebnikov even developed the concept of the *zvukopis'* (sound-painting) as a rival to *zhivopis'* (painting); 'painterly' concerns run through the whole of his work.

The influence of another west European artistic movement, that of Italian Futurism and its leading literary exponent Marinetti, is much more problematic and has already been the subject of considerable debate.[31] The Russian Cubo-Futurists themselves argued that Russian Futurism was entirely independent of its Italian counterpart.[32] However, recent commentators have remarked that 'Marinetti's Futurism was much more of an influence in Russia than is customarily thought and more than the Russian Futurists wanted to acknowledge.'[33] Almost certainly Khlebnikov would have been loath to acknowledge an Italian Futurist influence on his art, but commentators are quite right to point to Khlebnikov's early nationalism and glorification of war as points in common with Marinetti.[34] This is, however, surely more a case of parallel development or of shared attitudes than of influence.[35] Curiously, though, Khlebnikov did allow Marinetti a 'consultative vote' in his 'Martian Duma' in the 1916 *Trumpet of the Martians* (*Truba marsian*) manifesto (SP v 153).

One aspect of Italian Futurism which was shared by the Russian Cubo-Futurists (and other modernist movements elsewhere) was a tendency to engage in street-parading and to cause scandal. Leading Russian Cubo-Futurists painted their faces, wore outrageous clothes, exchanged insults with their audiences and, in general, tried to shock the bourgeoisie and to 'slap the face of public taste'. They took their art out on to the streets, in contrast to the Symbolists who held themselves and their art aloof from the crowd.

Here is not the place to discuss the complex literary phenomenon of Symbolism. Inevitably, as the dominant literary movement in the early part of the century it exerted some influence on the incipient Futurists and Khlebnikov was no exception.[36] Nevertheless, Symbolism's tendency towards mysticism and metaphysics, its focus of attention on the symbol and the musicality of verse was attacked by Futurist writers with considerable vigour. Opposition to the aesthetic tenets of Symbolism was a cornerstone of Russian Cubo-Futurism, but this negative aspect also had a positive side. The need to move away from the art of the past also entailed a desire which was 'Futurist' – a desire to create the art of the future. The Futurist movement had a great awareness of time and looked forward eagerly to a utopian leap into the future away from an unacceptable present.[37]

In answer to the Symbolists' concern with what lay beyond the word, the Cubo-Futurists favoured an emphasis on the word itself, on the 'new coming beauty' of the 'self-sufficient word'. Hence the title of the manifesto – the *Word as Such*. This manifesto attacked the mystical nature of contemporary literature; it criticized its preoccupation with the human soul and its 'pleasant' and 'sonorous' language. 'We think that language should be above all *language*,' the manifesto says, 'and if it should recall anything, then rather let it be a saw or the poisoned arrow of a savage.'[38] The Cubo-Futurists called for harsh words and sounds; for images which would shock. To the religious mysticism and metaphysics of the Symbolists they counterposed a 'card-game in hell'.[39]

In the collection accompanying the 'Slap' manifesto it was Khlebnikov's work which seemed, above all, to reflect the proclaimed literary programme. The collection included his neologistic short verse and prose and also the 'sound-painting' 'Bobeobi'. Khlebnikov's fellow Futurists were more than happy to help propagate precisely that aspect of his work which most establishment reviewers and literary figures found to their distaste. Khlebnikov was a gauntlet which administered the 'slap'. As Willem Weststeijn writes, 'the Futurists eagerly accepted Khlebnikov's experimental works because his experiments with words agreed with their own ideas about the necessary renovation of language'.[40] As a consequence, Khlebnikov, who in 1910 had already proved unacceptable to the literary establishment, rapidly found himself proclaimed the literary genius of the anti-establishment camp.

A result of this was that Khlebnikov was presented to the literary public largely as a *zaumnik* ('transrationalist') and experimenter and other aspects of his work did not receive much recognition, in spite of the fact that many were carried by Futurist publications. Few people, for example, would recognize Khlebnikov as the author of the stories 'The Hunter Usa-gali' ('Okhotnik Usa-gali') (SP IV 37–39) and 'Nikolay' (SP IV 40–46) with prose as 'semantically clear as Pushkin's',[41] even though they were published in the Futurist collection *The Three* (*Troye*). Equally, few would suspect that in 1913 Khlebnikov contributed articles and a story for the general readership of the slavophil newspaper *Slavyanin* (*The Slav*).[42] The Futurist collections seem to have left the reader with just a 'vague memory of Khlebnikov as some sort of transrational crank and conjurer';[43] yet these collections also contained work which was evidence of a much broader sweep of concerns. This was even true of the *Slap* collection which carried such works as 'Snake Train – Flight' ('Zmei poyezda – begstvo'), 'Monument' ('Pamyatnik') and 'Maiden God' ('Deviy bog'). By the end of 1912 Khlebnikov was already a writer of some maturity, and this maturity was further demonstrated in the deluge of Futurist publications which followed the *Slap* collection.

In 1913 and early 1914 Khlebnikov's work appeared in about 10 different collections. This was the most intensive period of activity for the Hylaeans as a group, and December 1913 saw the first productions of Futurist work on stage with performances in St Petersburg of Mayakovsky's tragedy *Vladimir Mayakovsky* and Kruchonykh's opera *Victory over the Sun* (*Pobeda nad solntsem*) for which Khlebnikov wrote the prologue. This is clearly why Khlebnikov's neologistic activity during the summer of 1913 was oriented towards the theatre.[44] As was the rule now, language was not the only area of concern for Khlebnikov. In September 1913 he wrote to Matyushin telling him that he was 'busy with numbers, calculating from morning until night'.[45]

Khlebnikov spent the summer months of 1913 in Astrakhan. When he returned north towards the end of that year, it was to an atmosphere of heated public debates and disputes on modern art and literature. The literary collections of the Futurists had only small circulations, and public lectures, readings and various street appearances enabled them to publicize their work more widely. Having spent the summer in the south, Khlebnikov had taken little part in these activities, and even after his return to Moscow and St Petersburg references to public readings by him are rare.[46] He seems to have been happy to allow his Futurist colleagues to promote his work, which they frequently did. David Burliuk, in particular, gave Khlebnikov's work much publicity, even reading lectures on the theme 'Pushkin and Khlebnikov'.[47] Nor did Khlebnikov take part in the celebrated Futurist tour of the provinces (December 1913–March 1914), which featured mainly David Burliuk, Mayakovsky and Kamensky.

Much is often made of Khlebnikov's 'shy and retiring' nature,[48] which made him an unlikely participant in Futurist publicity stunts. However, as Nadezhda Mandelstam points out, Khlebnikov was, at the same time, very quick to take offence.[49] His sister Vera said likewise, that, although at times 'gentle and quiet', he was also 'stubborn and capricious'.[50] In February 1914 the visit to Russia by the Italian Futurist Marinetti prompted one of the most public and publicized manifestations of Khlebnikov's temper. Inspired by nationalist sentiments and incensed at the homage being paid to this 'Italian vegetable' (NP 368), Khlebnikov distributed at one of Marinetti's lectures in St Petersburg a hostile leaflet which he had co-authored with Benedikt Livshits. Nikolay Kulbin tried to prevent the distribution and there was a confrontation.[51]

On the next day the impetuous Khlebnikov penned an angry letter to Marinetti, hurling back the insults he had received from

Kulbin and announcing his break with Hylaea (NP 368–9).[52] By the middle of the next month he had set off south again to spend the summer in Astrakhan.

Ironically it was this period which proved most fruitful for Khlebnikov in his associations with Hylaea, with the publication of three collected editions. At the turn of 1913 Kruchonykh published *Roar! Gauntlets: 1908–1914* (*Ryav! Perchatki: 1908–1914*); a little later he followed this up with *Selection of Verses: 1907–1914* (*Izbornik stikhov: 1907–1914*); and at about the same time David Burliuk brought out *Creations: 1906–1908* (*Tvoreniya: 1906–1908*).[53] Khlebnikov was not always happy at the treatment he received at the hands of Burliuk. When he had visited the Burliuk household he had left in their charge a number of manuscripts. Some of these works found their way into various Hylaean collections and the *Creations* and in 1914 (at about the same time as the dispute over Marinetti) Khlebnikov was prompted to write an open letter (SP v 257) attacking David and Nikolay Burliuk for printing works unfit for publication and for distorting them.[54] Khlebnikov's conflicts with Hylaea, however, were not long-lasting. He soon saw David Burliuk again and in the 1916 *Four Birds* (*Chetyre ptitsy*) collection his works were once more subject to editorial distortion.[55]

While the outbreak of the war with Germany in 1914 distracted the public from the domestic literary conflict, it gave Khlebnikov further incentive for the 'semi-scientific' (NP 370) numerological articles he was engaged on. He was particularly interested in plotting and predicting the dates of battles and at the turn of the year he published the pamphlet *Battles 1915–1917: A New Teaching about War* (*Bitvy 1915–1917: novoye ucheniye o voyne*). This was followed in 1916 by his *Time a Measure of the World* (*Vremya mera mira*).

By mid-1914 the spate of Russian Futurist publications had somewhat abated. Moreover, by 1915 the Futurist writers themselves were already being absorbed into the literary establishment. A sign of this was the publication in March that year of the first issue of *Archer* (*Strelets*) which featured not only almost all of the Hylaean writers, including Khlebnikov, but also four of the writers who had been consigned by them to a 'dacha by the river' in the 'Slap' manifesto – namely, Blok, Sologub, Kuzmin and Remizov. The Futurists were now appearing in print with their erstwhile adversaries.

Typically Khlebnikov spent much of 1914 and 1915 at his parents' house in Astrakhan, but by summer 1915 he was back in Moscow and the capital (by now renamed Petrograd), and, as we can see from diary entries (SP v 330–334), led quite an active social and literary life. Among those he saw were David Burliuk, Mayakovsky, Tatlin, Viktor Shklovsky and Osip Brik.

Still greatly preoccupied with his calculations to determine the 'laws of time', in December 1915 he decided to establish what he called his 'state of time'[56] a temporal power in opposition to the 'states of space'. A few months later he founded the union or society of the '317', a number which Khlebnikov chose because of the central role it played at that time in his attempts at mathematical prediction (SP v 175–6, 279, SS III 437–55). Khlebnikov viewed this society as a prospective world government and was also frequently to refer to its members collectively as the 'Chairmen of the Terrestrial Globe'.[57]

In April 1916, shortly after returning to Astrakhan, Khlebnikov was drafted into the army. After leading the life of a nomad for several years the regimentation of military life as a reserve infantryman in Tsaritsyn (now Volgograd) was little short of disaster for him. He directed appeals for assistance to various quarters, including Nikolay Kulbin who was a senior member of staff at the military medical academy. Khlebnikov's endeavour was to secure a discharge on medical grounds and it was probably with the aid of Kulbin's intercession that he was soon undergoing various medical checks to determine his suitability for military service. He managed to receive a month's furlough in August 1916 which he spent in Kharkov. Here he met up with the poets Aseyev and Petnikov, with whom he was involved in setting up the journal *Chronicle* (*Vremennik*). In grouping together with poets who were associated with the Futurist movement but who were not 'original' Hylaeans, Khlebnikov was now forming important new literary alliances.

Back in Astrakhan in September Khlebnikov underwent further tests, but at the end of the year he was in the 'trap' again (SP v 312) in a reserve infantry regiment near Saratov, where he was being 'unceremoniously' treated despite a document testifying to his nervous disposition.[58] It was his nervous condition, however, which apparently enabled him to receive, soon after the February revolution, a five-month furlough.[59] The enforced confinement of army life must have instilled in him a veritable hunger for space. He travelled north to Petrograd, but by the beginning of August he was back in Astrakhan, though not before visiting Kiev, Kharkov, Taganrog and Tsaritsyn. Two months later he was in Petrograd again, in time to witness the Bolshevik October revolution.

Although the war with Germany had dispersed the Futurist ranks (Kruchonykh and Kamensky had headed south to escape the draft), Khlebnikov had not entirely lost touch with his Hylaean comrades and their associates. He was, for example, in frequent contact with Matyushin, and in Moscow at the end of 1917 he was once more in the company of David Burliuk and Kamensky who even procured for him a wealthy patron. This 'domestication' of Khlebnikov was, however, shortlived.[60]

In the difficult conditions of 1918 he travelled extensively. After being held up along the Volga, mainly in Nizhny Novgorod (now Gorky), in August or September he reached Astrakhan on what was to be his last visit. Here he found work on the staff of a local Bolshevik military newspaper, *Krasnyy voin* (*Red Serviceman*),[61] and in early 1919 he also worked in the information section of a Red Army political department. He remained in Astrakhan for over six months, but in March 1919 he left for Moscow where plans were being made to produce a new edition of his collected works. Through Mayakovsky he received two advances for the planned publication, totalling more than a thousand roubles.[62] He then promptly took a train (his usual form of transport) for the south and soon arrived in Kharkov.

The Russian civil war was by now well under way and Khlebnikov was still in the region of Kharkov when the city was taken from the Bolsheviks at the end of June by the White Volunteer Army of Denikin. The Red forces did not retake the city until December. During this troubled time Khlebnikov was apparently detained on suspicion of being a spy by both the Red and White forces.[63] Moreover, he spent four months in hospitals; he suffered two bouts of typhus and he was again under psychiatric examination to ascertain whether he was mentally fit to be conscripted, this time into the White army. No doubt to Khlebnikov's great relief, the doctor who examined him found him unfit for military service.[64]

After the Bolsheviks had retaken the city and he had left hospital, Khlebnikov remained in and around Kharkov. Dressed in rags or makeshift clothing, he lived in considerable poverty, and, although engrossed in his writings and calculations, his spirits seem to have been at a low ebb. He had some contacts with a local Bolshevik educational organization, and it was during this period that he also came into contact with the Imaginist poets Yesenin and Mariengof. In April 1919 he appeared with them at a local Kharkov theatre where they staged a public ceremony electing him 'Chairman of the Terrestrial Globe'. According to accounts of the incident, the 'emaciated' Khlebnikov swore his oath in some seriousness, but for the Imaginists the performance was done in jest and they made a public laughing stock of him.[65]

By the end of the summer Khlebnikov was keen to travel south and in September he left Kharkov for the Caucasus. Stopping briefly for a *Proletkul't* conference in Armavir, a few weeks later he reached Baku where he worked for the local ROSTA[66] organization and also for the political department of the Bolshevik Volga and Caspian fleet. In Baku life was 'very good' (SP v 319) and he found there not only his old Hylaean colleague Kruchonykh, but also his old Symbolist mentor Vyacheslav Ivanov. Here he made what he saw as a breakthrough in his mathematical calculations on time and even lectured on them at the 'Red Star' University, though he felt his theories did not get the appreciation they deserved. 'If people do not want to learn my art of foretelling the future', he wrote afterwards, 'I shall teach it to horses' (NP 385).

In April 1921 Khlebnikov secured a place with the Red Army expeditionary force which was travelling to Iran to assist local revolutionaries in their struggle for power. Khlebnikov had been keen to travel south to Iran and even India for some time, and his letters home from Iran in spring 1921 are little short of euphoric. In tone they recall his best utopian writings. He appears at last to have found for himself on a personal level some of the harmony that he had elsewhere predicted for mankind as a whole.

Khlebnikov had always been attracted by the 'simple' life. Wherever he stayed, he always lived modestly, even ascetically, never surrounding himself with the trappings of bourgeois comfort. In Iran the unhappy, tramp-like but immobile figure of the year before was able to transform himself into something of an eastern 'dervish', wandering at will, happily dressed in simple clothing, and earning himself the epithet 'priest of flowers' (SP I 245). As he wrote in a poem at that time, he was at last able to bathe his tired and sore legs in the 'green waters of Iran' (SP III 127).[67]

Khlebnikov returned to Baku from Iran in July 1921. He spent the autumn in Zheleznovodsk and Pyatigorsk, where he arrived, according to his own testimony, half-dead, penniless and barefoot (SP v 322–3). The end of 1921 was marked by drought and famine, but fortunately he was able to secure boots, employment and a ration at the local ROSTA organization. Here he worked not as a poet but as a night watchman, a job which left him free to write. He took full advantage of this and many major works date from this period.[68]

Publication during the revolution and the civil war had been difficult. Khlebnikov had been placing his work in shortlived newspapers and journals, but he had not published a collected edition since 1914. The publication planned in 1919 had not materialized and so at the end of November 1921 he set off north to see what could be done. He was particularly interested in publishing his work on fate and time. He arrived in Moscow just before the new year of 1922 and immediately came into contact with his fellow-poets, Kamensky, Kruchonykh and Mayakovsky, but relations seem to have become strained. Mayakovsky has written of Khlebnikov being demanding and suspicious during this period.[69] Khlebnikov certainly felt some grievances, whether justified or not, over the failure to publish his work. He felt that he had been let down by his friends and even came to believe that manuscripts he had handed over for publication had been stolen and his works plagiarized.[70]

Where Khlebnikov's Hylaean colleagues failed, a new acquaintance succeeded. With the help of the artist Pyotr Vasilyevich Miturich, Khlebnikov prepared for publication both his 'supertale' *Zangezi* and some of the sections of his major work on fate and time, 'Boards of Fate' ('Doski sud'by').[71] Miturich, who had written to Khlebnikov in early spring 1922, expressing interest in his ideas, soon became a constant companion.

Life in Moscow at this time was difficult. Moreover, Khlebnikov's health was not good; some reports say he was now suffering from malaria (IS 62). He wanted to go south to Astrakhan. However, prior to his departure Miturich persuaded him to travel to the village of Santalovo in Novgorod province, where Miturich's wife worked as a teacher.[72] They reached there towards the end of May. Here Khlebnikov's health took a turn for the worse and his legs became paralysed. At the beginning of June Miturich managed to get him to what must have been a fairly primitive hospital in the nearby town of Kresttsy, but doctors were unable to prevent his condition from deteriorating. After three weeks Miturich took the seriously ill Khlebnikov back to Santalovo. Attempts were made to organize help from Moscow, but it was too late. Khlebnikov died on 28 June 1922.

III

It is becoming increasingly apparent that the point of departure for a critical examination of Khlebnikov's work should be the presumption that the text embodies not disorder and nonsense, but order and sense. This is not to say that Khlebnikov's works are always easily accessible to the reader. They are not. And no critic would deny the often complex nature of the Khlebnikov text. This does not mean, however, that they are incomprehensible. The Khlebnikov text can lie well within the bounds of comprehensibility.

It is probably Khlebnikov's predilection for word creation and experimentation which has been seen as the main barrier to comprehension associated with his work. It is this which elicits such epithets as 'gibberish' to describe his discourse and which can convey 'the impression of mental malfeasance or quaint poetic quackery'.[73] Word experimentation is, however, only one aspect of many in an extensive and varied opus. Nor, when it does occur, does it automatically represent an insuperable barrier to comprehension. Khlebnikov was systematic and methodical in his linguistic experimentation and his neologisms and 'transrational language' testify not to a preoccupation with nonsense, but to a preoccupation with sense. The words of Tynyanov, written in the article prefacing the first volume (1928) of Khlebnikov's *Collected Works*, still hold true today: 'those who talk about the "nonsense" of Khlebnikov must re-examine this question' (SP I 26).

If there is a barrier to comprehension in Khlebnikov's linguistic experimentation, then it is not in the destruction of meaning, but in the creation of meanings, and in their multiplicity. His neologisms are, as Willem Weststeijn has noted, 'nearly always semantically motivated'.[74] Khlebnikov created hundreds of new words out of legitimate formants, combining them in manifold ways. Words such as *smekhach* (from *smekh* meaning laughter), *krylyshkuya* (from *krylo* meaning wing), *vremir', smertir', zharir'* (based on *snegir'* meaning bullfinch), *mogatyy* (from a combination of *moch'* – to be able and *bogatyy* – rich) do not destroy meaning, but enhance it. Moreover, Khlebnikov would even explain what he was trying to create. He writes, for example, that a government (*pravitel'stvo*) which seeks to please (*nravitsya*) could be called *nravitel'stvo* (SP V 232–3).

The problems of comprehension in a Khlebnikov text can derive not so much from the impenetrability of the linguistic strata, as from the difficulties which arise in the text's conceptual framework. Khlebnikov's coinages can result in the juxtaposition of disparate elements, in a kind of verbal synaesthesia. Take, for example, the neologism *vremir'*, where a suffix associated with a bird (*-ir'*) is combined with the abstract concept of time (*vremya*):

> Tam, gde zhili sviristeli,
> Gde kachalis' tikho eli,
> Proleteli, uleteli
> Staya lyogkikh vremirey. (NP 118)

(There, where lived the waxwings, where the fir trees quietly swayed, there flew by, there flew away light time-finches in a flock.)

The result is, as Ronald Vroon puts it, a 'time-finch',[75] which embodies time in its passage. The neologism is metaphoric.

A similar juxtaposition occurs in the word *vremysh*, which appears in Khlebnikov's early prose fragment 'Temptation of a Sinner' ('Iskusheniye greshnika'): 'i bylo ozero gde vmesto kamnya bylo vremya, a vmesto kamyshey shumeli vremyshi' (SP IV 19). *Vremysh* is obviously formed from *vremya* (time) and *kamysh* (reed); again the abstract and the concrete coalesce and produce what we might (rather inadequately) call a 'time-reed' ('and there was a lake where instead of stone there was time, and instead of reeds there rustled time-reeds'). In bringing together 'time' and 'reed' Khlebnikov has also made use of the additional association of stone (*kamen'*) as an intermediary. Moreover, the sound element in the word *kamen'* is echoed in both *vremya* and *kamysh*, uniting all three disparate words within the same conceptual framework. Not only does Khlebnikov create new meanings with neologisms; by juxtaposition he can also enrich the meaning of already existing words. Meaning exists in abundance in Khlebnikov's works; it is up to the uncomprehending reader to grasp it.

If one of the problems of comprehension in a Khlebnikov text is conceptual, then another is contextual. To be understood *vremysh* has to be seen within the context of *kamysh*. Indeed, to understand the full implications of Khlebnikov's 'time-reed', the whole context of the prose fragment in which it occurs has to be taken into account. Here we see the portrayal not so much of a landscape, as of a 'timescape', which also features a 'time cottage' (*vremataya izbushka*) and a path which seems to stretch into the fourth dimension, bearing the prints of 'days, evenings and mornings' (SP IV 19). Nor in Khlebnikov's poetic world is context limited to a single work. *Vremysh* and the juxtaposition of time and stone (with the sound element particularly stressed) also occur in the short poem 'Time-reeds' ('Vremyshi-kamyshi') (SP II 275).[76]

Although certain texts can be analysed fairly adequately on an internal textual level, a broader understanding can be achieved by an inter-textual approach, by recourse to other texts of Khlebnikov. Without such movement from the text itself to the structure of Khlebnikov's poetic world as a whole, various levels of meaning in his work will remain unpenetrated and indeed often impenetrable. The notion of the 'timescape' and the comparison of time and stone run through the whole of Khlebnikov's work (see, for example, SP III 62, V 165); the early manifestations of it in 'Temptation of a Sinner' and 'Time-reeds' should be seen in this context.

Very often even inter-textual analysis can prove insufficient and an adequate interpretation of Khlebnikov's works can only be found with recourse to an extra-textual level, to factors which lie beyond the texts themselves. This 'open' approach to Khlebnikov's works is one which has been espoused and used successfully by Henryk Baran, who has demonstrated for example the usefulness of consulting botanical literature to explain references and allusions to plants in Khlebnikov texts.[77] Khlebnikov, we should recall, had a keen interest in the natural world. Indeed, he saw it as one of his artistic tasks 'to sing of plants' (SP V 298). Baran has also pointed to the myths of the Siberian Oroche tribe as an important source for some of Khlebnikov's works and has thereby shed light on several previously unexplained references.[78]

Such approaches to analysis may be applicable to other writers, but in Khlebnikov's poetic world it is a question of extent. There is a high frequency in his work of references and allusions which can be better elucidated inter-textually or extra-textually. As Henryk Baran has explained, 'Khlebnikov uses images and themes drawn from widely differing spheres of human experience as "building blocks" in his works'; these images and themes are taken from 'diverse cultural texts with which the general reader is not, as a rule, familiar'. When these materials are applied 'the poet used unfamiliar proper names, fragments of archaic or primitive myths, references to obscure rituals, etc. to convey complex trains of thought'.[79]

There are also formal or compositional elements which contribute to the complexity of the Khlebnikovian discourse; for example, shifting narrative stances, large-scale ellipsis, unstable narrative chronology and mixing of time-scales. The 'montage' effect of some of Khlebnikov's works and their disjointed structure is distinctly reminiscent of the 'shifted' perspective in Cubist paintings.[80] Difficulties in comprehending the linguistic strata of his works are in comparison quite minor. However, the formal elements of Khlebnikov's works are not to be seen in isolation. There is no form for form's sake in Khlebnikov. The form of a work is closely bound up with its content.

Accepting that order and sense lie behind the Khlebnikovian complexity, many scholars are now of the opinion that much obscurity is due to a deliberately cryptic presentation by the poet of his texts. The nature of the analysis of a Khlebnikov text approximates therefore to an act of decoding, where allusions and unexplained terms have to be tracked down with recourse to internal and external factors. Henryk Baran, for example, has written frequently of Khlebnikov's creation of 'poetic riddles' and Khlebnikov's 'orientation towards *encoding*'.[81] Barbara Lönnqvist's stimulating study of the long poem 'Poet' prompted her to reach much the same conclusion. She talks of 'the creation of hidden meanings' and she also points to the considerable importance for Khlebnikov of the riddle, noting that 'the hidden word is what Khlebnikov cherishes most of all'.[82]

Khlebnikov himself documented this view in his theoretical writings. 'A word is particularly expressive (*zvuchit*)', he wrote, 'when a different "second sense" shines through it, when it serves as a glass cover for the vague secret which it encloses, and which is hidden behind it.' And he adds: 'Everyday meaning is just clothing for the secret.'[83] He echoes these opinions elsewhere when he writes: 'words are particularly strong when they have two meanings, when they are living eyes for a secret and a second meaning shines through the mica of everyday meaning' (SP v 269).

Khlebnikov also wrote of the 'double life' of the word with reference to the two vying principles of 'sound' and 'reason' or 'sound' and 'name' which the word contains. At one moment, he wrote, it is the fruit or the 'vegetables of reason' which the 'tree of words' provides, at another it is the 'verbal blossom'. 'This struggle of worlds,' he wrote, 'this struggle of two powers, which is always taking place in the word, gives rise to the double life of language' (SP v 222).

Given Khlebnikov's declared interest in hidden meanings and the duality of language, it is not surprising that his texts can appear 'puzzle-like'.[84] Barbara Lönnqvist sees a possible explanation for the complexity in the 'strongly autocommunicative nature of Khlebnikov's poetry'. She continues:

> The poet writes for himself and can therefore leave out contexts familiar to him. Words in this sort of communication tend to become signs for special personal contexts that are not expressed in the text: a word or even a letter can stand for an entire semantic complex.[85]

Personal contexts are not, however, an unexpected departure in literature, particularly in lyric verse and are by no means peculiar to Khlebnikov's opus. However, for Khlebnikov the element of the personal context goes far beyond the lyrical presentation to encompass allusions to whole areas of the poet's private thought, experience and knowledge, for which extra-textual information can be of some importance. Ornithology, botany, mathematics, mythology, the visual arts and many other of Khlebnikov's preoccupations enter his works in various contexts, bringing with them a host of unspecified meanings, which are not explained directly within the text. Khlebnikov once wrote and told Matyushin that he was 'rummaging about' in the Brockhaus encyclopaedia (NP 372). To shed light on some of Khlebnikov's allusions, the reader may well have to do the same.

The problems of autocommunication in poetry are complex,[86] though to talk of Khlebnikov 'writing for himself' is somewhat misleading. If by this it is meant that Khlebnikov had no intention of directing his word towards a reading public, then there is much evidence to the contrary. The very idea of the riddle or the ciphered text seems to presuppose a reader who will attempt to solve the problems which have been set. It should be noted, too, that the Russian Futurist movement of which Khlebnikov was a part was highly audience-conscious. Even though Khlebnikov remained somewhat aloof from the public face of the movement, his written work reveals distinct elements of a declamatory style. He was the author or co-author of various manifestoes and declarations, including one entitled 'To All! To All! To All!' ('Vsem! Vsem! Vsem!') (SP v 164), which clearly have external addressees in mind.

Lönnqvist seems closer to the mark when she writes: 'the text assumes the character of secret writing structured according to the principle "understanding is for the initiated"'.[87] The implications are clear; Khlebnikov does have an addressee in mind, but to achieve an understanding of his work the reader has to decipher the text before him and thus become 'initiated' into his poetic world. Barbara Lönnqvist's study also makes the valid point that 'the rebus-like quality of many of Khlebnikov's poems ... derives from a conscious, aesthetically motivated desire for complexity: art should be artful'.[88] One should recall in this context that the production of the 'difficult' text was one of the aims formulated in the *Word as Such* manifesto ('so that it is written with difficulty (*tugo*) and read with difficulty').[89] Similarly, Aleksey Kruchonykh wrote in his 'New Ways of the Word' ('Novyye puti slova') that whereas the 'sleek Symbolists' were terribly afraid of being misunderstood by the public, the Hylaean poets 'rejoiced' at this.[90]

The 'artful' element of Khlebnikov's encipherment is on occasions only too apparent. Take, for example, the poem 'Isfahan Camel' ('Ispaganskiy verblyud') which includes a complicated encoding by Khlebnikov of the name of a friend. Notably, the code is elucidated by Khlebnikov himself in a commentary which he appended to the poem (SP III 379).[91]

The need to decipher a text can, of course, relate to a much greater range of literature than just Khlebnikov. It is not without relevance for avant-garde or modernist writing as a whole. It also has deeper associations. For example, the concept of the initiate to secret writing carries with it the implications of myth and magic, both of which play a considerable role in Khlebnikov's poetic world. The encoded word can be fundamental for such writings. Within the secret word lies a power which is not open to all. The difficult text as a facet of magical or religious writing was something of which Khlebnikov was well aware (SP v 225).

Khlebnikov, however, was not solely an encoder. Much of his activity as a writer was aimed not at encipherment but at decipherment. 'Everyday meaning', for example, was just 'clothing' for the secret meaning which lay hidden behind it. It was the desire to decode this secret meaning which provided the motivation for many of Khlebnikov's linguistic theories, ranging from ideas on the internal declension of words to his belief in the semantic weight which should be attached to individual letters. These are theories which are aimed not at disguising but at interpreting the codes of linguistic phenomena

His mathematical work, which became a main area of activity towards the end of his life, is also an exercise in interpretation and decipherment. His manuscripts, both published and unpublished, are filled with a multitude of calculations and proofs in algebraic and numerical formulas. He was, in fact, attempting to decode one of the greatest secrets of all, the workings of time and fate. His attempts to interpret diverse phenomena and so to penetrate the hidden meaning, which he felt lay concealed behind them, brought together into a single whole the disparate disciplines of language and number:

In the life of each phenomenon there is its midday full of strength, its dawn and its dusk. Some phenomena last moments, others – centuries. There is a basic law in that the rise of a phenomenon occurs under the sign of '*dva*' (two) and the setting of a phenomenon, its evening, is constructed in the country of the number '*tri*' (three). It is once again necessary to stress that language as a part of nature knew of this. This can be seen in such words as *doroga* (road) – a way for large, strong movement and *tropa* (path) – a way for weak, impeded movement, where it is 'difficult' (*trudno*) to walk and movement is expended fruitlessly . . .

And so *trud* (difficulty) relates to the possessions of the number *tri*, but *delo* (deed) constructs its world under the sign of *dva*. This is the difference which lies at the basis of the words *den'* (day) and *ten'* (shade). Existence in the course of d-time and non-existence in the course of t-time.[92]

And so into verse:

Trata i trud i treniye,
Tekite iz ozera tri!
Delo i dar iz ozera dva! (SS III 498)

(Loss and difficulty and friction, flow from the lake of three! Deed and gift from the lake of two!)

The scientific decoder and the artistic encoder come together in the desire of the visionary to help the reader to see the hidden significance which lies not only behind the 'everyday meaning' of the word, but also behind the everyday events of the world.

IV

In his article prefacing the first volume of Khlebnikov's *Collected Works* Yury Tynyanov wrote that Khlebnikov was 'our only epic poet of the twentieth century' (SP I 24). Numerous other scholars and critics, including Roman Jakobson, have also attested to Khlebnikov's epic status.[93] The number of Khlebnikov's long poems (Markov estimates over 30) is obviously some indication of his epic scope.[94] Nonetheless, the epic nature of Khlebnikov's writing is no simple matter and in the opinion of the Soviet critic Duganov in Khlebnikov 'epic works not only do not predominate, but actually numerically even cede place to the lyric and the drama'.[95]

Such things are difficult to quantify, but Duganov goes on to make the valid point that Khlebnikov's diverse production of drama, prose and poetry presents as its chief feature not so much the predominance of the lyric or the epic genre as the *mixing* of genres and their consequent relativity within the body of his work as a whole.[96] Tynyanov, too, recognized this rather fluid nature of Khlebnikov's writing, when he pointed out that Khlebnikov's short lyric works would also 'enter the epos' (SP I 24). Indeed, Khlebnikov would introduce his own lyric works into an epic context in, for example, his development of the genre of the 'supertale' or 'transtale' (*sverkhpovest'/zapovest'*). This was a cycle of individual works, combined together to form a larger composite text. Within the 'supertale' lyric works can acquire epic qualities.

As Duganov has shown, this relativity of genres can have certain consequences in the representation of the poetic I. When the poetic I, which is generally associated with lyric verse, occurs within the context of a larger composite work, it is imbued with a 'more complex content, as though it is receiving an additional dimension'. The personal I of the poet can merge with what Duganov calls the 'extra-personal I of mankind'.[97] The result is a mixture of the epic and the lyric.

This fluid nature of the poetic I (evident also in the shifting of narrative stances) and the mixing of the epic and the lyric is a significant feature of Khlebnikov's work. Nor is it restricted to Khlebnikov's composite works. Khlebnikov's poetic I also seems to acquire epic status even within the framework of an individual short lyric poem. Take, for example, 'I and Russia' ('Ya i Rossiya'), where the poet discovers within himself a whole 'state' (*gosudarstvo*) of people (SP III 304);[98] and the similar transformation in 'I went out a youth alone' ('Ya vyshel yunoshey odin') (SP III 306).

There is also a tendency (reminiscent of Mayakovsky) for Khlebnikov's poetic I to develop epic proportions by a transformation into various 'culture heroes' and poetic *personae*.[99] Like many poets, Khlebnikov was not averse to donning the masks of popular mythological heroes such as Prometheus or Theseus. His poetic I could also achieve a certain epic objectivity in the guise of alter egos such as Zangezi. Moreover, as if to underline the potential of the personal lyric I to assume epic status, Khlebnikov would even appear in his work in the third person under his own name (see, for example, SP II 168, III 306, V 141). Given such a predilection, it is perhaps not surprising that in the presentation of the Khlebnikovian poetic *persona* the autobiographical context can on occasion play a considerable role.

The presence of the personal context in Khlebnikov's work has already been noted, and the elucidation of such contexts can provide valuable clues to his poetic ciphers.[100] Autobiographical elements seem to be particularly notable in texts associated with his visit to Iran. Perhaps the most prominent example is the long poem 'Gul-mullah's Trumpet' ('Truba Gul′-mully') in which the poetic I dominates more than in any other Khlebnikov long poem (SP I 233–45). Letters Khlebnikov wrote home during his visit show (SP V 319–22) that information contained in the poem reflects not only poetic, but also biographical, facts (his journey to Iran on the military transport vessel the 'Kursk', his reading of Kropotkin). Even his christening as a 'Russian dervish' is biographical as well as poetic. Indeed, one of the key presentations of the poetic *persona* in the poem is as a prophet figure.

Whole parts of the poem are given over to relating incidents which may well have an objective autobiographical basis. Vladimir Markov has even dubbed Khlebnikov's poem a 'poetic diary of his visit to Persia'.[101] However, although the factual nature of some of the events can be confirmed from other sources, these events are seen through the prism of Khlebnikov's poetic vision and as such undergo a certain metamorphosis. In spite of the realistic autobiographical framework, the poem is clearly much more than a diary. It serves also as a forum for an autobiographical and lyric presentation of the poetic *persona* to merge with a presentation which has objective and epic qualities. One of the early references to the poem's poetic hero is, for example, not in the first person but in the third, as 'Khlebnikov child' (*chado Khlebnikova*) (SP I 233). Moreover, as well as the presentation of the *persona* as prophet, at one point the authorial poetic hero also transmutes into another, more objective *persona*, that of the epic figure Stepan Razin, famed leader of the Russian seventeenth-century peasant revolt. The portrayal of the Khlebnikovian poetic *persona* can reveal considerable complexity.

A similar mix of the lyric, the epic and autobiographical can be found in the portrayal of Zangezi (who is presented as the author of Khlebnikov's own 'Boards of Fate' – SP III 322). This prophet figure is one of Khlebnikov's most notable poetic *personae* and fittingly the 'supertale' in which he features provides a platform for some of Khlebnikov's most important preoccupations. It provides a platform for his linguistic theories, for an exposition of the power of the word and an explanation of its hidden meaning; it provides a platform for his theories on time and prediction and for his attempts to decipher the hidden meaning behind everyday events; and it also highlights another significant preoccupation of Khlebnikov, the problem of conveying these ideas and theories to others. Khlebnikov was well aware that his discourse did not exist within a void. The 'supertale' *Zangezi* is also a comment by Khlebnikov on his difficulties in communicating with the crowd.

Interestingly, these three preoccupations are close to those singled out by Willem Weststeijn when he noted that 'concern for *humanity* and its *future* and concern for a new *language* are the core of Khlebnikov's work and are closely connected with each other'.[102] We do not, however, have to rely solely on a critic to make this point. Khlebnikov himself had reached a similar conclusion. The poetic hero in his 'autobiographical tale' (SP V 346) 'Ka^2' tells us that: '. . . three sieges occupied my brain. The tower of the crowds, the tower of time, the tower of the word' (SP V 132). Notably, this triad of concerns appears in a similar form in the related text 'The Scythian's Skullcap' ('Skuf'ya skifa'), where the poetic hero says: 'I recalled the words of the grey priest: "You have three sieges: the siege of time, of the word and of the multitudes"' (SP IV 82). These are the three 'towers' to which Khlebnikov wished to lay 'siege'.

2
The tower of the crowds

I

A poet whose chief reputation has resided in incomprehensibility and for whom the coded text has become something of a hallmark might not be expected to manifest a life-long preoccupation with the crowd. However, the difficult nature of Khlebnikov's text should not conceal from view a poet who demonstrated a constant awareness of the significance of the crowd, in particular with regard to the poet and his tasks.

Such a preoccupation is, of course, well within the Russian literary tradition. In the nineteenth century, there had been considerable debate about the relations between the poet and the crowd and about the relative merits of 'pure' and 'civic' poetry. Nikolay Nekrasov, a keen advocate of the engaged 'civic' verse, summed up the conflict in the memorable lines – 'a poet you may not be, but to be a citizen you have an obligation'.[1] It is doubtful whether Khlebnikov would have posed the problem in such terms, but if Nekrasov 'devoted his lyre' to the Russian people (*narod*), and listened to their songs,[2] then there is something of this in Khlebnikov's work too.

Khlebnikov was by no means a large-scale imitator of folk art, but it certainly had some influence on his work. It was, for example, in folklore that he found an important thematic source for his creativity. The language of folklore has also been seen as relevant for his neologistic activity.[3] One of Khlebnikov's earliest extant pieces of verse (NP 244) is an imitation of a folkloric form; and Vladimir Markov points to one of Khlebnikov's late works, 'Washerwoman' ('Prachka') as still demonstrating a debt to popular forms with its use of *rayoshnik* verse (used by street traders) and the *chastushka* (from urban folklore).[4] Notably, this folkloric aspect of Khlebnikov's work may have contributed towards his rift with the 'Academy of Verse' and the writers grouped around the journal

Apollon. Nikolay Khardzhiev has written that the innovative tendencies in Khlebnikov's early work orientated towards non-canonical folkloric forms encountered a 'hostile' reception (NP 419). Khlebnikov himself has recorded the 'Academy's' rather ironic response to his use of such forms (NP 200).

Khlebnikov's satirical writings contain some sharp edges in their portraits of the capital's *literati*, though they do not particularly clarify the conflict which arose. Of some significance then is the pamphlet *Teacher and Pupil* written in the aftermath of Khlebnikov's rift with St Petersburg's distinguished literary circles. The second half of this pamphlet constitutes an attack on certain established writers (not all connected closely with *Apollon*), and it accuses them of various sins. The pamphlet, however, is not entirely negative. Khlebnikov contrasts the unsavoury concerns of these established writers with the positive attributes of folk art. The only literary creator which he sees in a consistently favourable light is the 'people' (*narod*).

Khlebnikov formulates his ideas in the form of tables, where aspects of popular art are juxtaposed with the preoccupations of contemporary literary figures:

'In our life there is horror'. I
'In our life there is beauty'. II

Demonstrates:	II	I
Artsybashev		+
Merezhkovsky		+
Andreyev		+
Kuprin		+
Remizov (insect)		+
Sologub		+
Folk song	+	

Consequently, writers are unanimous that Russian life is horror. But why is the folk song not in agreement with them?
Or are those who write books and those who sing Russian songs two different peoples?[5] (SP v 179–80)

Folk art is thus considered by Khlebnikov as having positive aesthetic qualities ('beauty' as opposed to 'horror') which were lacking in the art of some contemporary writers. When Khlebnikov abandoned the 'ivory tower' of the 'Academy of Verse', he appears to have chosen to align himself instead with the 'tower of the crowds'. However, the pamphlet does not only see folk art in aesthetic terms. Further explanatory tables give an indication of the positive ethical and ideological qualities which popular art possessed. According to Khlebnikov, it advocated 'life' instead of 'death' (SP v 180–1). This was clearly a reaction to the rather morbid preoccupations then prevalent in some contemporary literature. Artsybashev, one of those criticized by Khlebnikov, enjoyed a certain notoriety in this regard; and Khlebnikov styles the Symbolist writer Sologub here as a 'gravedigger' (SP v 180). It is in this context too that one might see Khlebnikov's notorious 'Incantation by Laughter'. Khlebnikov, who saw his fellow-writers 'cursing' the past, the present and the future (SP v 180–1), was issuing a different sort of invocation. The folk song was also regarded by Khlebnikov as being representative of patriotic sentiments, whereas 'writers' were firmly in the camp of 'non-Russia' (SP v 181). Khlebnikov's espousal of the art of the people was a manifestation of his opposition to the pro-western orientation of much of the literary elite.[6] Khlebnikov was propagating a national or Slavonic culture for which the 'folk song' (*narodnaya pesn'*) formed a basis.

It is this mixture of the ideological and the aesthetic which lies behind Khlebnikov's subsequent plan to 'expand' the frontiers of Russian and Slavonic literature.[7] Khlebnikov believed that there were lacunae in the literature which portrayed the popular heroes, the countries and the peoples of Slavdom. He saw it as his aesthetic task to fill in these gaps. In the intervals between the early rulers Ryurik and Vladimir or between Ivan the Terrible and Peter the Great it was as though the Russian people 'did not exist' for Russian literature, Khlebnikov wrote (NP 341). He sought to return Russian literature to its people. Basing his aesthetic outlook on popular art, Khlebnikov was at the same time fulfilling a literary mission for the people's benefit. His aesthetic relationship with the people was a two-way process.

Khlebnikov made a considerable attempt to implement this aesthetic programme and it provided the creative impulse for many of his works, ranging from the tale of the 'Slav' Emperor of Rome (NP 303–4) to the brief sketch of life in Montenegro.[8] And for Khlebnikov the frontiers of Russian and Slavonic literature stretched not only westwards into Poland and the Balkans but also looked eastwards towards India and felt the influence of the Persian and Mongol peoples (NP 341). These eastern countries are also portrayed in Khlebnikov's works (see, for example, 'Yesir' – SP IV 87–104).

It is in a formulation of this aesthetic programme, contained in a letter to Kruchonykh, that Khlebnikov again refers to the importance of the people for his own creative work. He regarded one of his artistic tasks as:

> To consult the dictionaries of the Slavs, the Montenegrins and others – the collation of the Russian language is not finished – and to choose many fine words, precisely those which are fine. One of the secrets of creative work is to see before oneself the people (*narod*) for whom one is writing, and to find a place for words on the axes (*osi*) of this people's life . . . (SP V 298)

Khlebnikov's linguistic activities have clear ties with his aesthetic programme.

It is of note that the propagation of his notion to expand the boundaries of Russian literature also afforded Khlebnikov an opportunity to write as a publicist and to appear before a wide readership. Far from 'writing for himself', it was texts relevant to these concerns which he published in 1913 in the newspaper *Slavyanin*, which espoused 'the spiritual, political and economic rapprochement of the Slavs'.[9] At the same time, some of Khlebnikov's verse also had a publicistic strain. Exhortations propagating a similar ideological line were directed outwards, towards a public (SP II 15, 23).

The significance of the *narod* (people) for Khlebnikov's writing can, however, be traced back to much earlier times. This is admirably demonstrated by Khlebnikov's 'dedication to the Russian peasantry' said to have been written as early as 1904. In it Khlebnikov wrote, in part:

> If there are those to whom I should ascribe a great and decisive role in my work, then it is those people with insignificant, somewhat weary, but always good and honest faces, who are bent over from their labours and deprivations . . . It is these, the Russian peasants . . . whom I consider to be my chief collaborators, and to whom I am exceptionally obliged in my work, for it is they who ploughed the earth for me, who sowed and baked the bread, they who brought it to me, whereas I just sat, doing nothing, except for eating the bread which they had baked . . . It is to them that I devote this work, as an inadequate testimony to the duty which weighs upon me.[10]

The actual work which bore this dedication has not, apparently, been preserved, but this eulogy of the Russian peasantry betrays considerable strength of feeling. It smacks of *narodnichestvo* (populism). In this dedication we can not only see an important early motivating factor for Khlebnikov's writing, but also gauge something of the sense of moral responsibility which he felt towards the simple people. The image of the people portrayed again suggests strong ethical overtones; the peasants have 'good and honest faces' and are selfless in their toil.

There is also something else present, however. While the author admires the peasants and feels sufficiently enamoured of their qualities to dedicate his work to them, he is, nonetheless, not one of them. There is a gap between the poet and the people which has to be bridged. Evidently, Khlebnikov's subsequent rejection of the western-orientated culture of his own literary class and his espousal of the cause of Slavonic folk culture should be seen as a step in this direction.

It is a step which can be seen against the background of the Futurist movement as a whole, in which the rejection of established literary values played a fundamental part. Vahan Barooshian summed up the negative attitude of the emerging Futurists to the established Symbolist writers as a desire 'to react against what they considered the lifeless and abstract language of the Symbolists and to reorient language to that of the street and daily life, to democratize poetry'.[11] This was certainly an important element of Mayakovsky's verse, and can be seen in the work of Kamensky and David Burliuk.[12]

Khlebnikov's aesthetics should also be seen in this context. He saw the existing literary elite as the purveyors of an alien culture in an alien tongue while the Russian earth cried out for lips with which to speak:

> And shall we remain deaf to the voice of the earth: give me lips! give me lips! Or shall we just carry on parroting western voices? (NP 323)

This article, written as early as the end of 1908 (six years before the writhings of Mayakovsky's 'voiceless street'),[13] also portrays Russia's 'dear lips' as being enchanted by the 'evil will of neighbouring islands' (NP 322).

In Khlebnikov's view the literary establishment propagated an art which was hostile to Russia, whereas the genuine 'art of the word' stemmed from nature, which had its base in the very 'soul of the people'.

. . . art is not enduring the cruel power of hostility towards Russia; a terrible icy wind of hate is blighting its plant.

. . . the freedom of the art of the word has always been limited by truths, each of which is a detail of life. These limits reside in the fact that nature, out of which the art of the word erects its palaces, is the soul of the people (*dusha naroda*). (NP 334)

While the Symbolists paid homage to the lofty figure of the eternal feminine, Khlebnikov's muse was distinctly more down to earth:

. . . 'Moya Muza bol'she promyshlyala izvozom
Iz zapada skital'tsev na vostok,
I yeyo nikto ne izoblichil v pochtyonnom zanyat'i vora.
Vprochem, ona inogda ne boyalas' navozom
Tyoplym zapachkat' odeyaniya bednyy tsvetok
Ili niz plat'ya, mimo skotnogo prokhodya dvora.' (NP 198)

(. . . 'My muse has made its living in the main by ferrying wanderers from west to east, and no one has accused her of the thief's honourable trade: she has, however, at times not been afraid to stain the poor flower of her attire or dress's hem on the farm yard's warm dung, as she passes.')

In this poem, which satirizes Ivanov's 'tower', the Symbolist vision of the beautiful lady is replaced by the portrayal of a coachwoman, not concerned at staining her dress with animal dung. It would seem, moreover, that an anti-westernist stance is again emphasized in the activity of this muse figure. Is she not engaged in ferrying the errant Symbolists back to the aesthetic wholeness of their own eastern soil?

In the context of Khlebnikov's 'populist' approach it was quite natural that he should support the popular revolt which erupted in Russia in 1917. The social and political democratization which the revolution had as its aim mirrored the aesthetic democratization which was associated with the Cubo-Futurist movement. Works with a populist frame of reference were firmly on the agenda of Russian literature and Khlebnikov did not have to sacrifice aesthetic principles to comply with this. His own work and the *narodnaya pesn'* were in one and the same camp. Blending his own voice with that of the 'washerwoman' and the 'voices from the street' he produced paeans to popular revolt:

Eto vremya kulachnykh boyov
Grudi narodnoy i svintsovoy puli.
Slyshite dikiy, beshenyy ryov:
Lyudi prosnulis'. (SP III 276)

(This is the time of fist fights between the people's breast and the lead bullet. Can you not hear the wild, furious roar: the people are awake.)

Khlebnikov's publicistic work was now connected with the revolutionary cause. This is reflected in his involvement with various Bolshevik propaganda organizations, for whom he produced work directed towards a broad public. He issued revolutionary exhortations; he wrote some captions for posters; he was even the author of verse appealing for food for the drought-stricken Volga region.[14]

The revolution certainly contributed towards an internationalist dimension in Khlebnikov's 'populist' concerns, though the term *narod* continues to feature prominently in his post-revolutionary writings.[15] One exhortation, for example, proclaims the *narod* as the future sovereign (SP II 253). Elsewhere, Khlebnikov's 'voices from the street' portray the *narod* as exacting its retribution like a 'butcher without restraint' (SP III 275). The 'washerwoman', in the poem of the same name, is described as a 'daughter of the people' (*doch' naroda*) (SP III 242) and her exhortations to revolutionary violence betray a considerable vehemence:

On, krasavets, dlinnyy nozh,
V serdtse barina khorosh!
Nozhom vas podchuyu
Prostaya devka:
Ya prachka, chornorabochaya!
Ay khorosh, ay khorosh!
Nozh. (SP III 233)

(He's a handsome fellow, the long knife, in the heart of the master just right! A simple girl I'll treat you to a knife: I am a washerwoman, an ordinary working girl! Just right, just right, the knife.)

The revolution may have brought another aspect of the people to the fore – the proletarian worker in whose name the Bolsheviks had taken power – but for Khlebnikov the revolutionary masses were seen mainly in terms of the poor and the unskilled, the beggars and the prostitutes, the capital's *Lumpenproletariat*. Nevertheless, he did make some attempts to develop proletarian themes in his work (see, for example, SP III 89–92).

The relationship between the poet and the crowd was now of some significance and Khlebnikov's writings reveal that he was not left untouched by the debates which surfaced in the revolution's aftermath. In particular, one untitled fragmentary article, written, according to Stepanov, in 1919–20, reads in part as follows:

It is said that the creators of songs of labour can only be the people <working> at the bench. Is this really so? Does not the nature of the song lie in a <departure> from oneself, from one's everyday axis? . . .
Inspiration has always <been a traitor to> the origins of the singer. Mediaeval knights sing of primitive shepherds, Lord Byron – of pirates, and that son of a tsar Buddha . . . glorifies poverty. Looking at it another way, Shakespeare, who was tried for theft, speaks in the language of kings, as does that son of a modest townsman Goethe, and their creative work is devoted to court life . . . Creative work, understood as the greatest declination of the string of thought from the life axis of the one who creates and as a flight from oneself, forces one to think that the songs of the workbench too will be created not by those who do the work, but by those who are outside the factory walls. (SP v 226–7)

This was almost certainly written in connection with the debates of the time which arose over the hegemony of revolutionary art, especially between the Futurists and the *Proletkul't*. Futurism took on a new lease of life after the revolution and acquired many new shades of meaning in rapidly changing circumstances. In short, the post-revolutionary Futurists saw Futurism as 'the most advanced art of the time, and therefore the only art worthy of and consonant with the proletariat'.[16] On the contrary, the *Proletkul't* believed that only proletarian writers could produce a true proletarian art.

Khlebnikov was away from the main centres of Russia (Moscow and Petrograd) for much of the post-revolutionary period and was therefore only on the periphery of the Futurist activities of this time. He will, however, have been associated in the public's mind with the Futurist movement. Whether he found himself drawn into the debates at the *Proletkul't* conference he attended in Armavir in September 1920 is not known, but, effectively, since he was by no means proletarian, his ability to create the new art of the people was under challenge. His theory of art as a 'flight from oneself' (*begstvo ot sebya*) is his response.

It is a spirited defence. Just because he is not a worker, he argues, does not mean that he cannot be a 'creator of songs of labour'; on the contrary, he says, it is a prerequisite for a producer of such songs that he does *not* belong to that class of people about whom his songs tell. Creation, Khlebnikov contends, involves a movement away from one's origins, and he suggests that the new art will be created by those 'outside the factory walls'.

It is difficult to imagine Khlebnikov as a true 'bard' of the proletariat, though in a sense some of his revolutionary poems are a vindication of his ability to make that 'flight' from himself which he felt was essential for inspiration. Khlebnikov became in his own right a chronicler of the popular uprising in those revolutionary years. It might be argued that this ability came rather from a closer contact with the people during that period.[17] But it is not the contact which Khlebnikov stresses here, so much as the separation. In his terms it seems to have been possible 'to see before oneself the people for whom one is writing', but yet stay detached 'outside the factory walls'. For Khlebnikov the identity of the poet here is distinct from that of the crowd.

The separation of the poet from the proletariat compares with the earlier separation of the poet from the peasantry. The classes of people have changed, but the distance of the poet is still apparent. It is a position which does not seem to offer the best formula for a harmonious relationship.

II

Given Khlebnikov's preoccupation with the crowd, it is not surprising to find the relationship reflected in his creative works and manifestoes. The paradigms of relations between poet and crowd which these works reveal can tell us a good deal more about how Khlebnikov viewed the relationship. They are worth dwelling on, at least in some detail.

Notably, an example of one such paradigm can be found in one of Khlebnikov's earliest known published texts, a youthful short prose sketch which begins with the words 'There was darkness . . .' ('Byla t′ma . . .'). This sketch tells of a 'black darkness', in which 'plain sticky beings, indistinguishable from the earth', live out their 'insignificant, tedious, quiet lives'. However, Khlebnikov writes:

> . . . in the same darkness there was one firefly, and he thought: 'what is better: to crawl around for a long time in the dark and in an unheard life, or to burn just once in a white flame, to fly like a white spark, to sing in a white song of another life, not of black gloom, but of the play and the streams of white light'. (NP 280)

The creatures portrayed have no conception of anything better than the dreary life which they lead. However, the firefly which lives among them is not only capable of perceiving 'another life', but, like a poet, longs to 'sing' of this life and thereby illumine the darkness in which the others exist. The firefly in the tale accomplishes this, and flies 'like a white spark in the black darkness', but as a consequence falls to earth dying with wings and legs burnt in the flames. Nevertheless, this heroic act, the tale tells us, awakens in the other creatures a 'yearning for light', and the memory of the dead firefly becomes an object of reverence.

While Khlebnikov's interest in natural history probably contributed to the choice of subject matter, it is obviously not just a story of insect life. The tale is allegorical and has clear implications for the relationship between the poet and the crowd. By 'singing his song', the firefly performs an individual act of sacrifice, which illumines the darkness of the unfortunate multitude and communicates to it a vision of a better life. The poetic hero is distinct from the other creatures, but is also a benefactor to them. Significantly, this theme of heroic sacrifice to provide relief for the suffering multitude occurs in another of Khlebnikov's early works. In 'Song of the Glooms' ('Pesn′ mrakov') two youths decide to die with others 'for the good of many' (NP 281).

The notion of the poetic hero as provider of light or as one who points the way towards it is present in many Khlebnikov texts. There are other early works, for example, which feature poetic *personae* with powers of illumination (SP II 266, 270). The warlike pan-Slav exhortation 'Battlesong' ('Boyevaya') urges the Slav people to go 'westwards, following the path of the sun' (SP II 23). Similarly, a later revolutionary exhortation, entitled 'Liberty for All' ('Volya vsem'), calls on people to hasten 'towards the sun and songs'.[18] Khlebnikov's unpublished proclamation, 'Indo-Russian Alliance' ('Indo-russkiy soyuz'), which calls for the 'wresting of India from the clutches of Great Britain',[19] includes the following proposition:

> We are lighting a lamp. Peoples of Asia, send your best sons to support the flame which has been lit. We are convening a congress of oppressed peoples . . .[20]

The bringer of light is also a bringer of liberty. Recalling 'There was darkness . . . ', the protagonists of this proclamation are also willing to consider self-sacrifice to advance their cause.

Interestingly, as well as portraying his *personae* as bringers of light and liberty, Khlebnikov also came to have the notion of the poet as a bringer of happiness to the crowd. In January 1922 he wrote an afterword for a book of verse by the artist Fyodor Bogorodsky, which begins:

> Creative work is the spark between the singer's surplus happiness and the unhappiness of the crowd.
> Creative work is the difference between someone's happiness and the general unhappiness. (SP v 260)

This again recalls the firefly in 'There was darkness . . .', which (over 15 years before) had flown 'like a white spark'. The spark is the act of creation, which momentarily bridges the gap between the poet and the crowd.

On occasion, the liberating mission of the Khlebnikovian poetic hero is associated with Khlebnikov's own attempts to determine the 'laws' of time and fate. For example, in 'Children of the Otter' ('Deti vydry') the crowds appeal to a select band of Futurists (*budetlyane*), who are armed with Khlebnikov's mathematical equations, to return peace to the world (SP II 165). Similarly, Zangezi, (who wears on his wrist the 'watch of mankind'), hopes, by means of Khlebnikov's theories of language and time, to be able to remove from the people the 'fetters of words' and to free them from the 'chains of their ancestors' (SP III 333). The hero of 'Storming of the Universe' ('Vlom vselennoy') attacks the 'skull of the universe' in order to seize the levers of fate and bring 'salvation to the people' (SP III 99). The benevolence which the Khlebnikovian poetic hero can provide for the crowd acquires cosmic proportions and the eminence of the poetic hero has to match the task in hand.

A characteristic example can be seen in the 'War in a Mousetrap' ('Voyna v myshelovke') cycle of poems, where Khlebnikov's poetic I is portrayed as carrying the whole of the earth on a ring on the little finger of his right hand (SP II 256–7). There is a tendency for the Khlebnikovian poetic hero to aspire to or to assume godhead. Khlebnikov's exhortatory poem 'Liberty for All' even considers bestowing freedom upon the gods: 'And if the gods are in chains, we shall give liberty to them too' (SP III 150).

One particular *persona* adopted by Khlebnikov which combines both the divine aspirations of the poetic hero and the altruistic nature of his enterprise is that of Prometheus, who stole fire from the gods in order to benefit mankind. Parts of 'Children of the Otter' demonstrate a particular reliance upon this ancient myth. The Promethean figure in this work (associated, moreover, with Khlebnikov's own name) utters the following words:

Ya, rastrogannyy, soshol
I zazhog ognyom doliny,
Zashatav nebes prestol.
Pust' znayet staryy vlastelin,
Chto s nimi ya – det'mi dolin. (SP II 168)

(Moved, I descended and set the valleys aflame, rocking heaven's throne. Let the old sovereign know that I am with them – the children of the valleys.)

In this portrayal theomachism is supplemented by an espousal of the popular cause; the hero's alliance is with the 'children of the valleys'. The altruism of Prometheus as a Khlebnikovian poetic hero is confirmed elsewhere when Khlebnikov refers to him as 'zashchityaz' cheloveka' ('protector of man') (SS III 393).[21]

However, in spite of the generally benevolent attitude of the Khlebnikovian poetic hero towards the crowd, the eminence of this hero can be matched by a correspondingly lowly presentation of the people. In one late lyric, for example, the poetic I merits the epithet 'great', whereas those who are allegedly his concern are described as 'poor and destitute in mind' (SP V 111). The juxtaposition is even more pronounced in 'War in a Mousetrap':

Ya, chtoby bol'she i dal'she khokhotat',
Ves' rod lyudey slomal, kak korobku spichek,
I nachal stikhi chitat'. (SP II 244)

(I, in order to laugh harder and longer, crushed the whole race of people like a matchbox, and began to read verses.)

This modifies somewhat the notion of poetic hero as benefactor.

Evidence of a rather unsympathetic portrayal of mankind can also be seen in the depiction of humanity at the mercy of the various monsters which inhabit Khlebnikov's poetic world. There is, for example, the giant bird in 'Crane' ('Zhuravl''), before which mankind is but a helpless 'trifle' (*pustyak*). The narrator in the poem laments that humanity has been but 'pulp, in which alien seeds ripened' (SP I 77). There is even a tendency to depict man in terms of passive domestic animals. Ka's 'friend' in the tale 'Ka' speaks of writing a book of 'people-breeding, while flocks of fine-fleeced people wandered around' (SP IV 48).

In the unpublished 'Union of Asia' ('Azosoyuz') manifesto, which purports to be the founding document of a union of the Asian peoples, Khlebnikov's attitude is quite dictatorial. He writes:

> Silence is the basic principle in relations between people. People can speak to each other when they have something to say.[22]

Nor does the declaration limit itself to trying to eradicate flippant utterances, it also issues strict sartorial guidelines:

> Man must be dressed lightly and simply. Man cannot be free internally if he is restricted by external conditions.[23]

Moreover, if the crowd has any doubt about the right of Khlebnikov to promulgate such edicts, among other unpublished writings he has provided us with evidence of his own birthright:

> Ya, Khlebnikov, 1885,
> Za (365+1)3 do menya
> Shankar'ya Achariya tvorets Ved
> V 788 godu.
> Za 365.9 do menya
> V 1400 Amenkhotep IV.
> Vot pochemu ya velik.
> Ya, begayushchiy po derevu chisel,
> Delayas' to morem to bozhestvom,
> To steblem travy v ustakh myshi.
> Amenkhotep IV – Yevklid – Achar'ya – Khlebnikov.[24]

(I, Khlebnikov, 1885, (365+1)3 before me Śaṅkarācārya creator of the Vedas in 788. And 365.9 before me in 1400 BC Amenhotep IV. That is why I am great. I, running along the tree of numbers, becoming now the sea, now divinity, now a blade of grass in the mouth of a mouse. Amenhotep IV – Euclid – Śaṅkarācārya – Khlebnikov.)

It is a fascinating example of a Khlebnikovian numerological poem. The pedigree which Khlebnikov establishes for himself is based on his own calculations concerning the laws which he believed governed the births of eminent people. Here he sees himself as continuing the traditions of the Indian philosopher Śaṅkara, the Egyptian pharoah Amenhotep IV and the ancient mathematician Euclid.

One work which reflects many of the elements of the relationship between the poet and the crowd is Khlebnikov's 1917 'Proclamation of the Chairmen of the Terrestrial Globe' ('Vozzvaniye predsedateley zemnogo shara') (SP III 17–23). Inspired, no doubt, by the February revolution, this work proclaims the takeover of the globe by Khlebnikov's prospective world government. It constitutes an attack on the frontiers which divide the world and on the 'states of the past'; it is a declaration of a *coup d'état* in defence of the people, who are being consumed by these states in their senseless wars. Yet in spite of these altruistic motives and in spite of the use of the French Revolution's motto ('liberty, fraternity, equality'), the portrayal of these Khlebnikovian rulers also reveals a self-laudatory stance and an attitude towards the people which is by no means flattering. Characteristically for Khlebnikov, these new world leaders aspire to divinity with smiles 'like gods'; they talk of their 'right of occupation' and refer to themselves as 'shepherds of people and mankind', whose 'flocks' can be rounded up at the sound of horns. With distinct Promethean overtones, mankind is also portrayed as 'moist clay' which can be fired in their kilns. Towns will be renamed in honour of them, the proclamation says, and the 'corpulent crowds of humanity' will follow in their tracks.

Nevertheless, this condescending attitude towards the people is tempered by the declaration's concluding lines. These read, in part,

> Comrade-workers! Don't complain about us: Like worker-architects, we tread along a special path towards a common goal. We are a special type of weapon.[25] (SP III 23)

It is a statement which confirms the separation from the crowd which the eminence of the poetic heroes entails. Khlebnikov's 'worker-architects' may share a common aim with the 'comrade-workers', but they are proceeding along their own special path. It is a statement which, however, also deflates somewhat the elevated status that the heroes have been given, since their plea to the workers not to complain about them is evidence of a certain lack of self-reliance. In spite of their 'supreme force' (SP III 21), these rulers must still look to the support of at least some of the subjects in their domain.

To counterbalance the grandiloquent claims of his 'rulers', Khlebnikov actually reveals in this work that the response of some of the crowd could be less than favourable. Having mounted the 'block' of themselves and their own names, the 'chairmen' proclaim their rule 'amid a sea of ... malicious eyes'. Some of the crowd acknowledge their divine status and revere them as 'saintly' (*svyatyye*); others, however, record their displeasure, calling the new self-styled rulers 'insolent fellows' (*nagletsy*).[26]

This dialogue between the Khlebnikovian poetic hero and the crowd receives further development in *Zangezi.* Here the reaction of the people is also portrayed as being mixed. At one point those who believe in Zangezi demonstrate great servility. 'We are the floor', they tell him, 'step upon our souls.' And they continue: 'We are believers, we await. Our eyes, our souls are the floor beneath your feet ...' (SP III 324). Yet at the same time the contemptuous attitude towards Zangezi of the non-believers is of unprecedented proportions. He is endowed with the epithets 'country bumpkin' (*lesnoy durak*) and 'crank' (*chudak*) (SP III 321–2) and his masculinity is called into question (SP III 322, 324). He is continually taunted about his linguistic and mathematical theories and when he gives the crowd a taste of some Khlebnikovian 'sound-painting' (*zvukopis'*) there is even a call for him to be burnt (SP III 345).

The contrasting adulation and abuse on the part of the crowd is reflected in the dual presentation of Zangezi himself, who combines the customary self-assertion of the poetic hero with traits of self-effacement. He refers to himself, for example, as 'great' or proclaims himself 'bozhestvar'' (a neologism meaning one who has the power to bestow divinity) (SP III 343–4).[27] Yet at the same time he can appear in the guise of a butterfly helplessly beating its wings against the window pane of human life (SP III 324). And although he can commune with his crowd with an incantatory force sufficient to frighten away the gods (SP III 339), he is nonetheless still a solitary figure (*odinok*) (SP III 343).

The elevated status of the poetic hero can be transformed from a position of power to one of isolation and rejection. In the poem 'Child!' ('Detusya!'), for example, the poetic I is no longer a leader of men, but a priestly outcast who laments his fate:

Mnogo mne zla prichinyali
Za to chto ne etot,
Vsegda ne lyudim,
Vezde ne lyubim. (SP III 149)

(They caused me much harm for not being of this world, always solitary, everywhere unloved.)

Nor is it simply a case of the poetic hero being spurned by others. The rejection can be reciprocated. In a short lyric poem, appropriately entitled 'Rejection' ('Otkaz') (SP III 297), Khlebnikov's poetic *persona* specifically rejects the role of 'ruler' to which it previously aspired. The poem reflects Khlebnikov's concern at the slaughter in the civil war and reveals a poetic I who would rather commune with nature than be instrumental in the killing which then predominated in human affairs.

The contradictory elements of self-assertion and self-effacement are also evident in the complex presentation of the poetic *persona* in 'Gul-mullah's Trumpet'. On the one hand Khlebnikov, as we have seen, invoked the figure of the rebel leader Razin, yet on the other hand he is also a 'priest of flowers' (SP I 245) happier sharing his food with a dog than with people (SP I 241).

There is even a certain Khlebnikovian legitimacy in this 'seesaw' of roles which the poetic hero adopts. Khlebnikov also seems to have related it to his 'discoveries' in the 'laws of time', which, he thought, every so often dictated a change of fortunes. He called it the 'law of the seesaw' (*zakon kacheley*).[28] This can be seen in the previously cited 'birthright' poem, where the poetic I runs along the 'tree of numbers', becoming in turn 'divinity', 'sea' (associated with the 'people' elsewhere in Khlebnikov's work), and 'a blade of grass in the mouth of a mouse'.[29] It can also be seen in 'War in a Mousetrap' in the ease with which a poetic I can change from a 'king' into a 'wild and frightened rabbit' (SP II 246); there is a similar contrast elsewhere, where the poetic I is described as 'now like a beggar, now like a tsar' (SP V 116).[30]

The status of the Khlebnikovian poetic *persona* thus moves through various permutations. The reverence of people can be replaced by hostility; and the poetic hero can be reduced from leader of men to outcast. This array of contradictory images can be seen further in the following lines:[31]

Vshi tupo molilisya mne,
Kazhdoye utro polzli po odezhde,
Kazhdoye utro ya kaznil ikh,
Slushaya treski,
No oni poyavlyalis′ vnov′ spokoynym priboyem.
Moy belyy bozhestvennyy mozg
Ya otdal, Rossiya, tebe:
Bud′ mnoyu, bud′ Khlebnikovym.
Svai vbival v um naroda i osi,

Sdelal ya svaynuyu khatu
'My budetlyane'.
Vsyo eto delal kak nishchiy,
Kak vor, vsyudu proklyatyy lyud'mi. (SP v 72)

(Lice offered up blind prayers to me, each morning they crawled across my clothes, each morning I executed them, listening to them crunch, but they kept on breaking over me in calm waves. My white divine brain I have given up to you, Russia: be me, be Khlebnikov. I have driven piles into the mind of the people, axis lines too, I made the 'We Futurists' hut on piles. I did all this as a beggar, as a thief, everywhere cursed by people.)

Images of the poetic hero's godlike stature are set here against images of his beggarly status. The poetic hero is initially portrayed as an object of worship and an arbiter of life and death. He exercises this power, however, not over the human inhabitants of the terrestrial globe, but over the lice which inhabit his body, and he is not even able to keep these creatures at bay. Subsequently, the poetic hero's brain is described as 'divine', but his sacrificial act of surrendering this divinity to Russia is not so much self-effacing as self-enhancing. It becomes an act of 'self-mythologization', an invocation to the poetic I's own exalted personage. Russia is told to 'be Khlebnikov'. Moreover, although the poetic hero claims to have built his Futurist household aloft upon piles driven into the 'people's mind', this image of popular foundations is countered by the final images of rejection and isolation. The 'divine' poetic hero has performed all his tasks 'as a beggar, as a thief, everywhere cursed by people'. Exalted or cursed, king or beggar, Khlebnikov's poetic *persona* is separated from the crowd which surrounds it.

III

The exaltation of Khlebnikov's own name in his work means that we are dealing not only with possible autobiographical contexts (we know, for example, that Khlebnikov was suffering from lice at about the same time as he wrote the 'lice' poem),[32] but also with an 'automythical' context. This is an aspect which is characteristic of his work and which can be seen in his many declarations and proclamations, where reality, fiction and fantasy intermingle, and the boundaries between real and imaginary worlds become rather blurred. One example has already been seen in the 'chairmen of the terrestrial globe' proclamation, in which Khlebnikov's notions of establishing a world government achieve 'poetic' fulfilment. This proclamation at least had a collective hero (reflecting the literary manifestoes of the time), though Nikolay Khardzhiev maintains that Khlebnikov was its sole author.[33] Elsewhere, however, Khlebnikov could elevate his poetic *persona* individually to the position of 'chief of the terrestrial globe' (SP v 139–41); and this self-styled leader of mankind could also sign one of his edicts as 'king of time Velimir I' (SP v 153).[34]

This self-assertion was not merely a facet of Khlebnikov's egocentricity. In many ways he was only following the lead of his Cubo-Futurist colleagues, who at the end of 1915 had pronounced him not only 'king of poetry' but also 'king of time' (SP v 333). Since Khlebnikov was frequently being proclaimed a genius by some of his fellow writers (a fact which Khlebnikov himself proudly noted – NP 353) it is not surprising that he developed a certain sense of self-importance. However, while for Khlebnikov's literary associates his 'coronation' as 'king of time' may have been a playful masquerade, for Khlebnikov the enterprise of controlling time and destiny had been embarked upon in some earnest. What for some was clearly an 'imaginary' world, could be for Khlebnikov very 'real' indeed.

The whole question of the 'real' or 'imaginary' nature of the Khlebnikovian *persona* is made even more complex by his adoption of pseudonyms. The name Velimir, bestowed upon him in 1909 at the gatherings of Ivanov's literary salon, was clearly more than a *nom de plume.* As well as its Slavonic element (as opposed to the Latin-based Viktor), it also contained important semantic aspects; *velet'* means to order, *mir* means world and the prefix *veli-* is associated with 'greatness'. But Velimir was not the only name which Khlebnikov used. His pseudonyms were numerous and varied and some may well have been geared towards specific types of writing.[35]

If the eminence of the hero in Khlebnikov's poetic world could go unwanted and unrecognized by the crowd, the same could also be true for Khlebnikov the poet in the real world. The Cubo-Futurists' espousal of Khlebnikov as their poetic genius was accompanied by an adverse public reaction. Burliuk's lectures on 'Pushkin and Khlebnikov', we are told, 'evoked fierce attacks on the part of the "yellow" press of the capital and the provinces' (NP 466). Nor was Khlebnikov capable of approaching his public himself to redress the balance. While Mayakovsky, David Burliuk and

Kamensky were noted for the bold and strident tones of their public performances, the case of Khlebnikov was exactly the opposite. Not only did he rarely take part in these public events, but when he did so, he demonstrated a clear inability to impress himself upon his audience. What was probably the only public reading given by Khlebnikov in 1913 prompted one reviewer to note that 'it was impossible to make out what he was saying' (NP 467).[36]

Accounts of public appearances made by Khlebnikov several years later in the post-revolutionary period paint a similar unflattering picture:

> He read several verses, read them very quietly so that almost nothing could be heard. There were catcalls. People decided that it was some sort of fraud.[37]

> . . . Khlebnikov's appearance did not evoke any particular excitement. Moreover, he read quietly and timidly – he was unable to perform successfully.[38]

> I remember him once on the stage of the cafe, as though he had been driven into a corner by the rays of the electric light. He mumbled something to himself. The audience immediately turned away. There was the clatter of crockery, conversations started up. He stood, hands behind his back, silent and in thought. Finally, they took him off.[39]

Similar scenes are described at a reading Khlebnikov gave for the Union of Poets. His voice, initially loud, was said to have become a 'quiet murmur and indistinct mumbling', as one by one the audience, mainly of other poets, 'quietly but resolutely began to leave the hall' until only two or three people remained.[40]

Khlebnikov was not at ease performing in public, which is why poets such as Mayakovsky would read his verse for him. The contrast between the public self-effacement which Khlebnikov endured and the stentorian self-assertion of Mayakovsky's appearances is quite pronounced. Mayakovsky and Khlebnikov's other literary colleagues were clearly, sometimes painfully, aware of this. Kamensky, for example, attributes the following words to Mayakovsky:

> It sometimes seems to me that Vitya himself doesn't understand what a brilliant poet he is. A scholar! A genius! But he doesn't understand a thing of our bustling, everyday life. He's like some sort of saint, and this irritates me terribly. A kangaroo! Why, for instance, hasn't he got a voice? Well,

he hasn't a voice and that's it. He purrs something only half-intelligible. A real miracle maker! Without a voice. And is it possible in our idiotic days to be a poet without a voice . . . [41]

Kamensky goes on to add his own remarks about the inability of Khlebnikov to recite his verse. He would, Kamensky writes, break off a reading, simply saying 'and so on'; and his quiet murmuring would evoke the comment 'not of this world'.[42] Notably, however, this 'otherworldliness' of Khlebnikov's public face could serve as a positive aspect in his relations with the crowd.

One of the traits in the presentation of Khlebnikov's poetic heroes is their 'saintly' or divine attributes. Zangezi, it will be recalled, is accompanied by his believers as well as his detractors. The poetic heroes in the 'chairmen of the terrestrial globe' proclamation are even given the epithet 'saintly'. One of Khlebnikov's poetic guises is the 'priest of flowers'; another is as a 'hirsute priest' (SP III 149). The presentation of the poetic *persona* as 'otherworldly' can transform an image of isolation and rejection into one of respected holy asceticism. Likewise, in the 'real' world, while Khlebnikov may not have coped successfully with public performances, he was in the eyes of many of his contemporaries a kind of 'holy fool', the visionary and ecstatic 'dervish' of Russian poetry.[43]

It was this quality which was noted by Osip Mandelstam's wife, Nadezhda, when she encountered Khlebnikov in the last months of his life. She recalls that when the destitute Khlebnikov came to have meals with them the old woman who cooked their meals 'greeted Khlebnikov not just affably, but even with joy, treating him as a wandering "man of God" – this pleased him and brought a smile to his face'.[44] Nadezhda Mandelstam subsequently adds that she suspected Osip felt the same way about Khlebnikov as this old woman and that he also 'looked upon him as a "man of God" '.[45]

Judging by the following comment of Sergey Spassky, Khlebnikov's image of himself as the revered 'otherworldly' figure may not always have been sufficient compensation for being ridiculed as a freak and for the neglect and catcalls of the crowd:

. . . Khlebnikov did not like being considered a crank. He had a different notion of himself – bold, adept, with a loud voice, leading the crowd behind him, – in short, very similar to Mayakovsky . . . [46]

It is this conflict between his perception of himself and how others perceived him which is embodied in some of his texts. He strives to make up for inadequacies in real terms by aspiring to eminence in poetic terms. This helps to explain the repeated appearances of his own name within his texts and the strong 'automythical' presence of the Khlebnikovian *persona*.

There are very few accounts by contemporaries of readings by Khlebnikov which seem to have made some impact upon his listeners. There is, however, one account which particularly stands out. In the difficult period Khlebnikov spent in Kharkov in 1920, he occasionally gave readings for a local Bolshevik club. Many years later one such reading was recalled by Aleksandr Leytes:

> I remember only one gathering at which the poet arrived in an agitated mood and read a new poem in a way that was unusual for him. He began animatedly: 'I have seen the black Vedas, the Koran and the Gospels and the books of the Mongols in their silken boards . . . form a fire . . . to speed up the coming of the single book.' Citing in a song-like fashion the names of the Nile and the Ob, the Mississippi and the Danube, the Zambezi and the Volga, the Thames and the Ganges, gradually filling with inspiration, he sharply raised his voice: 'Yes, you read without care. Pay more attention! You are too distracted and your gaze is idle, as if it were your scripture classes. Soon, soon, you shall read these mountain chains and great seas, this single book!'
>
> This time he was listened to with concentration. There was a motley crowd for an audience. Students, members of the regional committee, staff from the Ukrainian Bolshevik Communist Party Central Committee, young workers from the locomotive building depot. There were even noisy adolescents, formerly of the lower forms of the old schools, who had now become pupils of 'united labour', and who had come along to the club for the greatest treat of those evenings – the jam sandwiches, even they fell silent.[47]

It is a distinct change from the catcalls and inattentiveness normally associated with a Khlebnikov performance. On Khlebnikov's part the approach is somewhat unusual too. He is agitated, inspired, declaiming in an enthusiastic and rhythmic manner. The nervous confusion and mumbling have been replaced by a forceful 'Mayakovskian' voice.

It is of considerable note that the poem Khlebnikov is reciting here is the important work 'Single Book' ('Yedinaya kniga'). It is a poem which has a direct bearing on the dialogue between the poet and his public and which moves towards its climax in the following lines (several of which were highlighted by Leytes):

Rod chelovechestva – knigi chitatel′,
A na oblozhke – nadpis′ tvortsa,
Imya moyo – pis′mena golubyye.
Da, ty nebrezhno chitayesh′.
Bol′she vnimaniya!
Slishkom rasseyan i smotrish′ lentyayem,
Tochno uroki zakona bozhiya.
Eti gornyye tsepi i bol′shiye morya,
Etu yedinuyu knigu
Skoro ty, skoro prochtyosh′! (SP v 25)

(Mankind is the reader of the book, and on the cover is the name of the creator, my name, in blue letters. Yes, you read without care. Pay more attention! You are too distracted and your gaze is idle, as if it were your scripture classes. Soon, soon, you shall read these mountain chains and great seas, this single book!)

This poem is an indictment not of an inadequate poet, but of an inadequate public. It is a reprimand for the inattentive and careless reader, who, the poem predicts, will, nonetheless, soon be reading this poet's 'single book'. It is a prediction which bears the force of a threat. Khlebnikov, a poet so often ignored by his audience, is venting some of his frustrations upon his crowd and is reaffirming his own position as poet.

The poem begins, like several others by Khlebnikov, with the words 'I have seen . . . '; Khlebnikov's poetic message arises from a mental image, a vision. It is this vision which he found difficult to communicate to his crowd. There is, however, no self-deprecation or remorse in the poem. The poet is not chastising himself for his inability to bridge the gap between himself and his public; he is, on the contrary, chastising his reader for being unable to perceive the harmonious vision which the poet is privileged to witness.

Nonetheless, despite the appearance of this 'single book', the poet and the crowd are still allotted their respective hierarchical positions. Faceless humanity is the reader of the book; Khlebnikov's poetic I is its creator, his name etched in blue letters on its cover. Despite its title, the 'single book' divides into both poet and crowd.

IV

Towards the end of Khlebnikov's life, the conflicts evident in the portrayal of relations between poet and public became something of a major poetic theme. In their presentation of the poetic hero the poems of this period highlight the juxtaposition between images of eminence and images of neglect and rejection. Moreover, on a personal level, tensions were heightened at this time for Khlebnikov as a result of the strained relations with some of his literary colleagues, such as Mayakovsky and Brik. This was as a result of Khlebnikov's suspicions that his manuscripts had been stolen and his work plagiarized. This rift is reflected in some of his texts, and becomes part of the more general lament concerning the alleged disregard for his work.

One short lyric poem of this period where such preoccupations surface (it was, apparently, written in the last two months of his life) is the poem which begins 'Not like a Shrovetide devil' ('Ne chortikom maslyanichnym'). One of the first images to appear in this work is of a kind which is already familiar to us. It is the portrayal of the poetic *persona* as the 'Bell of Liberty':

> Kolokol Voli,
> Ruku svoyu podymayu
> Skazat′ pro opasnost′.
> Dalyokiy i blednyy
> Mnoyu ukazan vam put′ . . . (SP III 311)

(The Bell of Liberty, I raise my hand to tell of the danger. I have shown you the way, distant and pale . . .)

There is, however, an additional element here to this customary image of the poet-liberator. The 'Bell of Liberty' is also something of a tocsin. The poetic I speaks of pointing out 'danger'. Furthermore, it would appear from the images of effacement which follow that it is a tocsin which has been unsuccessful. The poetic I speaks of 'falling', of being covered by 'dark clouds' ('Da, ya sryvalsya i padal,/Tuchi menya zakryvali . . . '); and this is followed by expressions of bitterness at rejection:

> Ne raz vy ostavlyali menya
> I unosili moyo plat′ye
> Kogda ya pereplyval prolyvy pesni
> I khokhotali, chto ya gol.
> Vy zhe sebya razdevali
> Cherez neskol′ko let,
> Ne zametiv vo mne
> Sobytiy vershiny,
> Pera ruki vremyon
> Za dumoy pisatelya.[48] (SP III 311–12)

(More than once you deserted me and carried off my clothes when I was swimming across the straits of song, and laughed because I was naked. But after a few years you ended up stripping yourselves, failing to note in me the summit of events, the pen of the hand of times beyond the thought of the writer.)

As in the poem 'Single Book', the disregard which the poetic hero experiences is related to his creative activities as a writer, his swimming across 'the straits of song'. Moreover, the reference to the failure to note in him 'the summit of events' and 'the pen of the hand of times beyond the thought of the writer' gives some indication that the disregard is also connected with Khlebnikov's own work on the 'laws of time'. (Hence, perhaps, the earlier reference to the unheeded prophecy of danger).

The last few lines of this poem serve, however, as a reassertion of the poetic I when faced with such neglect:

Ya odinokim vrachom
V dome sumasshedshikh
Nyos svoi pesni – lekarya. (SP III 312)

(Like the only doctor in a madhouse, I took my songs as helpers on my rounds.)

Despite rejection and humiliation, the image of the poetic I as benefactor still persists. The 'literary' mission of the hero is also a mission of healing – an attempt to put an end to the madness around him. Khlebnikov, who had himself frequented asylums as an inmate, uses this poem to reverse the roles.

As with many of the lyrics of this period it is difficult to determine with any certainty precisely to whom the poem is addressed. However, the general character of the lament of the poetic I and the archetypal imagery involved are mixed with images which may involve allusions to specific personal slights. The possibility cannot be discounted, therefore, that the poem has a specific addressee or addressees in mind.

The combination of general lament and specific complaint is a feature of another important late lyric poem 'To All' ('Vsem'), which was written at about the same time as 'Not like a Shrovetide devil'. The title gives some indication as to the catholic nature of its theme. Yet this poem also contains specific references which indicate that it may well be directed towards certain individuals in particular. One of the subjects Khlebnikov touches upon here is the appropriation of his manuscripts. The poem is quoted in full:

> Yest′ pis′ma – mest′.
> Moy plach gotov,
> I v′yuga veyet khlop′yami,
> I nosyatsya besshumno dukhi.
> Ya prodyryavlen kop′yami
> Dukhovnoy golodukhi,
> Istykan kop′yami golodnykh rtov.
> Vash golod prosit yest′,
> I v kotelke izyashchnykh chum
> Vash golod prosit pishchi – vot grud′ nadarmaka!
> I posle upadayu, kak Kuchum
> Ot kopiy Yermaka.
> To golod kopiy prokolot′
> Prikhodit rukopis′ polot′.
> Akh, zhemchuga s lyubimykh mnoyu lits
> Uznat′ na ulichnoy torgovke!
> Zachem ya vyronil etu svyazku stranits?
> Zachem ya byl chudak nelovkiy?
> Ne ozorstvo ozyabshikh pastukhov –
> Pozhara rukopisey palach –
> Vezde zazubrennyy sekach
> I lichiki zarezannykh stikhov.
> Vsyo chto tryokhletnyaya godina nam dala,
> Schot pesen sotney okruglit′,
> I vsem znakomyy krug lits,
> Vezde, vezde zarezannykh tsarevichey tela,
> Vezde, vezde proklyatyy Uglich! (SP III 313)

(Letters are vengeance. My cry is ready, and the blizzard's snowflakes swirl, and spirits pass by noiselessly. I am pierced by the lances of a spiritual hunger, run through by the lances of hungry mouths. Your hunger calls for food, and in the pot of fine plagues your hunger calls for its meal – take my breast for nothing! And afterwards I fall like Kuchum from the lances of Yermak. It is the hunger of lances to pierce that comes to weed out a manuscript. Oh, to recognize on a street trader pearls from the faces that I loved! Why did I let that bundle of pages go? Why was I such a clumsy crank? This is not the mischief of shepherds grown cold – it is the butcher of a fire of manuscripts – everywhere a blade's serrated edge and the little faces of verses hewn down. All that these three years have given us, it can be rounded off at a hundred songs, and the circle of faces known to all, everywhere, everywhere the bodies of tsareviches hewn down, everywhere, everywhere the cursed Uglich!)

The development of the imagery in this poem is complex. The theme of the poet offering up his body for consumption to satisfy what he terms a 'spiritual hunger' merges into a lament over the destruction of his verse. Images of self-sacrifice are followed by the bitterness of self-reproach. This time it is not the crowd which is voicing the epithet 'crank' (*chudak*), it is the poet's own poetic I. He recognizes on a 'street trader' pearls from his own work and he chastises himself for letting his manuscripts go.

The mutilation of his verse is compared to the mutilation of the Tsarevich Dmitry, the son of Ivan the Terrible, murdered during the 'Time of Troubles' in Uglich in 1591 and whose identity was later assumed by several pretenders to the Russian throne. The implications are that Khlebnikov's verse has suffered a similar fate. It has been butchered and appropriated by a host of pretenders to his throne. However, the assertive nature of the poetic I is evident again; this 'Time of Troubles' results in a desire for retribution. The poem's first line is a call for vengeance.[49]

The assertive nature of the poetic I when subject to maltreatment by others is also a feature of another late lyric (probably 1921–2), which begins in the following manner:

> Russkiye desyat′ let menya pobivali kamen′yami . . .
> I vsyo-taki ya podymayus′, vstayu . . . (SP v 109)

(The Russians have been stoning me for ten years . . . And still I rise, get up on my feet . . .)

And once he has picked himself up, this poetic I is ready for retribution to proceed:

> I iz glaz moikh na vas l′yotsya pryamo zvyozdnyy uzhas
> Zhestokiy poyedinok.
> I ya vstayu kak prizrak iz peny
> Ya dlya vas zvezda.
> Dazhe kogda vy ukrali moi shtany ili platok
> I mne nechem smorkat′sya . . .
> Ya zhestok, kak zvezda . . .
> Dvoyku buri i kol podvodnogo kamnya
> Stavit ona moryaku za neznaniye,
> Za oshibku v zadache . . . (SP v 109)

(And from my eyes the terror of the stars streams directly at you, a cruel duel. And I rise like a spectre from the foam, I am for you a star. Even when you stole my pants or handkerchief and I had nothing to blow my nose with . . . I am cruel, like a star . . . For his ignorance, for a mistake in calculation, it gives the sailor the bad mark of a storm and the stake of an underwater rock . . .)

Once again the generalized nature of the lament is modified by what appears to be a reference to a particular personal slight – the theft of clothing, similar to that voiced in 'Not like a Shrovetide devil'. In addition, specific imagery, connected with Khlebnikov's own mathematical theories (*dvoyku buri*), is combined with an image which has archetypal qualities, the presentation of the hero as a star. The message of the poem is that this star shines in the night sky and if the sailor on earth takes a wrong bearing from it his voyage is liable to meet with disaster. It is, of course, allegorical; Khlebnikov is expressing concern and voicing threats over the neglect of his work.

The imagery in the poem recalls the warning of danger in 'Not like a Shrovetide devil'. Furthermore, like that poem, this work contains the mixed imagery of self-assertion and self-effacement. The guiding star of the poetic I is 'distant, great and immovable', but at the same time he could 'die and become unneeded' (SP v 110). These contrasting elements persist through to the final lines of the poem:

Ne khokhochite, chto ya
Ozaryayu myortvuyu glupost'
Slabey mayaka na shatkoy korme vashego sudna.
Ya slab i tuskl, no ya nepodvizhen,
On zhe opishet za vami
I s vami krivuyu krusheniya sudna.
On budet padat' krivoyu zhara bol'nogo i s vami na dno.
On vash, on s vami – ya zh bozhiy.
Pust' moya tuskla zarya . . .
No ya nepodvizhen! ya vechen.
I okolo osi mirov, gde kruzhitsya mir
Boytes' byt' zlymi ko mne,
Shemyakoy sud'ey moyey mysli.
Pust' ya ne ryov, a <polunochnyy svist yele slyshnyy,
nevynosimykh ukhu komet>.[50] (SP v 110)

(Do not laugh at me for illuminating fatal stupidity more weakly than the beacon on the unsteady helm of your ship. I am weak and dim, but I am immovable, whereas the beacon will describe after you and with you the curve on the graph of your shipwreck. It will sink to the bottom with you like the curve on the chart of a fever. It is yours, it is with you – but I am of

God. My glow may be dim . . . But I am immovable! I am eternal. And around the axis of the worlds, where the world spins, beware of bearing me malice, of bearing false witness to my thought. I may not be a roar, but <the hardly audible whistle at midnight of comets, unbearable to the ear>.)

The confident warning which the poetic I issues to those who might treat him badly ('beware of bearing me malice') is combined with images which betray a marked vulnerability ('I am weak and dim'). Furthermore, this vulnerability is underlined when the 'dim' light of the star is said to shine 'more weakly than the beacon' on the helm of the ship. However, the benefit of the star is that it is fixed in the sky and 'eternal', whereas the beacon will sink along with the ship that bears it. Claims of divinity re-emerge: the star of the poetic I is of God (*bozhiy*), but the ship's beacon is of men (*on s vami*).

This comparison of the different types of light is supplemented in the last line of the poem by an implied comparison in another sphere of the senses, specifically the sphere of sound. The heavenly body into which the poet has transmuted his poetic *persona* does not 'roar' but rather emits that 'barely audible whistle of comets unbearable to the ear'. Not only does the Khlebnikovian heavenly body give off a weak light, but it also has an almost inaudible voice.

Who then, if anyone, emits the 'roar' which could blot out Khlebnikov's 'barely audible whistle'? One is tempted to suggest that it is a fellow-poet whom Khlebnikov clearly liked to describe in riddle form elsewhere with reference to his 'powerful voice' (SP v 112) and with the epithet 'leader of the crowds' (SP v 97). This is, of course, Mayakovsky, whose 'iron chin', in Khlebnikov's words, 'cut through the crowds like an ice-breaker' (SP v 112). Can we see confirmation for this in the other comparison which Khlebnikov makes in the poem, that between the dim light of the Khlebnikovian star and the beacon which shines on the helm of the ship? The Russian for beacon is *mayak*; it is certainly not beyond the bounds of credibility that for *mayak* Khlebnikov meant us to read Mayakovsky.[51]

The problem in deciphering the complex imagery (as well as the problems in deciphering Khlebnikov's rough manuscript) make 'The Russians have been stoning me . . . ' a difficult poem. It is so saturated with semantic possibilities that, as V. P. Grigoryev has pointed out, Khlebnikov could have developed further almost every phrase in it in turn.[52] But Khlebnikov did exactly the opposite. Rigorously eliminating images and associations superfluous to his main thought, he produced on this theme a short lyric poem, which is rightly considered among his best. I quote it in full:

Yeshcho raz, yeshcho raz,
Ya dlya vas
Zvezda.
Gore moryaku, vzyavshemu
Nevernyy ugol svoyey lad′i
I zvezdy:
On razob′yotsya o kamni,
O podvodnyye meli.
Gore i vam, vzyavshim
Nevernyy ugol serdtsa ko mne:
Vy razob′yotes′ o kamni
I kamni budut nadsmekhat′sya
Nad vami,
Kak vy nadsmekhalis′
Nado mnoy. (SP III 314)

(Once again, once again, I am for you a star. Woe to the sailor, who has taken the wrong angle of his ship and a star: he will smash to pieces on the rocks, in the shallows. Woe to you too, who have taken the wrong angle of my heart: you will smash to pieces on the rocks and the rocks will laugh long at you, as you laughed long at me.)

The poet is 'once again' telling his public that he is a star and that those who do not guide themselves correctly by this star will break up on the rocks. It is the bitter and assertive response of a poet maligned; a further warning by Khlebnikov to his readers to pay attention to his works. It is a poem which echoes the retributive tone of 'To All'; those who have mocked the poet will themselves in turn be mocked. The mockery which Khlebnikov threatens, however, is much more ominous; those who have 'taken the wrong angle' to the poet's heart will be mocked by the very rocks with which they collide. It is as though the poetic hero is in league here with the forces of nature against his detractors. It is a forceful presentation of the poetic *persona*, but one which again reveals the solitary nature of the poet's task. Embodied in the heavens as a star, he is still well apart from the rest of humanity.

The solitary nature of the poetic *persona* can also be seen in the title of another lyric of this period, 'Lone Performer' ('Odinokiy litsedey') probably written towards the end of 1921. It is a poem which has clear mythological overtones, since the action it depicts is the slaying of an 'underground bull'. The model for the poetic hero derives in part from the Greek hero Theseus.[53] This portrayal of the liberation of man from monster echoes similar acts of benevolence by other Khlebnikovian poetic heroes, in particular the attack on the 'people-eating' states by Khlebnikov's 'chairmen of the terrestrial globe' (SP III 20). The Minotaur-like bull in 'Lone Performer' is depicted as follows:

> A mezhdu tem kurchavoye chelo
> Podzemnogo byka v peshcherakh tyomnykh
> Krovavo chavkalo i kushalo lyudey . . .[54] (SP III 307)

(And meanwhile in dark caves the curly brow of the underground bull bloodily champed its dish of people . . .)

It is, however, no match for the poetic hero, who kills it and proceeds to demonstrate his victory by displaying to the world his trophy of the severed bull's head:

> I bych'yu golovu ya snyal s moguchikh myas i kosti
> I u steny postavil.
> Kak voin istiny ya yeyu potryasal nad mirom:
> Smotrite, vot ona! (SP III 307)

(And I removed the bull's head from the mighty flesh and bone and placed it by the wall. Like a warrior of truth I shook it above the world: look, here it is!)

Nevertheless, although the 'warrior of truth' has fulfilled his task with distinction, his victory is not crowned with the success that should be its due. For, although the hero may call upon the crowd to look upon his triumph, the people cannot see him. He is invisible to them:

> I s uzhasom
> Ya ponyal, chto ya nikem ne vidim:
> Chto nuzhno seyat' ochi,
> Chto dolzhen seyatel' ochey idti! (SP III 307)

(And with horror I understood that I was seen by no one: that it was necessary to sow eyes, that a sower of eyes was needed!)

The fears of the 'dim star' are expressed in a much more forthright manner. The hero, himself depicted earlier in the poem as blind ('slepoy ya shol'), is not so much unseeing as unseen. The allusion is quite evidently again pointing to the poet's concern for a lack of recognition by the crowd. What is the use of fighting for the 'truth' if people have no eyes to see it? It reflects Khlebnikov's perception of his own position. He accomplishes his feats and no one notices them; he is the 'lone performer'.

The poem does not, however, end on a note of despair. A solution is put forward. If the crowd has no vision then eyes must be 'sown' for them so that they can see. The lone performer, detached from the crowd, is yet determined that his performance shall not pass unnoticed. It is again allegorical; the poet as visionary is also faced with the task of making his crowd 'see'.

Khlebnikov reflected on this theme again elsewhere. In a short prose piece written at about the same time as 'Lone Performer', which deals with 'sardine tin cities' and conjures up a vision of an alternative city ('a primaeval forest of the other truth' – SP IV 300–1), he writes:

'Fine!' I thought. 'Now, I am the sole player, and the rest of them – the whole huge nighttime city with its blazing lights – are the spectators. But there will come a time, when I shall be the only spectator, and you – the performers.' I shall subject these infinite crowds of the city to my will.

(SP IV 301)

The hero aspires to a reversal of the roles, where he is no longer the single performer, but the single spectator able to watch the endless crowds of the city play out their parts subject to his will. It is a familiar vision of eminence, yet be it solitary spectator or solitary performer, the poetic hero is still alone, the gulf between him and the crowd has not been bridged.

The solitary nature of the poetic *persona* and his detachment from mankind is also evident in the lyrical passage on the butterfly in the 'supertale' *Zangezi*:

Mne, babochke, zaletevshey
V komnatu chelovecheskoy zhizni,
Ostavit′ pocherk moyey pyli
Po surovym oknam, podpis′yu uznika,
Na strogikh styoklakh roka.
Tak skuchny i sery
Oboi iz chelovecheskoy zhizni!
Ya uzh styor svoyo sineye zarevo, tochek uzory,
Moyu golubuyu buryu kryla – pervuyu svezhest′,
Pyl′tsa snyata, kryl′ya uvyali i stali prozrachny i zhostki,
B′yus′ ya ustalo v okno cheloveka.
Vechnyye chisla stuchatsya ottuda
Prizyvom na rodinu, chislo zovut k chislam vernut′sya.

(SP III 324)

(It is for me, a butterfly, flown into the room of human life, to leave the writing of my dust across the stark windows, like the signature of a prisoner, on the stern window panes of fate. So dull and grey is the wall-paper of human life! The windows' transparent 'no'! I have already rubbed away my blue glow, the patterns of dots, my blue storm of wing – the first freshness, the dust has gone, my wings have withered and grown transparent and brittle, wearily I beat against man's window. The eternal numbers beckon from the other side summoning me home, calling a number to return to the numbers.)

The butterfly is a 'prisoner' in the room of human life. Wearily it beats its wings against the window of fate and in the process leaves its 'signature'. In the act of 'writing', however, the butterfly loses the dust from its wings and cripples itself. It is a revealing portrait. 'Literary' images are again significant; the act of writing becomes self-sacrificial. The portrayal recalls the sacrifice by another winged creature, the firefly in 'There was darkness . . . '. Moreover, both these Khlebnikovian *personae* perceive the life in which they find themselves as 'tedious' and their self-sacrifice is an attempt to reach out towards 'another life'. For the butterfly in *Zangezi* this involves overcoming the 'window panes of fate' and returning to the home of numbers (clearly a reference to Khlebnikov's attempts to discover the 'laws' of time and fate). The true home of this Khlebnikovian poetic hero lies outside 'the room of human life'.

Within the context of the 'supertale', the self-sacrificial act looks forward to the suicide of the hero, Zangezi. It is a suicide in which, once again, 'literary' enterprises are implicated:

Povodom bylo unichtozheniye
Rukopisey zlostnymi
Negodyayami s bol′shim podborodkom
I shlepayushchey i chavkayushchey paroi gub. (SP III 368)

(The reason was the destruction of manuscripts by malicious scoundrels with a large chin and a smacking and champing pair of lips.)

The reason cited for Zangezi's suicide (the 'destruction of manuscripts') brings to mind the bitter lines which Khlebnikov penned in 'To All' and the allegations that towards the end of his life his own manuscripts had been stolen and plagiarized. These associations acquire even more ominous proportions if we recognize in the portrait of the culprit depicted here the 'large chin' which was also a feature of one of Khlebnikov's periphrastic portraits of Mayakovsky (SP v 116). It appears that Zangezi/Khlebnikov has killed himself because Mayakovsky has destroyed his manuscripts.

However, Zangezi is ultimately not to be defeated by such a rival. Like the numbers which beckon the butterfly and the pale star which vied with the beacon, Zangezi seems to be eternal. The hero may die, but he is quickly resurrected. The 'supertale' concludes in the following manner:

Zangezi (*vkhodya*): Zangezi zhiv,
Eto byla neumnaya shutka. (SP III 368)

(Zangezi [*enters*]: Zangezi is alive, it was a stupid joke.)

Zangezi's suicide ends not in death, but in a type of rebirth.

The quest for rebirth or resurrection is a significant feature of Khlebnikov's poetic world. Like many other aspects of his verse, it is a quest which has strong archetypal qualities, evidence of which can be seen in the frequent portrayal of the process by means of such fundamental elements as water and fire.[55]

Such rebirths provide the Khlebnikovian poetic *persona* with an opportunity to reassert itself after neglect or abuse. In one short poem (SP v 72), for example, Khlebnikov describes how some young women teased him with the unflattering epithets 'old man' and 'grandfather'. But he also describes how he was able to rejuvenate his prematurely ageing body by an almost ritual bathing in the 'stream of Narzan', ('I grew vigorous and strong and gathered myself together').[56]

A similar regeneration, this time by fire not water, can be seen in the following lyric (dating probably from 1921):

Ya vyshel yunoshey odin
V glukhuyu noch',
Pokrytyy do zemli
Tugimi volosami.
Krugom stoyala noch'
I bylo odinoko,
Khotelosya druzey,
Khotelosya sebya.
Ya volosy zazhog,
Brosalsya loskutami kolets,
Zazhog polya, derev'ya –
I stalo veseley.
Gorelo Khlebnikova pole.
I ognennoye ya pylalo v temnote.

Teper' ya ukhozhu,
Zazhogshi volosami,
I vmesto Ya
Stoyalo – My!
Idi, varyag surovyy!
Nesi zakon i chest'.[57] (SP III 306)

(I went out a youth alone into the dead of night, covered to the earth with stiff hair. The night was all around and it was lonely, friends were wanted, self was wanted. I set fire to the hair, scattering scraps of rings, set fire to the fields, the trees – and it became merrier. Khlebnikov field was ablaze. And a fiery I burned in the darkness. Now I leave, hair alight, and instead of I there was – We! Onwards, stern Varangian! Take with you law and honour.)

The regeneration which this poem portrays represents a significant advance for the poetic hero in terms of his relations with the crowd. At the outset of the poem, the customary solitary nature of the poetic I is stressed ('I went out a youth *alone*', 'and it was *lonely*'). The hero's isolation is underlined even further by his alienation not only from friends, but also from self. The response of the poetic hero is to indulge in a ritual self-immolation. He sets fire to his hair, the countryside around him catches light, and the conflagration brings with it some relief ('and it became merrier'). The fire burns like a liberating force. With the image of 'Khlebnikov field was ablaze' the poem even hints at the battle of Kulikovo field, the scene of the celebrated Russian victory against the Tatar hordes.

The 'fiery I' of the hero blazes in the darkness, but the transformation which takes place is not solely one from dark to light. It is also one from solitude to multitude. The battle of 'Khlebnikov field' to which the reader is witness seems to be connected with the poet's own siege of the 'tower of the crowds'. The result of the fire is the transformation of the individual *I* into a collective *We*; it is a portrayal of communion with the people.

However, even in the portrayal of this absorption into the collective, the poetic I is still able not only to retain a unique individual nature but actually to strengthen it. In what is almost certainly a reference to the Viking Ryurik, generally accepted as Russia's first ruler, the poem's last lines portray the hero as the 'stern Varangian', ready to carry forth 'law and honour'. Through this rare achievement of unity with the crowd and an apparent end to solitude the poetic hero also undergoes the regeneration and the reaffirmation of his own individual being.

The concept of a universal being was reiterated elsewhere by Khlebnikov. One late, unpublished, manuscript talks of the construction of mankind into 'a single whole', and refers to the 'discovery of a common denominator for the fractions of mankind, a goodworld (*ladomir*) of bodies'.[58] Similarly, a late poem has reference to a 'world body' (*mirskoye telo*) and to 'a tree of Mr People' (*derevo Gospodina Naroda*) which can be divided into a 'multitude of I's' (SP V 113).

This notion was also the subject of the important late lyric (probably 1921), entitled 'I and Russia' ('Ya i Rossiya'):

Rossiya tysyacham tysyach svobodu dala.
Miloye delo! Dolgo budut pomnit' pro eto.
A ya snyal rubakhu
I kazhdyy zerkal'nyy neboskryob moyego volosa,
Kazhdaya skvazhina
Goroda tela
Vyvesila kovry i kumachovyye tkani.
Grazhdanki i grazhdane
Menya-gosudarstva,
Tysyacheokonnykh kudrey tolpilis' u okon,
Ol'gi i Igori,
Ne po zakazu,
Raduyas' solntsu, smotreli skvoz' kozhu.
Pala temnitsa rubashki!
A ya prosto snyal rubashku:
Dal solntse narodam Menya!
Golyy stoyal okolo morya. –
Tak ya daril narodam svobodu,
Tolpam zagara. (SP III 304)

(Russia gave freedom to thousands upon thousands. A fine deed! Long will it be recalled. But I just took off my shirt and each reflecting skyscraper of my hair, each pore in the city of my body hung out its rugs and its calico covers. Citizens, men and women, of the state of Me, crowded at the windows of the thousand-windowed curls, Olgas and Igors, under no order to do so, rejoicing at the sun, looked through my skin. The dungeon of the shirt has fallen! And I simply took off my shirt: gave the sun to the peoples of Me! Stood naked by the sea. – Thus did I grant freedom to the peoples, a suntan to the crowds.)

The poem uses for an archetypal image of liberation the removal of clothing – the very thing for which Khlebnikov elsewhere chastises his detractors. Here, however, it is not a case of clothing being stolen by others, but a wilful disrobement by an assertive poetic I and an act which again reveals this *persona* as a bringer of light and liberty. The poem equates two activities: the liberating mission of the Russian revolution and the poetic I's removal of clothing on a sunny day by the sea. The revolution gave freedom to 'thousands upon thousands' of people; when the poetic I discards the 'dungeon' of his shirt he accomplishes a similar act of liberation. For his body is revealed not just as an individual 'I', but as a veritable man-state, populated by whole peoples. Thousands of 'Olgas and Igors' crowd at the 'windows' in the pores of his skin joyfully taking in the sun which he has now 'given' to them. It is finally a vision of harmony. The *persona* of the poet and the crowd form a single whole.[59]

Not surprisingly, perhaps, it is an image which recurs in one of Khlebnikov's utopian visions:

> We must not forget about man's moral duty towards the citizens who inhabit his body. This complex star of bones.
> The government of these citizens, human consciousness, must not forget that the happiness of man is a bag of sand containing grains of the happiness of his subjects. We shall remember that each of the hairs of a man is a skyscraper, out of whose windows thousands of Sashas and Mashas gaze at the sun. We shall lower our world into the past on piles (*svayami*).
> That is why sometimes simply taking off one's shirt or bathing in a stream in spring can give more happiness than becoming the greatest man on earth. (SP IV 297)

The poetic hero is 'once again' a star, but he is here not distant, neglected or threatening retribution, but the star of a 'man-state' which contains within itself thousands of individual citizens. The moral duty of the poetic hero as benefactor is still firmly maintained, but it is not simply a duty. The happiness of the hero and his subjects is interconnected and interdependent. Assertive forays at external cosmic control have been replaced by a humble inner harmony. The simple act of removing a shirt can give 'more happiness than becoming the greatest man on earth'. Through an image of personal regeneration the poetic *persona* liberates not only himself, but also his people. In the final analysis it is the poet's own body that forms the tower which the crowds inhabit.

3
The tower of the word

I

It is probably Khlebnikov's assault on the 'tower of the word' which is regarded by most as his major battle. Although he may have had a fear of 'sterile, abstract discussions about art' (NP 367), he certainly did not fear discussions about the word and about language. He left several articles dealing with this subject and providing an exposition of his views. These views were of crucial importance for the Russian Futurist movement.

Khlebnikov was in the vanguard of experimental work on language and, as Willem Weststeijn has pointed out, even 'several years before the first Futurist manifesto was published ... had already formulated some of the principles of the Futurists' language renovations'.[1] Long before Russian Futurism with its programme of word creation had been thought of, Khlebnikov had coined scores, if not hundreds, of new words. If the Futurist 'Slap' manifesto had expressed a 'hate' for the existing literary language, then Khlebnikov was already attempting to reshape this language. Although Khlebnikov called for a siege of languages (SP v 259) and for their destruction (SP v 157), his approach was also constructive.[2]

Like his Cubo-Futurist colleagues, Khlebnikov was keen to see the word assume its rightful place in the literary arts after what was regarded by them as some years of neglect. As Kruchonykh put it, hitherto there had been only 'the pityful attempts of slavish thought to recreate its own way of life, philosophy and psychology ... verses for all sorts of domestic and family use', but there had been no 'art of the word'.[3] And a 'work of art is the art of the word,' a joint Khlebnikov–Kruchonykh declaration proclaimed (SP v 247).

Given this, there has been a tendency to identify Khlebnikov as a leading exponent of that cornerstone of Russian Cubo-Futurist aesthetics, the 'self-sufficient word' (*samovitoye slovo*). This is generally understood as the notion of the word as the primary fact and hero of poetry with an emphasis not on meaning but on form, texture and sound. That such a notion has been applied to Khlebnikov's work is not, perhaps, surprising. He once wrote, for example, that 'the word remains not for worldly use but for the word' (SP v 157) and he described his attitude towards the word as 'the self-sufficient word beyond daily life and everyday uses' (*samovitoye slovo vne byta i zhiznennykh pol'z*) (SP II 9). However, in spite of the implications of such statements (especially when taken out of context), Khlebnikov's notion of the 'self-sufficient word' was, in fact, somewhat different.[4]

In the article, 'Our Foundation' ('Nasha osnova'), first published in Kharkov in 1920, he explained himself as follows:

> The word can be divided into the pure word and the everyday word. One can think of the word as concealing within itself both the reason of the starlit night and the reason of the sunlit day. This is because any single everyday meaning (*bytovoye znacheniye*) of a word also obscures from view all the word's remaining meanings, just as the daytime brings with it the disappearance of all the shining bodies in the starlit night ... In separating itself from everyday language (*bytovoy yazyk*) the self-sufficient word differs from the living word just as the revolution of the earth around the sun differs from the everyday passage of the sun around the earth. The self-sufficient word renounces the spectres of a particular everyday situation and in the place of this self-evident lie constructs a twilight of the stars. (SP v 229)

In Khlebnikov's view, therefore, the word is both 'pure' and 'everyday'. Concealed behind its 'everyday meaning' are 'remaining meanings' which can be likened to stars in the sky, unseen during the hours of daylight, but, nonetheless, still there. It is this notion of unseen, but more fundamental, meanings residing behind an illusory 'everyday meaning' which Khlebnikov then links to the 'self-sufficient word'. The simile he now uses is the way in which it appears to people on earth that the sun revolves around the earth, whereas, in fact, the reverse is the case and, in spite of appearances, the earth revolves around the sun. Khlebnikov equates the former, the appearance of the sun going round the earth, with 'everyday language', and the latter, the physical reality of the earth revolving around the sun, with the 'self-sufficient word'. He juxtaposes the 'spectres', the 'self-evident lie' of the 'everyday situation' with the 'starry twilight' of the 'self-sufficient word'.

For Khlebnikov then, the 'self-sufficient word' was not so much a word devoid of 'everyday meaning' as one which transcended it, one which disclosed 'remaining meanings'; it was not so much a word detached from everyday life, as one which revealed life's processes at a more fundamental level. It is clearly associated with the notion of the hidden or secret aspect of the word, which, Khlebnikov believed, could 'shine through the mica of everyday meaning'.[5]

He expressed a similar viewpoint elsewhere with considerable irony when he wrote: 'those who accept words in the form in which they are served up for us in conversation are like people who believe that hazel grouse live in the woods plucked and covered with butter and cream . . .'.[6] The implication is that these 'grouse-words' lived meaningful, 'self-sufficient' lives long before they were ever served up as 'everyday meaning' on the human plate. Far from being a proponent of words devoid of sense, Khlebnikov was greatly preoccupied with meanings, and it was his search for these meanings which formed the basis for his linguistic experimentation.

II

Writing in 1919, in an introduction to an edition of his works which was never to appear, Khlebnikov defined his 'first attitude towards the word' as follows:

> To find, without breaking the circle of roots, the philosophers' stone (*volshebnyy kamen'*) for transforming all Slavonic words, one into another – freely to fuse Slavonic words – that is my first attitude towards the word. This is the self-sufficient word beyond daily life, and everyday uses.
>
> (SP II 9)

Leaving aside for a moment the reference to 'fusing' Slavonic words, the deeper level of meaning here which provides a framework for the 'self-sufficient word' to operate is the 'circle of roots'. The roots of words are key bearers of meaning, foundation blocks in the semantic system of language. Within the 'circle' of these roots lay, for Khlebnikov, the 'philosophers' stone' of language, the pivotal point through which the meanings of everyday language could pass and be transformed. Elsewhere, Khlebnikov had written that while words were 'of man', their roots were 'of God' (NP 323); and it was the root of the word, this 'divine' implement of word construction, which Khlebnikov saw as one of the basic building blocks for his own work on word creation. How he used such building blocks can be seen immediately in the famed neologistic poem 'Incantation by Laughter':

O, rassmeytes', smekhachi!
O, zasmeytes', smekhachi!
Chto smeyutsya smekhami, chto smeyanstvuyut smeyal'no,
O, zasmeytes' usmeyal'no!
O rassmeshishch nadsmeyal'nykh – smekh usmeynykh
smekhachey!
O, issmeysya rassmeyal'no smekh nadsmeynykh smeyachey!
Smeyvo, smeyvo,
Usmey, osmey, smeshiki, smeshiki,
Smeyunchiki, smeyunchiki.
O, rassmeytes', smekhachi!
O, zasmeytes', smekhachi!
(SP II 35)

This 'incantation' is not only a demonstration of the 'self-sufficiency' of the word, it is also a demonstration of the richness of meaning which can be built from a single root in the Russian language. It presents a conglomeration of neologisms (verbs, nouns, adjectives, adverbs), all based on the Russian root word for laughter (*smekh*). It uses to the full the possibilities inherent in the Russian language for word-building, with each new word developing different semantic nuances. Although Vladimir Markov has said that 'the result can only be suggested in English',[7] he has by no means been the only person to attempt translation. These translations have come up with such coinages as 'laughniks', 'laughathons', 'laughiness', 'laughicate', 'belaughably', 'laughadors' etc.[8]

Khlebnikov produced, particularly in his early work, hundreds of similar neologisms based on the roots of words which already existed in the Russian language. The 1913 collection *Croaked Moon* (*Dokhlaya luna*) contains, for example, four pages of words which Khlebnikov had derived from the root of the Russian word for 'love' (SP IV 317–18). In a less concentrated form such neologisms are scattered throughout many of his works (for example, *nebich, nebinya, nebistel'* from the root of *nebo*, meaning sky; *lyudnyak, lyudosh'* and *lyudel* from the root of *lyudi*, meaning people).[9]

It is clear, however, that the building of words from such roots could not take place without the use of another significant building block in word creation – the suffixes and prefixes which abound in the Russian language. This is evident to a large degree in 'Incantation by Laughter' where one can find nominal (*smekhachi, smeyunchik*), verbal (*issmeysya, usmey, smeyanstvuyut*) and adjectival/adverbial (nadsmeynykh, smeyvo) examples, to name but a few. It was the combination of these two elements (root and affix) which Khlebnikov was able to use to such effect, and it was a pattern which he repeated in many other neologisms, all of which expand the frontiers of meanings which are already present in 'everyday language'.

Frequently, in his coinages Khlebnikov would follow the normal laws which govern word formation. He would, however, also violate these laws, joining, for example, verbal stems with suffixes which required substantival stems (*budetlyanin* would fall into such a category).[10] Nor was Khlebnikov averse to employing 'pseudo-derivational' procedures, using in his coinages 'suffixes' which were not really suffixes at all in 'everyday language'. Khlebnikov, for example, saw *-bro* (from *serebro* meaning silver) as a suffix and created words by (what is really 'false') analogy (*lobzebro, volebro*).[11]

Establishment literary critics viewed this neologistic activity as nonsense or as a sign of madness,[12] but for a fellow artist and writer such as Benedikt Livshits Khlebnikov had made the Russian language come alive, he had allowed new meanings to be born and dormant ones to be awoken. Livshits wrote how on first encountering Khlebnikov's manuscripts his head had spun and all accepted notions about the nature of the word had been swept aside. 'I felt on my face', Livshits wrote, 'the breath of the primaeval word.'[13]

The principle of word creation was associated in Khlebnikov's mind with the language of the common Russian people (*narod*). For him it was the 'will of the people' which could grant the 'right to create words' (NP 323). But, as we have seen, his 'first attitude towards the word' went beyond the Russian language to encompass 'all Slavonic words', and their transformation 'one into another'.

Khlebnikov's interest in the Slavonic language is well-documented. One of the artistic tasks which he set himself was, we should recall, 'to consult the dictionaries of the Slavs, the Montenegrins and others ... and to choose many fine words' (SP v 298). And

Khlebnikov practised what he preached. His sketch about Montenegrin life, 'Tempered Heart' ('Zakalyonnoye serdtse'), makes use of Montenegrin words and sayings;[14] and Khlebnikov called on Kruchonykh to provide himself with vocabulary in Czech, Polish and Serbian (SP v 302).

Khlebnikov's borrowings from other Slavonic languages were part of his general appetite for word creation. He himself noted that when he used the Polabian word for moon (*leuna*), the poet Bryusov mistakenly saw it as a neologism (SP II 7).[15] Such an error is hardly surprising. Many of Khlebnikov's borrowings from other languages or dialects can be similarly mistaken. Nor was the choice of Khlebnikov's vocabulary limited to geographical locations; he would also choose freely throughout time as well as space, and certain words which appear at first sight to be coinages are in fact archaisms. Moreover, Khlebnikov frequently used archaic formants in his own neologisms, thus giving the impression of an old Russian or even Common Slavonic language.

The affinity of the Slavonic languages particularly attracted Khlebnikov. His desire to expand the bounds of Russian literature so that it encompassed the whole of the Slav world was also accompanied by a vision of the unity of the Slavonic languages. Notably, it was this vision of a pan-Slav language which prompted him to make his first contact with Vyacheslav Ivanov. In the letter which he sent to Ivanov in March 1908, asking him to comment on some of his verse, Khlebnikov wrote:

> Reading over these verses, I recalled the 'pan-Slav language', whose shoots would sprout through the thick layer of modern Russian. That is why it is your opinion about these verses in particular which is dear and important to me and why it is to you that I am deciding to turn. (NP 354)

In an article a few months later Khlebnikov was again referring to the need to direct attention to the 'single common circle' of the 'common Slavonic word' (NP 323). The 'circle of roots' which provided him with the framework for his 'self-sufficient word' was the same 'circle of roots' which formed a common basis for all the Slavonic languages. He aspired towards creating the means whereby all Slavonic words would be able to 'fuse' freely together.

This, however, as he tells us, was only his first attitude towards the word. He describes his second attitude as follows:

> Seeing that roots are just spectres behind which stand the strings of the

alphabet, to discover the unity in general of world languages, a unity formed from the units of the alphabet – this is my second attitude towards the word. The path towards a universal transrational language. (SP II 9)

Khlebnikov may have thought initially only in terms of a pan-Slav language, but his horizons later broadened substantially and he came to believe firmly in the possibility of evolving a universal tongue. He began to see even the roots of words as 'spectres', and through these 'spectres', as the basic implements for a projected universal language, he began to catch sight of 'units of the alphabet', individual letters. In linguistic terms he was coming to see the phoneme as semantically significant, as a morpheme in its own right.

The development of these ideas occurred over a period of time, though indications that Khlebnikov was thinking in terms of the semantic potential of individual letters or sounds were already apparent in the 1912 *Teacher and Pupil* dialogue. It was here that he formulated his theory of 'internal declension':

... if the genitive case answers the question whence, and the accusative and dative the question whither and where, then the declension of a stem in these cases should give the resulting words meanings which are opposite. Thus, kindred words should have distant meanings. This can be demonstrated. For example, *bobr* (beaver) and *babr* (Siberian tiger), signifying a harmless rodent and a terrifying beast of prey, and formed from the accusative and genitive cases of the common stem 'bo', show by their very structure that the *bobr* is to be pursued, to be hunted as game, and the *babr* is to be feared, since here man himself may become the object of the hunt on the part of the beast. Here the most simple body, by changing its case, changes the sense of the verbal construct. (SP V 171)

Khlebnikov's *Teacher and Pupil* goes on to provide further examples, such as *bog* (God) who evokes fear and *beg* (flight) which is evoked by fear.[16] It is the alteration of the individual vowel within the words which, Khlebnikov contends, governs their sense.

As Ronald Vroon has pointed out, Khlebnikov did not, however, believe that the word and the object it denoted were identical.[17] If the real sun disappeared, Khlebnikov writes in 'Our Foundation', and we were left simply with the word 'sun' then the earth would freeze. The word could not shine in the sky like the real object to which it referred (SP V 234). Rather, Khlebnikov saw language, to quote his own words, as a 'game of dolls'. In this game dolls for all the world's 'things' could be sewn up out of scraps of sound. Khlebnikov writes:

> People who speak the same language take part in this game. For people who speak a different language, such dolls of sound are simply a collection of sound scraps. And so the word is a doll of sound, and a dictionary is a collection of toys. (SP v 234)

Nor did Khlebnikov believe that the linguistic sign was arbitrary. His view on the 'internal declension' of words demonstrates this. In opposition to one of the basic tenets of Saussurian linguistics, Khlebnikov perceived an inherent connection between the sound of a word and its meaning, between the signifier and the signified.[18]

Khlebnikov was to pursue such ideas much further and the dialogue in *Teacher and Pupil* gives us some idea of the direction they would take. Following the description of the 'internal declension of words',[19] the dialogue suggests:

> Perhaps the forces in ancient reason simply sounded in a language of consonants. Only the growth of science will allow us to divine the whole wisdom of language, which is wise because it was itself a part of nature. (SP v 172)

This passage encapsulates two of the most fundamental notions of Khlebnikov's view of language. One is the 'language of consonants', which was to develop eventually into Khlebnikov's projected universal tongue;[20] and the second is the expressed belief in the natural wisdom of language.

The 'language of consonants' was soon to surpass by far in importance the vowel-centred theory on 'internal declension', though it seems to have sprung from the same source. An article said to have been written at the beginning of 1912 (NP 459) which contains further reflections on the 'internal declension' of vowels also shows considerable interest in the role of consonants, and, in particular, the initial consonant. Noting, for example, the 'internal declension' which operates in the words *les* (forest) and *lysyy* (bald), Khlebnikov also points out that it is the letter *l* 'in the sense of striving upwards' which begins both words (NP 327–8).

As well as recording the divergent but associated meanings of similar sounding words which 'declined' internally, Khlebnikov was now starting to gather together clusters of words which began with the same consonant, identifying in these words related semantic elements. He links together *les* (forest), *luk* (bow) and *luch* (ray).

He equates *lit'* (to pour) with *lug* (meadow) and *luzha* (puddle) and develops general axioms which he feels might be applicable to the initial consonant *l*. He sees it, for example, as being connected with 'independent movement' (NP 326) or as signifying 'movements in which the cause of movement is a moving point' (NP 459). And he also supplies definitions for *d* (NP 459) and *t* (NP 325). By 1912 Khlebnikov had already embarked upon the path of 'semanticizing' the initial letter of the word.[21]

Within the next few years he had formulated an opinion on the 'special nature' (SP v 188) of initial letters and had produced further definitions for the meanings of these letters. One such list of definitions tells us, for example, that *m* involved 'the disintegration of a whole into parts'; on the other hand, *s* stood for 'the collection of parts into a whole' (SP v 189). He frequently compiled lists of words, which, he believed, had similar basic meanings because of their identical initial letter. He could link the words for a seal's flipper (*last*), a boat (*lad'ya* or *lodka*), a ski (*lyzha*), a leaf (*list*), and the palm of the hand (*ladon'*), to name but a few, because, '*l* begins those names where the force of gravity, travelling along a certain axis, is dispersed along a plane transverse to this axis' (SP v 198).

It was possible to name, Khlebnikov points out, 'twenty types of human structures' which begin with the letter *kh*, for example, *khram* (temple), *khlev* (cow-shed), *khoromy* (mansion). The reason being that 'buildings serve as protection, consequently *kh* can be defined as the plane of a barrier between one point, within the circle of this protection, and another point moving towards it' (SP v 200). The initial letter *ch* meant a cover or casing (*obololochka*), 'a surface empty within, which has been filled or which encompasses another volume', for example, *cherep* (skull), *chasha* (goblet), *chulok* (stocking) (SP v 207). These were the 'strings of the alphabet' which stood behind the 'spectres' of roots and constituted Khlebnikov's second attitude towards the word.

Khlebnikov was also interested in the 'national' implications of a given letter or sound. He noted the importance of *r* for Russia (*Rus'*, *Ryurikovichi*) (SP v 192); and of *g* and *sh* for Germany (*Germaniya, Gyote, Shopengauer, Shelling*) (SP v 188). Since he did not take accounts of the vagaries of transliteration (Heine and Hegel become in Russian *Geyne* and *Gegel'*), he was probably right to talk, however, of the possible 'fury' of 'comparative linguistics' (SP v 189). In a rare excursion into the semantic potential of initial vowels, he also reflected on the fact that the letter *a* was associated with continental land masses (as it is, arguably, in English – Asia, Africa, America, Australia). Perhaps, he wrote, 'these words revive the syllable *a* of a protolanguage, meaning dry land' (SP v 192). As the phoneme becomes, in Khlebnikov's view, a morpheme, it begins to assume the semantic identity of a root word.

The notion that the semantic qualities of the individual letter were somehow related to a common protolanguage brings us to another important aspect of Khlebnikov's linguistic beliefs. For, as well as believing in the possibility of a universal language arising in the future out of his 'units of the alphabet', he also believed that such a universal language had once existed in the past, in primitive times. The present Babel of languages, he wrote, was a betrayal of the 'glorious past'. Languages now 'served the cause of hostility', whereas once they had 'united people'; 'savage understood savage and laid aside his blind weapon' (SP v 216). Khlebnikov looked forward to the re-establishment of this social and linguistic harmony. 'What is better?' he jotted down in a notebook not long before his death, 'universal slaughter or a universal language?'[22] This utopian potential of language was an important factor in the development of his linguistic theories. As he writes in the visionary long poem *Goodworld* (*Ladomir*):

Leti, sozvezd'ye chelovech'ye,
Vsyo dal'she, daleye v prostor,
I pereley zemli narech'ya
V yedinyy smertnykh razgovor. (SP I 186)

(Fly, human constellation, ever onwards, further into space, and recast the dialects of earth into a single dialogue of mortals.)

Khlebnikov referred to his notion of the semantic significance of the initial letter under various names. As well as his references to the 'strings' or 'units' of the alphabet, he talked of the 'simple names of language', the 'alphabet of concepts' and the 'alphabet of the intellect'.[23] He also came to refer to it as the 'language of the stars' (*zvyozdnyy yazyk*) (SP III 75). In using this latter term for his projected universal language he was imparting to it a certain aesthetic quality. Khlebnikov's partiality for the image of the star has already been noted and the term 'language of the stars' reinforces this. The name may derive in part from an image which Khlebnikov used in order to portray the words in one of his initial-letter clusters. After giving a list of (allegedly) semantically associated words beginning with *l*, he writes: 'all of these words are stars in the sky of *l*, they are flying towards a single point' (SP v 199). Yet the star of Khlebnikov's 'language of the stars' also relates to a particular star, it was a language which he saw as 'common for the whole of the star inhabited by people' (SP III 376), in other words, a world language for the planet earth.

Moreover, the term 'language of the stars' also has another important connotation. Explaining the nature of his 'self-sufficient word', Khlebnikov wrote, it will be recalled, that this word constructed, in place of the 'self-evident lie' of the 'everyday situation', a 'twilight of stars'. The 'language of the stars' is another aspect of Khlebnikov's 'self-sufficient word', and its concomitant 'starry meaning' (SP v 229) operates at a deeper level than 'the everyday meaning of a word'.

By 1919 Khlebnikov had worked out specific axioms for all the consonants in the Russian alphabet except for *f* (SP v 217–18). Ronald Vroon suggests that Khlebnikov seems to have known instinctively that this phoneme did not exist in Common Slavonic.[24] Certainly, words beginning with *f* in Russian include a high quantity of western loan words.[25] It is perhaps this which made Khlebnikov keep his distance.

In the article 'Our Foundation', which contains the last extensive exposition of his 'alphabet of the intellect', Khlebnikov enumerated as follows the two premises which formed its basis:

1. The first consonant of a simple word governs the whole word, ordering those which follow.
2. Words which begin with the same consonant are united by the same concept . . . (SP v 235–6)

It has been frequently pointed out that while Khlebnikov provides some ingenious examples to back up the tenets of his 'language of the stars', it is not difficult to discover examples which do not appear to fit in with them. There are two important things to note here. Firstly, irrespective of its general merits, Khlebnikov's 'language of the stars' operates as an important semantic system within the body of his own works. It can be seen as a self-contained system. Secondly, however, the fundamental proposition underlying his semanticization of the initial consonant – that is, the relationship between sound and meaning – is by no means irrelevant for modern linguistics. Tests have frequently and consistently shown that people *do* associate certain sounds with certain concepts.[26] Khlebnikov was a poet, not a specialist in linguistics, but his poetic vision of language may well have something to offer to the study of the science of language.

If Khlebnikov saw his 'language of the stars' as being able to reveal for us the 'deep meaning' (SP V 199) of the word, then this was because of his belief, already formulated in the 1912 *Teacher and Pupil* dialogue, in the natural wisdom of language. In his view 'language is just as wise as nature and we are only learning to read it with the growth of science'; furthermore, 'the wisdom of language has preceded the wisdom of sciences' (SP V 231). Elsewhere, Khlebnikov writes, 'language is an eternal source of knowledge' (SP IV 49).

Similar to the way in which the diverse trees in a forest stem initially from seeds which can be held in the palm of the hand, so, for the 'new sower of languages', the whole variety of words can, according to Khlebnikov, be reduced to the 'basic units of "alphabetical truths"' (SP V 228). From these basic units, Khlebnikov maintains, it should be possible to draw up a type of Mendeleyevian periodic table, and, using this, to train engineers to lay down the tracks of language. He continues:

> How frequently the spirit of language permits a direct word, the simple substitution of a consonantal sound in an already existing word, but instead of this the whole nation uses a complex and fragile descriptive expression and increases the time wasted by world reason on reflection. Who will travel from Moscow to Kiev via New York? And yet what line of the modern literary language is free from such journeys? This is because there is no science of word creation. (SP V 228)

It was precisely such a science of word creation which Khlebnikov believed he was establishing in his 'language of the stars' with its 'basic units of "alphabetical truths"'. Nor was this, in Khlebnikov's view, an arbitrary system, but one which reasserted the neglected but inherent wisdom of language. It was possible to make use of language's own creative potential.

This inherent wisdom which Khlebnikov perceived in language also makes itself felt in his notion that running through language, 'more ancient' than the 'verbal' (*slovesnyy*) aspect of the word, was an 'arch of reason' (*rassudochnyy svod*), which remained constant while language itself changed around it (SP V 192). For Khlebnikov this 'life of reason', as he called it elsewhere, was associated with his 'mute language of concepts from units of the intellect' and formed a counterpart to the 'language of words' (SP v 188). It is a duality which takes its place alongside (and may be equated with) the other dualities evident in Khlebnikov's view of language, such as sound and meaning, and the 'language of the stars' and 'everyday language'. Yet Khlebnikov's view of the word was not restricted to dualities.

In one of the articles where he formulates some of the first axioms for his 'language of the stars', he writes: 'running past the sound-leaves and the root-thought in words (via the initial sound) is the thread of fate . . .' (SP v 189). He confirms this view elsewhere in the same article: 'the word has a triple nature: for the ear, for the intellect and as a pathway for fate' (SP v 188).[27] The knowledge which resided in these 'basic units of "alphabetical truths"' was considerable. The initial consonant served as a 'bearer of fate' (SP v 188), as a 'channel for the currents of fate' through which it was possible 'to hear the future in indistinct murmurings (*v neyasnykh govorakh*)' (SP v 192). The destiny of mankind was, in Khlebnikov's view, not so much written in the stars, as written in his 'language of the stars'.

It is not, therefore, surprising that he saw the word as a source of some power. If the initial consonant was able to 'govern' the rest of the word, then at a higher level:

> . . . the word governs the brain, the brain – the hands, the hands – kingdoms. The bridge to the self-sufficient kingdom is self-sufficient speech. (SP v 188)

III

There is, perhaps, one aspect of the word's power which stands out above others in Khlebnikov's vision of language. This is the word's potential to be moulded into the shape of an international tongue. For, however artificial Khlebnikov's projected international discourse may seem, it was for him not something which he imposed on language from without but which arose organically from within. In his 'second attitude towards the word' Khlebnikov did not speak of 'inventing' a universal language, but of discovering it.

One of the primary aims in elucidating definitions for initial consonants was the compilation of a type of dictionary which could serve as a basis for this international tongue. In Khlebnikov's view his 'language of the stars' did not merely relate to the Russian language alone:

> If it turns out that *Ch* has one and the same meaning in all languages, then the question of a universal language is resolved: all types of footwear will be called *che* foot, all types of cups – *che* water – it is clear and simple. In any case *khata* means a hut not only in Russian but also in Egyptian; *v* in Indo-European languages signifies rotation. (SP v 236)

One of the most notable aspects of Khlebnikov's definitions of individual letters in his 'language of the stars' is their geometrical or spatial quality. This will already be apparent from some of the definitions which have been cited above. It will be even more evident if we cite further definitions for this 'common alphabet', which he also called a 'concise dictionary of the spatial world' (SP v 219):

> . . . *Z* means the reflection of a moving point from the line of a mirror at an angle equal to the angle of incidence. The impact of a ray on a hard plane. (SP v 217)

> . . . *K* means the absence of movement, a network of n points at rest, the retention of their positions as regards each other; the end of movement. (SP v 218)

> . . . *B* means the meeting of two points moving along a straight line from different directions. Their struggle, the recoil of one point from the impact of the other. (SP v 218)

These definitions, which occur in the 1919 article, 'Artists of the World' ('Khudozhniki mira'), reflect Khlebnikov's continuing interest in geometry and provide some indication as to why he viewed himself as sharing the birthright of the geometers Euclid and Lobachevsky.[28] They also reflect something about the way Khlebnikov perceived not only language, but also the world; the formulas are not abstract, but concrete and visual.[29]

Khlebnikov sometimes viewed his 'language of the stars' in terms of 'sound "images"' (SP v 220) or 'songs' (SP III 332), but since he also visualized it in terms of such graphic 'spatial configurations',[30] it is not surprising to find that he was also interested in its potential as a 'written language, common for all peoples' of the earth (SP v 216). It is the need to discover written signs for his universal language which lies at the basis of his 1919 appeal to the world's artists. He saw it as the 'task of artists to provide graphic signs for the basic units of reason' (SP v 217).[31]

Khlebnikov saw the written language as having a greater potential of universality than the Babel of spoken languages. He wrote:

> Let a single written language be the companion for the future destinies of mankind and let it be a new collecting vortex, a new collector (*sobiratel'*) of humankind. Mute graphic signs will reconcile the polyphony of languages. (SP v 216–17)

Khlebnikov provides some suggestions in his article as to the form the signs for his universal language should take. For example, *v*, which has the definition 'the rotation of one point around another', he sees 'in the shape of a circle and a point within it'; *z*, which is defined in terms of the reflection of a moving point, Khlebnikov sees as a 'fallen *K*: mirror and ray'; *ch*, which is defined as a container or casing, is seen 'in the shape of a goblet' (SP v 219). The typescript of the article provides representations of these new signs.[32] Not only, therefore, did Khlebnikov perceive a link between sound and meaning, but he also wished to establish a link between the *visual form* of the written character and its meaning. Moreover, in Khlebnikov's view, this link was not artificial but had its roots in the primaeval origins of language:

> ... in the beginning the sign of a concept was a simple sketch of this concept. And it was from this seed that grew the tree of the special life of the letter. (SP v 219)

He clearly had in mind the ideographs of Chinese or the hieroglyphics of ancient Egypt. He believed, for example, that the Chinese and Japanese people 'speak a hundred different languages, but write and read in a single written language' (SP v 216).[33]

The concentration on the written character brought together Khlebnikov's interests both in mathematics and in the visual arts. On one level he came to speak of his world language not only in geometrical terms but also in terms of an 'algebraical language'.[34] Yet on another level, with the idea of signs as picture-writing, he also saw it as an extension of painting, which, he wrote, 'has always spoken in a language accessible to all' (SP v 216).

Notably, in the 'Artists of the World' article, Khlebnikov actually tried to provide practical examples of his international language, producing the following text and its 'translation'. Khlebnikov writes:

Instead of saying:
'The hordes of Huns and Goths, having joined together and gathered round Atilla, full of enthusiasm for battle, moved onwards together, but having been met and defeated by Aetius, protector of Rome, they dispersed into many bands, halted and settled peacefully on their land, after spreading out into the steppes, filling up their emptiness' – should one not say:
'Sha+so (Huns and Goths), ve Atilla, cha po, so do but bo+zo Aetius, kho Rome, so mo ve+ka so, lo sha steppes+cha'.[35] (SP v 220)

As V. P. Grigoryev has pointed out, this 'translation' (one of two which Khlebnikov offers) begs many questions.[36] The semantics of these 'units of the alphabet' are diffuse. The fate of parts of speech (verbs, nouns, etc.) and of the categories of time and number is unclear. Nor has 'everyday language' been entirely dispensed with. Also the conjunction 'but' seems to remain untranslated in spite of its similarity in Russian (*no*) to the translated 'units'. There is, too, the question of the use of vowels, which, Khlebnikov notes here, are 'coincidental and serve euphony' (SP v 220). Such attempts to produce an international language are quite primitive and Khlebnikov was the first to admit this. He called them the 'first cry of a young child' (SP v 221).

Notably, Khlebnikov saw such attempts to produce a universal tongue in terms of his 'transrational language' (*zaumnyy yazyk*). This was evident in the description he gave for his 'second attitude towards the word' when he spoke of his search for a 'universal transrational language' (SP II 9). It is also evident in the address to the 'artists of the world', where, despite the primitive nature of his attempts at 'translation', he declares: 'the general model (*obraz*) for a future universal language has been given. This will be a "transrational" language' (SP v 221).

In a sense, though, it was not so much the end result, the universal language itself which was 'transrational', as the process, the potential of language to transform itself into it. Khlebnikov elsewhere referred to the semanticization of the initial consonant as 'a way to make transrational language rational' (SP v 235), a view which was echoed in the 'Artists of the World' address, when he talked of his 'attempt to transform transrational language from a wild into a domesticated state, to force it to carry a useful load' (SP v 220).

'Transrational language' meant different things to different people at different times. In the *Word as Such* manifesto (which bears the names of both Khlebnikov and Kruchonykh) 'transrational language' was associated, it will be recalled, with the dissection of words. Elsewhere in the same year (1913) Kruchonykh saw 'transrational language' in terms of the word's 'irrational parts'.[37] Earlier that year, however, Kruchonykh had already published his poem, 'Dyr bul shchyl', which was soon seen as the 'transrational' poem *par excellence* and which Vladimir Markov regards as the inauguration of 'transrational language'.[38] According to Kruchonykh, this poem was written in his 'own language' and in words which did not have a 'definite meaning'.[39] Yet, despite the 'private' nature of this language, Kruchonykh also saw it as 'free' and 'universal' (*vselenskiy*).[40] Its universality was not, however, of the systematic 'language of the stars' variety, but was rather related to the language of emotions, with which Kruchonykh closely associated his 'transrational language'.[41]

Khlebnikov's fullest presentation of his ideas on 'transrational language' occurs in the article 'Our Foundation', where the term serves as a subheading for a small section given over to a discussion of its meaning. It is here that Khlebnikov develops his theory of language as a game of dolls. He then continues:

> But language has developed naturally from a few basic units of the alphabet; consonantal and vocal sounds were the strings for this game of sound dolls. But if one takes combinations of these sounds in any order, for example: bobeobi, or dyr bul shchol [sic], or manch′! manch′! chi breo zo! – then such words do not belong to any language, but they still say something, something elusive, but, nonetheless, something which is real. (SP v 234–235)

Such 'scraps of words', Khlebnikov reiterates, 'do mean something':

> But since they do not give anything directly to the consciousness (they are unsuitable for the game of dolls) these free combinations, the play of the voice beyond words, are called transrational language. Transrational language means lying beyond the bounds of reason. (SP v 235)

It is clear from this that Khlebnikov's concept of 'transrational language' was not restricted to his theory of universal communication. Indeed it was broad enough to go beyond his own works and to encompass Kruchonykh's 'Dyr bul shchyl', which, although not the bearer of any 'definite meaning', was for Khlebnikov by no means devoid of meaning entirely. Khlebnikov even remarked on 'Dyr bul shchyl' that it was able to 'calm the most ungoverned passions' (NP 367).[42] Khlebnikov also cites as examples of *zaum'* not only the words of the dying Amenhotep (Akhenaton) from his tale 'Ka' (SP IV 67), but also the opening word of his 'sound-painting' (*zvukopis'*) 'Bobeobi sang the lips' ('Bobeobi pelis' guby'). Given this broader view of *zaum'* it is worth looking in greater detail at how Khlebnikov's 'transrational' discourse becomes reflected in his creative works.

The few 'sound-paintings' which Khlebnikov wrote can serve as one example. 'Bobeobi' is perhaps the most famous of them and reads in full as follows:

> Bobeobi pelis′ guby
> Veeomi pelis′ vzory
> Pieeo pelis′ brovi
> Lieeey – pelsya oblik
> Gzi-gzi-gzeo pelas′ tsep′,
> Tak na kholste kakikh-to sootvetstviy
> Vne protyazheniya zhilo Litso. (SP II 36)

(Bobeobi sang the lips, veeomi sang the gazes, pieeo sang the brows, lieeey sang the aspect, gzi-gzi-gzeo sang the chain, so on a canvas of some sort of correspondences, beyond this dimension there lived a Face.)

Khlebnikov's 'language of the stars' may have come to associate individual consonants with 'spatial configurations', but this early 'sound-painting' (first published in the 1912 *Slap* collection) had already associated them with colour. Khlebnikov was later to specify: the lips are bright red (*bobeobi*), the eyes are blue (*veeomi*), and the brows are black (*pieeo*) (SP V 276). A further brief glossary (SP V 269), headed 'sound-painting' and again equating consonants and colours, shows considerable consistency with *b* again described as red and *p* as black with a tint of red. Moreover, the face of the portrait is recognizable in this glossary in the colour white, which is attributed to the letter *l* and the chain becomes identifiable too, since the letters *g* and *z* are coloured respectively yellow and golden. Khlebnikov did, however, on this occasion, attribute blue not to *v* but to *m*.

'Bobeobi' is clearly not an exercise in Futurist gibberish, but an attempt at the representation of colour in terms of sound, a type of synaesthesia. Such experimental work had at the time a considerable pedigree. The Russian Cubo-Futurists were by no means the first or only poets to respond to painting in their verse. Khlebnikov himself even points to an authority for such poetry in Mallarmé and Baudelaire, who, he writes, had already 'spoken of the sound correspondences of words' (SP v 275). It is probably no coincidence that Khlebnikov portrays his own early 'sound-painting' on a 'canvas of some sort of *correspondences*'.[43]

Khlebnikov also linked this type of 'transrational language' with that other type of *zaum'* – universal language. He described the 'art' of 'sound-painting' as 'a means of nourishment, from which it is possible to grow the tree of a universal language' (SP v 269). It is, perhaps, not surprising then to find yet another passing reference to the alleged connection between colours and individual consonants in his address to the artists of the world (SP v 219). Here *m* is again seen in terms of the colour blue and *v* (blue in 'Bobeobi') becomes green. These changes are reflected in Khlebnikov's other major 'sound-painting' which occurs in *Zangezi*:

V*e*o-veya – zelen′ dereva,
Nizheoty – tyomnyy stvol,
Mam-e*a*ṃi – eto nebo,
P*u*ch′ i chapi – chornyy grach.
Mam i emo – eto oblako. (SP III 344)

(V*e*o-veya – green of tree, nizheoty – dark trunk, mam-e*a*mi – this is sky, p*u*ch′ i chapi – black rook. Mam i emo – this is cloud.)

As Ronald Vroon has pointed out, the glossaries which Khlebnikov provided make the decipherment of his few 'sound-paintings' 'an elementary task'.[44]

Interestingly, unlike Rimbaud, Khlebnikov did not assign colours to vowels. In fact, as Khlebnikov himself put it, at least as far as he was concerned, vowels were 'less studied than consonants' (SP v 237). This can be seen in his 'translations' into 'universal language', where, as has been pointed out, vowels were merely 'coincidental' and 'served euphony'. Vowels do, however, play some semantic role in his language theories (this is evident in his views on 'internal declension'). He once also gave them the following definitions: '*i* connects/*a* against/*o* increases growth/*e* decline, to fall/*u* submissiveness'; which led him to conclude that 'a poem full of vowels alone is full of sense' (SP v 189).[45]

It is within the context of Khlebnikov's 'sound-paintings' that one should also view such works as 'Storm in the Month of Au' ('Groza v mesyatse Au'). This begins as follows:

Pupupopo! Eto grom.
Gam gra gra rap rap.
Pi-pipizi. Eto on.
Bay gzogzigzi. Molniy blesk.
Veygzogziva. Eto ty.
Goga, gago – velichavyye raskaty.
Gago, goga!
Zzh. Zzh. (SP v 73)

(Pupupopo! It is thunder. Gam gra gra rap rap. Pi-pipizi. It is he. Bay gzogzigzi. Flash of lightning. Veygzogziva. It is you. Goga, gago – majestic thunderclaps. Gago, goga! Zzh. Zzh.)

There is clearly an onomatopoeic principle at work here with the poem attempting to convey the sounds of a summer storm. However, the development of the sounds released in this poem by the storm may also be seen to have reference both to Khlebnikov's 'colour coding', and to the spatial configurations of his 'language of the stars'.[46]

An onomatopoeic principle is also evident in Khlebnikov's 'bird language' (*ptichiy yazyk*). Although this is generally considered in the context of Khlebnikov's *zaum'*, it is really an attempt by Khlebnikov to reproduce the sounds of birds, which, as an experienced ornithologist, he was able to do with some accuracy. As with his 'sound-paintings', Khlebnikov makes what he is doing quite explicit to the reader. In the two works where his 'bird language' occurs, the brief 'Wisdom in a Snare' ('Mudrost' v silke' – SP II 180 – first published in 1914) and *Zangezi* (SP III 318–19), the names of birds are given, and in *Zangezi* there are also descriptions of the birds' activities in 'everyday language':

Bunting, rocking on a branch: Tsy-tsy-tsy-sssyy.
Chiffchaff, flitting alone through the green sea, through the upper waves of the topes of the trees, forever shaken by the wind: Pryn'! ptsir*e*p-ptsir*e*b! Pts*i*reb! – tseses*e*.
Bunting: Tsy-sy-sy-ssy (rocking on a reed). Jay: Pi*u*! pi*u*! p'yak, p'yak, p'*y*ak!
Swallow: Tsiv*it*'! Tsiz*it*'! (SP III 318–19)

Nor should one neglect the semantic implications of this bird language, since Khlebnikov was well aware that different bird sounds reflected different moods.[47]

Another aspect of Khlebnikov's 'transrational language' (and one to which he referred as such)[48] is his 'language of the gods'. Like the 'sound-painting' and the 'bird language', it consists of non-derivational coinages (words which are not derived from 'everyday language'), and it is generally considered as the 'most extreme example' of his *zaum'*.[49] This 'language of the gods' appears not only as a section in *Zangezi* (with its main presentation following on from the 'bird language') (SP III 319–21) but also forms the basis for a late short dramatic piece, entitled, appropriately, 'Gods' ('Bogi') (SP IV 259–67). Here is an example of this 'divine' discourse:

Juno: Bal'dur, come here!
Zam, gag, zam!
Unduri: Dekh, mekh, dzupl.
Tuki, paki sitsoro
Migoanchi, mechepì'!
Rbzuk kvakada kvakira! khlyam!
T'ien: Sioukin sisisi.
Siokuki sitsoro!
Khryuryuryuri chitsatsò.
Pech', pach', poch'.

(SP IV 266–7)

As Ronald Vroon has pointed out this 'form of neology . . . is the most impenetrable and least referential of all'. It is, however, Vroon continues, 'an anomaly' because (contrary to his usual practice) 'Khlebnikov provides no glossary, no models, no clues which would lend meaning in the ordinary sense of the word to the coinages'.[50] One should, nevertheless, point out that, similar to his 'sound-painting' and 'bird language', Khlebnikov does combine the neology with 'everyday language', thereby giving it a certain contextual framework. In *Zangezi*, for example, the main exposition of the 'language of the gods' is introduced by an extensive passage in 'everyday language' which sets the scene. In the short drama 'Gods' (as can be seen from the first line in the above quotation) Khlebnikov intersperses the 'transrational' divine utterances with a discourse which is accessible. There are also stage directions. As a result of this the outline of a plot becomes discernible.

One aspect of this 'language of the gods', which stands out, is its 'objective' nature. It is associated not with the 'subjective' language of the poetic I but with the speech of 'characters'. In this sense it is similar to the 'language of the birds'.[51] It is also dialogic, which implies that meaning is present in the discourse, even if it is not apparent to the reader (who perceives it like a conversation in a foreign language). A further point which should be made is that such non-derivational 'transrational' neology is comparatively rare in the context of Khlebnikov's overall word creation and it affects only a tiny percentage of his creative output.

Like both the 'sound-painting' and 'bird language', however, this 'language of the gods' does have a pedigree which is not restricted to Khlebnikov's later works. 'Night in Galicia' ('Noch′ v Galitsii'), for example, first published in 1914, includes the following passage:

Water nymphs: Io, ia, tsolk,
Io, ia, tsolk.
Pits, pats, patsu,
Pits, pats, patsa.
Io ia tsolk, io ia tsolk,
Kopotsamo, minogamo, pintso, pintso, pintso!
Witches (stretching out into a flock like cranes and flying away):
Shagadam, magadam, vykadam.
Chukh, chukh, chukh.
Chukh. (SP II 201)

As Khlebnikov informs us earlier in this poem, the source for this 'transrational' chant of the water nymphs is not non-derivational neology created by the author but a 'text-book' (as Khlebnikov ironically refers to it) by a certain Sakharov (SP II 200). The book in question is the impressive *Skazaniya russkogo naroda* (*Tales of the Russian People*) compiled by I. A. Sakharov in the mid nineteenth century, which includes a number of magical chants, witches' songs and incantations and which was brought to Khlebnikov's attention in 1913 by none other than Roman Jakobson.[52] It is this magical language which can serve as an analogue for Khlebnikov's 'language of the gods' and which represents another important aspect of Khlebnikov's *zaum′*.[53]

As Khlebnikov explained in the article 'Our Foundation':

The fact that transrational language predominates in invocations and charms, driving out rational language, goes to show that it has a special power over the consciousness, special rights to life alongside rational language. (SP v 235)

In another article, written at about the same time (1919–1920), he was more specific:

They say that verses should be comprehensible. For example ... <a signboard on a street>, on which is written in a clear and simple language: 'We sell ...' ... but a signboard is still not poetry. Though it is comprehensible. On the other hand, why are charms and invocations in so-called magical speech, the sacred language of paganism, these 'shagadam, magadam, vygadam, pits, pats, patsu' – why are they successions of syllables collected together which reason can make no sense of, so it seems like a transrational language of folklore? Yet attributed to these incomprehensible words is the greatest power over man, spells of sorcery, a direct influence on man's destiny. The greatest charms are concentrated in them. They are regarded as having the power to control good and evil ... (SP v 225)

Khlebnikov is speaking in defence here of a magical 'transrational' discourse. This apparently non-communicative language does in fact communicate something and seems to exercise 'the greatest power over man'. It is a language, Khlebnikov says further on in this article, which can bypass the 'head (*golova*) of the government' and address itself 'directly to the people of the feelings' (SP v 225). It is also associated in Khlebnikov's view with the 'people' (*narod*) on a real plane as well as a metaphoric one. These charms and invocations seem to him like a 'transrational language of folklore' (*v narodnom slove*).

Khlebnikov's interest in the magical trappings of folklore was considerable. Thematically his works abound in wood demons, water nymphs, wizards and witches, and reflect their rites and rituals. It is important, however, to see such preoccupations within the context of the time. Symbolist writers such as Blok and Balmont also wrote works on poetry and magic, as did Andrey Bely.[54] Moreover, in the first decade of this century Slavonic mythology was 'in high fashion' with works by Aleksey Remizov and Sergey Gorodetsky enjoying particular success.[55] Both of these writers exerted some influence on the early work of Khlebnikov, who held Gorodetsky's collection of verse, *Yar'*, in high esteem.[56] The mythological and incantatory elements of Gorodetsky's verse will have found in Khlebnikov a sympathetic ear.

Incantatory elements are spread throughout the whole of Khlebnikov's verse. Notably, Khlebnikov's renowned poetic debut, the *smekhachi* poem, was published under the title 'Incantation by Laughter', which immediately placed even his derivative 'non-transrational' verse in a magical context. The hero of the late 'supertale', Zangezi, also utters his own incantation (SP III 344). Since Khlebnikov's poetic *personae* could fulfil magical roles, it is not surprising that Khlebnikov was himself seen by some of his contemporaries as a wizard or magician.[57] Moreover, it was quite legitimate for the language of such a 'magician' to be in a coded form. The poet as a magician is also the poet as bearer of a coded text; and it is by virtue of this coded text that the magician maintains his power.

A related aspect of this magical 'transrational language' was identified by Khlebnikov as the language of prayer. Following his comments (cited above) on the 'sacred language of paganism', Khlebnikov also wrote:

> The prayers of many peoples are written in a language which is incomprehensible to those who pray. Does a Hindu really understand the Vedas? Old Church Slavonic is incomprehensible to a Russian. Latin – to a Pole and a Czech. But a prayer written in Latin works just as effectively as a signboard. Thus, the magical speech of charms and invocations does not wish to have everyday reason as its judge. (SP V 225)

Of course, whether prayers can 'work as effectively as a signboard' may be open to dispute, but for the believer this type of 'magical' discourse certainly cannot be judged by 'everyday reason'. However, 'magical' language of this kind is different in that it has a specific referential meaning which is unknown to the listener solely because the language is foreign or ancient. Even though the words may be incomprehensible to the worshippers, their meaningful nature is not in doubt. One would expect a similar type of response to some of Khlebnikov's own work.

To discover another factor contributing towards the development of Khlebnikov's magical 'transrational language' one should turn to a less canonical form of worship. Khlebnikov will have been well aware of the interest manifested by some of his friends and literary colleagues in the activities of the schismatic religious sects and in particular their glossolalia. The formalist critic Shklovsky, for instance, cited examples of schismatic glossolalia in his 1915 article on the preconditions for Futurism.[58] Kruchonykh also cited from the chants of the schismatics in his manifestoes outlining

Cubo-Futurist theory. His 'New Ways of the Word' article, printed in the Futurist miscellany *The Three* alongside Khlebnikov's works, contained the following examples of glossolalic utterances:

"namos pamos bagos" . . .
"gerezon drovolmire zdruvul
dremile cherezondro fordey"[59]

Kruchonykh actually called such neologistic chants 'transrational language'.[60]

Unlike prayers in Latin or Old Church Slavonic, glossolalia is essentially non-referential, though Kruchonykh associated it with an ability to speak in foreign languages.[61] At its roots, of course, this 'speaking in tongues' is ultimately connected with the descent of the Holy Spirit and the universal communication of the word of God ('every man heard them speak in his own language' Acts 2–6). As such it bears a certain similarity to some of Khlebnikov's (and Kruchonykh's) own linguistic aspirations: it is at the same time 'transrational' and universal. One might say that speaking in tongues is a 'real' divine language and, indeed, Ronald Vroon has pointed to what he calls 'a number of remarkable similarities' between glossolalic utterances and Khlebnikov's own 'language of the gods'.[62]

Another of the analogues which Ronald Vroon points to for the 'language of the gods' and which is also of a more general relevance for Khlebnikov's magical 'transrational language' (though it is not 'transrational' *per se*) is the use of proper names. Vroon points out the 'striking parallel . . . between the names of the gods or heroes and their subsequent utterances' and suggests that they are 'apparently trying to utter their own names and those of their fellow deities, perhaps in an attempt to define their own essence'.[63]

The potential sound play of exotic names can be seen in the passage which Khlebnikov uses as an epigraph for the play 'Gods' (a passage which he also used in his long poem *Goodworld*):

Tuda, tuda,
Gde Izanagi
Chitala Monogatori Perunu,
A Erot sel na kolena Shang-Ti,
I sedoy khokhol na lysoy golove boga
Pokhodit na kom snega, na sneg;
Gde Amur tseluyet Maa Emu,
A Tiyen beseduyet s Indroy;

Gde Yunona i Tsintekuatl′
Smotryat Korredzhio
I voskhishcheny Murill′o;
Gde Unkulunkulu i Tor
Igrayut mirno v shakhmaty . . . (SP IV 259)

(To there, to there, where Izanagi read Monogatori to Perun, and Eros sat on Shang Ti's knees, and the grey tuft of hair on God's bald head is like a ball of snow, like snow; where Cupid kisses Maa-Emae, and T′ien talks to Indra; where Juno and Tsintekuatl look at Correggio and are delighted by Murillo; where Unkulunkulu and Thor play peacefully at chess . . .)[64]

It is quite evident that the names of some of these gods, and, perhaps, also of the painters Correggio and Murillo, would be rather mysterious for the average Russian (and, for that matter, foreign) reader. Attention will consequently be shifted on to the sound of the name rather than its unknown referent. As Vladimir Markov said in his comments on *Goodworld*: 'in some passages these names almost lose their denotative quality, and are used rather like abstract colour stains'.[65] In Khlebnikov's own terms, they bypass 'the head of the government' where reason presides and directly affect 'the people of the feelings'.

This 'transrational' use of proper names is even more pronounced when Khlebnikov actually uses names as derivatives for coining new words:

Usad′ba noch′yu, chingiskhan′!
Shumite, siniye beryozy.
Zarya nochnaya, zaratustr′!
A nebo sineye, motsart′!
I sumrak oblaka, bud′ Goyya!
Ty noch′yu oblako, roops′! (IS 380)

(Country house by night, Genghis Khan! Make noise, blue birch trees. Glow of night, Zarathustra! And blue sky, Mozart! And cloud's twilight, be Goya! You cloud at night, Ro-ops!)

The names of Genghis Khan, Zarathustra, Mozart and the painter Rops[66] have been made into verbal imperatives and the poem calls upon aspects of nature and the physical world to assume their qualities. Another short poem, 'O dostoyevskiymo begushchey tuchi!', (which has been translated as 'O the racing cloud's Dostoyevskitude!'), containing a similar combination of neology and proper names, has been called by one critic an 'incantation by name' and referred to in terms of 'an act of magic'.[67] Moreover, an 'incantation by name' lies at the basis of one of Khlebnikov's most remarkable long poems 'Razin'. It is remarkable because it is a work comprising over 400 lines of palindromes, which Khlebnikov himself called 'an incantation by double flow of speech' (SP I 318).

The poem begins with a two-line palindromic epigraph:

> Ya Razin so znamenem Lobachevskogo logov.
> Vo golovakh svecha, bol′; mene man, zasni zarya. (SP I 202)

(I am Razin with the banner of Lobachevsky's lairs. In the heads a candle, pain; of enticements for me, sleep dawn.)[68]

Its first section, entitled 'Path' ('Put′'), then continues:

> Setuy utyos!
> Utro chortu!
> My, nizari, leteli Razinym.
> Techot i nezhen, nezhen i techot.
> Volgu div nesyot, tesen vid uglov.
> Oleni. Sinelo.
> Ono. (SP I 202)

(Lament cliff! A morning for the devil! We, the low ones, flew like Razin. It flows tender, tender it flows. Carries the Volga of wonders, narrow is the aspect of corners. Deer. It has grown blue. It.)

The form as such does not demand neology. But, despite Khlebnikov's evident versatility, he was not averse to expanding palindromic possibilities by means of coinages (the apt *nizari*, 'the low ones' – in terms of class or topography – serves as an example here).[69] The palindrome has strong magical connotations as a form for spells and incantations. It is a dual flow of sound which conceals words within words and doubles the word's power. The fact that the poem illustrates Khlebnikov's 'poetic' relationship with Stepan Razin is no coincidence. Khlebnikov regarded himself, after all, as 'Razin in reverse' (SP I 234). He viewed the palindrome as having a prophetic potential, once describing his palindromic lines as 'reflected rays of the future' (SP II 9). The reflection of the sounds evident in the palindromes is matched by the reflection of the dual fates which are involved. Khlebnikov is not only incanting Razin in this poem, it is also an invocation to himself.[70]

Similar to the palindrome is Khlebnikov's tendency to encode names and key words as anagrams. Recognizing a potential here for the hidden meaning, Khlebnikov himself once wrote that the short poem beginning 'Krylyshkuya' was 'fine' because it contained within it 'like the Trojan horse' the word *ushkuy*, (the name given to the boats used by the pirates who plied the Volga river) (SP V 194). Other anagrams can be found in abundance in Khlebnikov's works, and he was particularly fond of encoding the name of Razin. An example of this can be seen in the poem '*Ra* ...' (SP III 138) which presents several anagrams of the rebel hero's name before actually citing the name in full.

This is a poem which also demonstrates the multiplicity of meanings present in a Khlebnikov text. *Ra* is not only associated with the name of Razin but is also the name of the Egyptian sun god and the ancient name of an area adjacent to the Volga river, which is where the Razin in the poem washes his feet. In addition to this, the *Ra* of the poem also relates to the letter *r* in Khlebnikov's 'language of the stars'.[71] Strictly speaking, palindromes and anagrams, although involving an element of coding, are not within the sphere of Khlebnikov's magical 'transrational' language. But when the anagram relates to the 'language of the stars' it can clearly acquire a 'transrational' aspect. This is a direction which can lead into an area of polysemantics where every key word in a Khlebnikov text might be seen with regard both to its 'everyday meaning' and to the 'starry meaning' of its initial letter.

Indeed, ultimately, Khlebnikov even viewed his magical, incantatory language in terms of this 'starry meaning'. In the same article in which he talks of 'the charms and invocations in so-called magical speech ... these "shagadam, magadam, vygadam, pits, pats, patsu"', he also writes how the 'strange wisdom' of this magical speech can be broken down 'into truths contained in the individual sounds: *sh, m, v*, etc.' 'We do not yet understand them,' Khlebnikov continues. 'Let's be honest. But there is no doubt that these sequences of sound represent a series of universal truths which are passing before the twilight of our soul' (SP V 225).[72]

When Khlebnikov makes use of his 'language of the stars' in his creative work, he usually provides at least some clues as to how one should interpret such a coded discourse. For example, as with his 'language of the gods', his 'bird language' or his 'sound-painting', he mixes the 'transrational language' with 'everyday language', thereby providing an important explanatory context. A prime instance of this is his 'Scratch Across the Sky' ('Tsarapina po nebu'), whose first section 'A Breach into Languages' ('Proryv v yazyki') also has the descriptive subtitle 'combination of the language of the stars and everyday (*obydennogo*) language' (SP III 75).

The scene depicted in this passage is that of a joyful peasant dance. It reads in part:

Pi bega po kol'tsu tropy,
Sha nog bosykh,
Kak kratki *Ka* pokoya!
I *Ve* volos na golove lyudey,
Ve vetra i lyubvi,
Es radostey vesennikh . . . (SP III 75)

(*Pi* running along the ring of the path, *Sha* of bare feet, how short the *Ka* of rest! And the *Ve* of hair on the head of people, *Ve* of wind and love, *Es* of spring joys . . .)

In addition to the mixing of 'languages' Khlebnikov also goes as far as to append a glossary of this 'language of the stars' to assist the reader further (SP III 376–7). According to this glossary, *Pe* records the movement of a point in a straight line away from an unmoving point; *Sha* is the 'merging of surfaces', the greatest area within the least confines; *Ka* is the halting of many points at one unmoving point; *Ve* – the movement of a point around an unmoving point; and *Es* – paths of movement which have a common starting point (like the rays of the sun radiating outwards). In these few lines we have a graphic portrayal of the dancers coming together, halting and moving apart again with their hair swirling around their heads. It is possible to take any of the lines from this section and, using the glossary provided, reach some interpretation of the 'coded' text.[73]

'Scratch Across the Sky' also reveals another aspect of Khlebnikov's 'language of the stars'. As well as being able to function as an autonomous unit with its own 'meaning', in combination with 'everyday language' it has the potential to act as an instrument for neology. The end of a section entitled 'To the Terrestrial Globe' ('Zemnomu sharu') reads:

Go lyudi, smotrite na nebo:
Che zori tak velyat!
Mne goum povelel
Vvesti *Go* nravy
Letuchego pravitel'stva
Zemnogo shara,
Kak motylyok porkhayushchego
Po lugu imyon. (SP III 80)

(*Go* people, look at the sky: *Che* dawns thus command! Goum has bid me to introduce the *Go* customs of the terrestrial globe's flying government, fluttering like a butterfly across a meadow of names.)

Here we can see how the phoneme *Go* has combined with the 'everyday' word it qualifies, *um* (meaning mind or intellect), to form the compound neologism *goum*. This neologistic tendency of the 'language of the stars' manifested itself as early as 1916 (curiously, with the coinage *chezori*, which Khlebnikov keeps separate in the quote above).[74] It is a potential which is also evident in Khlebnikov's own attempts at 'translations' into his universal language, which themselves are a type of 'combination of the language of the stars and everyday language' (SP V 220–1).

Since Khlebnikov defines *Go* in his glossary as the 'highest point' (SP III 377), *goum* can be interpreted as a 'supreme intellect'. Such an interpretation is confirmed in *Zangezi*, where this coinage occurs again among many similar ones (*vyum, noum, laum*, etc.) as part of Zangezi's 'sounding of the bells of the intellect' (*blagovest uma*) (SP III 334–6). Following his usual practice of facilitating the task of the reader, Khlebnikov once more provides a glossary for all these words; *goum* is defined as a type of intellect which is as 'high' as the stars (SP III 336). Interestingly, the *Zangezi* glossary again lists *chezori* (and other such *che* words) by analogy with *cheum*.

Khlebnikov also seems to have been prepared to create new 'compound' words based entirely on the units of his 'language of the stars', producing, for example, *viel'* (from *v* and *l*).[75] Although Khlebnikov directed his attention primarily at the initial consonant, he was also prepared to consider the semantic potential of consonants elsewhere in the word. This tendency was present as early as 1912 in the article beginning 'Let us take two words . . .' ('Izberyom dva slova . . .') (NP 325–9). The notion receives more detailed attention several years later in 'Scratch Across the Sky', where, among other things, Khlebnikov muses on the combination of the consonants *kh* and *m* in the word *khlam* (meaning junk or trash). Khlebnikov notes here that the beginning of the word, *khla*, contains the 'strength of the cow-shed and comfort' ('sila khleva i kholi'), whereas *am* conveys the 'strength of the grave, and of pestilence' ('sila mogily i mora') (SP III 80–1). He goes on:

> *KHA* – eto pregrada mezhdu ubiytsey i zhertvoy,
> Volkom, livnem i chelovekom,
> Kholodom i telom, morozom i kholey.

EM – razdeleniye obyoma, nozhom i tsel′yu
Na mnozhestvo malykh chastey.
Khlam – razrushennoye nachalo kholi . . . (SP III 81)

(*KHA* is the barrier between killer and victim, wolf, downpour and man, between cold and body, frost and comfort. *EM* is the division of volume, by knife and aim, into a multitude of small parts. Junk – the principle of comfort destroyed . . .)

The meaning of the word *khlam* is governed, according to Khlebnikov, not only by the initial consonant *kh*, but also by the final consonant *m*. The protective barrier formed by *kh* is rendered into 'junk' by the destructive power of the letter *m*. The meaning of a word can become the result of an interaction between the different consonants within it. This provides an 'everyday language' model for neologisms such as *viel′*.

Khlebnikov developed the notion of the word as an arena of conflict, where one consonant could vie with another for supremacy. Thus, by changing the second consonant of *khlam* (*l*) into an *r*, 'junk' can be transformed into a 'temple' (*khram*) (SP III 328, V 104). Similarly, the master (*pan*) may rule, but, with the change of the final consonant *n* into an *l*, the 'master has fallen' ('pan pal') (SP III 84–5).

This type of word-play (reminiscent of the 'reverse meaning' in the theory of internal declension) is also associated with the 'duel of words' which Khlebnikov saw in *Zangezi*. V. P. Grigoryev has identified this in terms of the struggle between *m* and *b*, where the *m* has ousted *b* from 'everyday words' such as *bogatyr′* (hero), *bogach* (rich man), and *bogi* (gods) to produce neologisms such as *mogatyr′*, *mogach* and *mogi* (from *moch′* – to be able).[76] A similar process can be seen in the renowned example which Khlebnikov provides in *Goodworld*, where the revolution achieves a linguistic fulfilment with the replacement of the 'landlords' (*dvoryane*) by the 'creators' (*tvoryane*) (SP I 184).

This initial mutation is often associated with the 'language of the stars'. Moreover, the creation of such words as *tvoryane* is what Khlebnikov viewed as an expression of the natural wisdom of language. Clearly, this type of opposition was also associated with neology, but not always. Khlebnikov could, for example, make the same point using the 'wisdom' of existing 'everyday language', contrasting *bratvy* (brothers) and *zhratvy* (guzzlers) (NP 61).[77]

With the emphasis being placed on initial consonants in such cases, even 'everyday language' in Khlebnikov's creative works can take on a certain 'starry' aspect. This is, perhaps, not surprising, since he would, of course, explain the definitions of the initial consonants in his 'language of the stars' by recourse to 'everyday' words. As he wrote in 'Our Foundation':

> ... take two words, *lad'ya* (boat) and *ladon'* (palm of the hand). The starry meaning of this word, which comes out in the twilight is: an enlarged surface, against which is directed a path of force, like a spear striking armour. (SP v 229)

In short, both words have the same 'starry meaning', because they are governed by the same consonant *l*. Because of this stated connection, one cannot, henceforth, dissociate such canonical words entirely from their 'starry meaning'. As Ronald Vroon has rightly pointed out, this again leads into the area of polysemy, where 'canonical words are selected to demonstrate the validity of Khlebnikov's conclusions concerning the semantic field of the consonant in question'.[78] In the final analysis, the canonical words themselves become part of the 'language of the stars'.

Khlebnikov saw, in particular, certain proper names in such terms. For example, the names of many White leaders in the civil war began with *k* (Kaledin, Krymov, Kornilov, Kolchak), a letter which, for Khlebnikov, was already associated with the end of movement and thus with death.[79] This is an extension of an earlier notion that *g* was associated with Germany and *r* with Russia. Not surprisingly, *l* could become associated with Lenin (SP III 84) as well as with the concept of harmony (*ladomir*), the restoration of equilibrium (SP v 230) and even the arrival of popular power in Russia (SP v 237). Such letters demonstrate some flexibility in their semantic scope, although they function within certain parameters. *G*, for example, can acquire the general connotations of ruler and authority and *r* the struggle to overcome such authority.[80] These individual letters assume almost mythological status and can figure as 'self-sufficient' entities, 'warriors of the alphabet', acting out historical events:

> *Er, Ka, El'* i *Ge* –
> Voiny azbuki, –
> Byli deystvuyushchimi litsami etikh let,
> Bogatyryami dney ...
> I tshchetno *Ka* neslo okovy, vo vremya draki *Ge* i *Er*,
> *Ge* palo, srublennoe *Er*,
> I *Er* v nogakh u *Elya*! (SP III 330)

(*Er, Ka, El'* and *Ge* – warriors of the alphabet, – were the *dramatis personae* of those years, the heroes of days . . . And in vain was *Ka* in chains, during the battle of *Ge* and *Er*, *Ge* has fallen, felled by *Er*, and *Er* is at the feet of *El'*!)[81]

However, in Khlebnikov's view, such scenarios reach beyond mere representation, since his initial consonant was, after all, a 'bearer of fate and a path for wills' (SP v 188):

> Vzdor, chto Kaledin ubit i Kolchak, chto vystrel zvuchal.
> Eto *Ka* zamolchalo, *Ka* otstupilo, rukhnulo na zem'.
> Eto *El'* stroit moryu mora mol, a smerti smelyye meli.
> (SP III 329)

(It is nonsense that Kaledin has been killed and Kolchak, that the shot has resounded. It is *Ka* that has fallen silent, *Ka* which has retreated, crashed to the ground. It is *El'*, building a breakwater for the sea of pestilence, and bold shallows for death.)

Ultimately, language itself is seen by Khlebnikov as a determining factor in the unfolding of human destiny. As he writes in *Zangezi*, after depicting the battle between the 'warriors of the alphabet':

> Pust' mglu vremyon razveyut veshchiye zvuki
> Mirovogo yazyka. On tochno svet. (SP III 330)

(Let the prophetic sounds of universal language disperse the mist of time. It is like light.)

IV

Khlebnikov's preoccupation with the potential of language was enormous. He identified for himself over fifty different types of 'languages'[82] ranging from the familiar and well-used 'language of the stars' and 'magical speech' to the less developed 'rainbow speech' and 'personal language'. Moreover, these many 'languages' do not restrict themselves solely to words. The list of Khlebnikov's different discourses also reveals a fascination with the 'linguistic' potential of that other great love of his – mathematics and the number. We can find, for example, references to the 'number-word' (*chisloslovo*), 'number-names' (*chisloimena*), 'number language' (*chislovoy yazyk*) and 'number-speeches' (*chislorechi*).[83]

This interest in the interplay between language and number manifests itself in various ways. One early dialogue (published

1913), developing the familiar notion of the relationship between sound and meaning, attempts to establish etymological connections between the names given to numbers and other words. For example, there is a suggestion that the Russian word for 'seven' is related to the Russian word for 'family'. 'Is not the number seven (*sem'*) a truncated form of the word for family (*semya*)?' one of the interlocutors in the dialogue asks. A connection is even drawn between the word for 'unit' (*yedinitsa*) and 'food' (*yeda*), the alleged justification being that 'primaeval man' would eat his food as an individual 'unit' without the help of others (SP v 184). These rather limited notions do not appear to have been developed further by Khlebnikov, though a similar idea is apparent in his later connection between the numbers two (*dva*) and three (*tri*) and clusters of words which began with the initial consonants of these numbers – *d* and *t*.[84]

The early dialogue which included these suggestions also linked numbers and words in a very different way. Commenting on one of Khlebnikov's own short poems, 'Grasshopper' ('Kuznechik'), the dialogue noted that in the first four lines of the poem 'the sounds "u, k, l, and r" are repeated five times each'. A similar five-fold 'structure' is also identified in the long poem 'I and E' (SP v 185). Khlebnikov was clearly interested in the mathematical symmetry which seemed to him to operate in his own verse. It is a further insight into the kind of hidden meanings which Khlebnikov perceived.

He pursued such ideas in a brief article published in *Chronicle* in 1916, this time, though, applying the mathematical principles to verse by Pushkin and Lermontov. Here, as well as pointing out a numerical pattern in the distribution of certain letters, he also linked the individual letters in question with his 'language of the stars'. Thus he was able, in his view, to establish a correlation between the struggle of life and death in Pushkin's 'Feast during the Plague' ('Pir vo vremya chumy') and the interplay between the letter *m* (which he associated with death) and the letter *p* (which he associated with vitality). He accorded the work the 'number name (*chislovoye imya*) 5m+p', and referred to this 'language' as 'the second language of songs' (SP v 210–11). As he wrote elsewhere at about this time, 'the light of numbers' was now falling on the sphere of 'linguistics' (SP v 203).

That the potential of the number was already of some importance for Khlebnikov by 1914 can be seen in the letter which was written to him in February of that year by Roman Jakobson. This letter quotes Khlebnikov as saying that the alphabet was 'too poor for poetry', that it would lead into a 'blind alley' and that he (Khlebnikov) had arrived at 'the number'.[85] Such dissatisfaction would seem to imply that Khlebnikov was contemplating using the number as a means of artistic expression. Indeed, Jakobson expresses the view in his letter that poetry from numbers was possible and he asks Khlebnikov to provide him with a small sample. Khlebnikov did not, however, to our knowledge, write a 'poem of figures', (*poema tsifr*) (though, apparently, Kruchonykh did).[86]

On the contrary, Khlebnikov seems at this stage to have been looking at numbers in terms of practical rather than poetic language. For example, one of his aphoristic 'Proposals' ('Predlozheniya') first published in December 1915 in the collection *Took: the Futurists' Drum* (*Vzyal: baraban futuristov*), put forward the following suggestion:

> All thoughts on earth (there are so few of them) should be given a special number, like the houses of a street, and conversation should be carried out and thoughts exchanged by means of a language of sight. Numbers should be attributed to the speeches of Cicero, Cato, Othello, Demosthenes and the unnecessary imitative speeches in the courts and other institutions should be replaced by a simple signboard bearing the number of the speech. This is the first international language. (SP v 158)

It is not so much the aesthetic function of numbers as their communicative function, their potential as an international discourse, which interests Khlebnikov here.

Khlebnikov expressed a similar notion in 1916 when he suggested that 'a language of numbers' could serve as a pan-Asian 'dictionary'. Numbers could be attributed to each action and each image (*obraz*), and 'number-speeches' created. 'The mind will be freed from the senseless waste of its strength on everyday speeches,' he concludes (SP v 157).

Moreover, as well as freeing the mind from everyday chores, these 'number-speeches' would, Khlebnikov claimed, free language from 'an insulting burden'. 'Languages will remain for the arts' (SP v 158). His *Time a Measure of the World* (published in 1916) confirmed this opinion when it stated: 'an obsolete instrument of thought, the word will nonetheless remain for the arts' (SS III 447).

It would be greatly misleading, however, to give the impression that Khlebnikov did not perceive any aesthetic merit in number. Although he does not appear to have espoused the idea of a 'poem of figures', numbers do appear in his works on many occasions. Such appearances are usually connected with his developing interest in mathematically predicting the course of history. His poems include figures which relate to years and dates or to the equations which he used to determine these dates (take, for example, the 'birthright' poem, quoted earlier). In addition, number features prominently both as a poetic image and as the subject of some important works.[87]

One notable consequence of Khlebnikov's preoccupation with his mathematical predictions was the association of number with an historical pattern or symmetry. In being able to represent historical or temporal processes in terms of numbers or equations, Khlebnikov was able to reach a point where the numbers and equations could be perceived 'aesthetically'. Take, for example, the following description (in *Time a Measure of the World*) of the relationship between the earth and its 'number of numbers' 365:

> . . . the terrestrial globe should be perceived as a finished work of pure art, of sounds, where Scriabin[88] is the earth, strings form the year and the day, and the predominant harmony (*sozvuchiye*), placed at the head of the whole work, is the numbers 365, 1, 25 (the sun's day being taken as 25 earth days) . . . (SS III 445)

Consequently, in spite of his view of language remaining for the arts, number was by no means without an important aesthetic merit for Khlebnikov. This was so evident towards the end of his life, in particular, that number became for him an aesthetic rival to the word. In 1919 he wrote how he had 'recently gone over to numerical writing (*chislovoye pis'mo*), like an artist of number' (SP II 11). Elsewhere he confirmed: 'the artist of number is coming to replace the artist of word'.[89]

Two roles, one as the author of mathematical calculations and the other as the poet, vied with each other for supremacy, but Khlebnikov saw both roles in aesthetic terms – either way he was an 'artist'. His carefully structured calculations on time and fate are to be seen in a similar light to his lines of verse. His writings on time and fate might, in fact, be considered 'poems of figures' in their own right.

Or, perhaps, one should say 'figure-sculptures', since, as Khlebnikov wrote in one of the sections probably intended for his 'Boards of Fate':

> Number is like the only clay in the fingers of the artist. From it we want to shape the blue-idol face of time! The face for which mankind has for a long time yearned in all its dreams . . .[90]

Nor was sculpture the only form of art which Khlebnikov associated with number. He also spoke of the 'desire to move from the hazy word to the precise *architecture* of numbers'.[91] Similar to the way in which he could identify 'piles' (*svai*) for structures in the geometrical shapes of letters, he saw in his numbers the physical shapes of buildings and constructions. They could even take on the appearance of a whole town in the 'steppes of time':

> Where previously the remote steppes of time had been, there suddenly rose up orderly polynomials (*mnogochleny*) built upon the numbers three and two, and my consciousness was like that of a traveller before whom there suddenly appeared the jagged towers and walls of a town which no one knew existed. (SS III 473)

A mathematical expression could become for him a 'street of towers disappearing into the distance'.[92] Numbers began to rise up before him in the shape of the very 'tower of time', to which – like the 'tower of the word' – he was also laying siege:

> Yest' bashnya iz troyek i dvoyek
> Khodit po ney starets vremyon. (SP III 351)

(There is a tower of threes and twos, the elder of times paces on it.)

4

From warrior to prophet – the siege of the tower of time

I

As early as 1904, in a self-styled epitaph 'Let them read on a tombstone ...' ('Pust′ na mogil′noy plite prochtut ...') Khlebnikov had already outlined many of his future concerns. He included as one of his prospective achievements the fact that he had 'linked time and space' (NP 318). Many years later, not long before his death, Khlebnikov testified to the strength of this prediction, announcing in his 'Boards of Fate' that he had provided 'a quantitative link between the principles of time and space' (SS III 477).[1]

The nature of the relationship between these two principles was for long a major preoccupation. Khlebnikov was concerned at the neglect that the study of time was suffering. Time, in his view, was a 'cinderella' (SS III 443); it was a 'serf' (SP V 105), a 'kitchen boy'[2] in the service of space. Khlebnikov wished to correct the imbalance. He wished to find physical laws which operated in the 'state of time' just as they did in the 'states of space'. He saw the movement of time 'visually' (SS III 473). He had, in effect, a vision of time as a kind of three-dimensional entity, 'a vision of time in stone' (SP V 104). Osip Mandelstam formulated this dimensional synaesthesia succinctly when he spoke of Khlebnikov as, 'a kind of idiotic Einstein, unable to distinguish which was nearer – a railway bridge or the *Lay of Igor's Campaign*'.[3]

Moreover, time and space were more than just linked in Khlebnikov's vision, they were also, to all intents and purposes, interdependent. His 'laws of time' could not exist in a void, they were irrelevant unless applied to the world of space. Ultimately, if Khlebnikov came to besiege the 'tower of time', then many of his early battles were fought in the 'states of space' and it was through these battles that he began to pinpoint his final objective.

When Khlebnikov spoke of 'besieging' his 'tower of time' (and his other 'towers'), the image of battle was not fortuitous. War and conflict were one of the major concerns of his writing and this is reflected in his calculations aimed at discovering his 'laws of time'. The dates of battles were one of the key factors in his attempts to plot the future. Nor was Khlebnikov interested solely in contemporary conflicts. His interest encompassed a whole plethora of wars and battles spread throughout history and over much of the globe. His preoccupation with war was both temporal and spatial; it was demonstrative of the 'link' between the third and fourth dimensions which he claimed to have established.

Undoubtedly, one of the reasons for what one might call the 'polemocentric' aspect of Khlebnikov's works was the troubled time in which he lived. The Russo-Japanese war was closely followed by the tensions in the Balkans, which eventually gave rise in turn to conflict on a huge scale with the outbreak of the First World War. On the domestic front the frequent eruptions of revolutionary violence culminated in the collapse of autocracy and the Bolshevik takeover. Foreign intervention and civil war rapidly followed. The times in which Khlebnikov wrote were not peaceable; neither were his works.

II

Amid the annals of large scale violence and individual conflict which Khlebnikov's works chronicle, the figure of the warrior becomes a most important poetic hero. This will already have become evident to a certain degree in the discussion of the poet and the crowd, where the portrayal of the poetic hero as benefactor or liberator could often involve warrior-like feats. It will also be evident that Khlebnikov did not view such warrior-like feats in a negative light. Indeed, the opposite seems to be the case.

This view can be confirmed if one looks at some of Khlebnikov's early (pre-1914) works. Some of these reveal an ethos of considerable aesthetic admiration for the warrior. There is, for example, the portrayal of the cossack warrior Palivoda in 'Children of the Otter' (SP II 153–7); of the Amazon 'bold beauties' in 'The Seven' ('Semero') (SP II 116–18); and of the 'glorious commanders' in 'Alferovo' (SP II 114–15). A positive aesthetic response is also evoked from Khlebnikov by a similar figure, that of the hunter. This can be seen in the sympathetic depiction of the hunter and brigand Usa-gali (SP IV 37–9) and in the portrayal of the hunter

Nikolay (SP IV 40–6); as it also can in the dedication of the long poem 'Snake Train – Flight' to the elk hunter Popov, whom Khlebnikov compares with the hero of Russian epic poetry Dobrynya. 'Dogs followed him like tame wolves', Khlebnikov writes. 'His stride was equal to two strides of ordinary men' (SP II 106).

The attraction which Khlebnikov felt towards the eastern or Slav warrior and hunter is a reflection of the pan-Slav stance which was prevalent in his aesthetic outlook. The Montenegrin tale 'Tempered Heart', which arose out of his desire to 'consult the dictionaries of the Slavs, the Montenegrins and others' (SP V 298) highlighted the warrior-like qualities of this people in its struggle against the Turks. It is a tale on a par with the positive aesthetic depiction of Nikolay and Usa-gali. Khlebnikov's expressed mission to expand the frontiers of Russian literature (of which the Montenegrin tale forms a part) included as potential subjects specific areas of Slav military history. Khlebnikov noted that the era in which the battles at Kulikovo, at Kosovo and Grunwald occurred 'was quite unknown' to Russian literature and was awaiting its Przhevalsky.[4] Khlebnikov saw it as his task to be such a figure, and his two short poems which deal with the battles of Kosovo and Grunwald (SP II 274) are to be seen in this light.

Certainly, the struggle for Slav unity, for pan-Slavism, was one of the most important of Khlebnikov's early campaigns among the 'states of space'. The combination of the two positive aesthetic preoccupations of warrior and Slavdom produced a major motivation for his early writings. Elements of nationalism also mingled on occasion with the broader Slav concerns. It is in the militant espousal of the cause of nationalism or pan-Slavism that Khlebnikov's warrior *persona* makes some of its first appearances. Several works of this early period manifest precisely these concerns. The authorial *persona* assumes the role of warrior leader exhorting fellow Slavs, or fellow countrymen, to take up arms for the good of the cause. The short poem 'We want to be familiar with the stars' ('My zhelayem zvyozdam tykat''), in which the legendary hero Dobrynya is again mentioned, is just such an exhortation. The poem catalogues a whole host of national heroes worthy of emulation, (recalling the incantatory use of proper names seen elsewhere in Khlebnikov). It reads in part:

O, upodob'tes' Svyatoslavu, –
Vragam skazal: idu na vy!
Pomerknuvshuyu slavu
Tvorite, severnyye l'vy.
S tolpoyu pradedov za nami
Yermak i Oslyabya.
Veysya, veysya, russkoye znamya,
Vedi cherez sushu i cherez khlyabi!
Tuda, gde dukh otchizny vymer
I gde neveriya pustynya,
Idite grozno kak Vladimir,
Ili s druzhinoyu Dobrynya. (SP II 15)[5]

(Oh, be as Svyatoslav, – he told his enemies: I come at you! Create the glory that has faded, northern lions. A crowd of ancestors behind us, Yermak and Oslyabya. Swirl on, swirl on, Russian banner, lead on over land and sea! To where the spirit of the fatherland has died out and where there is the wilderness of unbelief, go as sternly as Vladimir, or as Dobrynya with his retainers.)

The poem is an exhortation to the Russian people to do battle, to wage a campaign of expansion where the 'spirit of the fatherland has died out'. The way to regain Russia's 'faded glory' is seen in the examples of the (real and mythical) heroes of the past.[6] The past is invoked in order for the present to be transformed. The temporal aspect was already making its mark in Khlebnikov's battles in space.

Perhaps the most renowned pan-Slav exhortation is the poem 'Battlesong', which laments the 'wave of Germans from the west'[7] (SP II 23) and the alien influences and customs (*inobyt'*) it brings with it. The poem calls on the Slavs to unite, to rise up, to push back the German wave and move westwards to victory:

Ya i sam by skazal, ya i sam rasskazal,
Protyanul by na zapad klyanushchuyu ruku, da vsyu
gorech' svoyu, da vse yady svoi sobirayu, chtob
kliknut' na zapad i yug svoyu vest', svoyu
veru, svoy yar i svoy klich.
Svoy gnevnyy, pobednyy, voinstvennyy klich:
"Napor slavy yedinoy i tsel'noy na nem'!" (SP II 23)

(And I myself would tell, I myself relate, would stretch out my hand in an oath towards the west, and I gather together all my bitterness and venom in order to shout out to the west and the south my news, my faith, my fury and my call. My angry, victorious, belligerent call: 'the pressure of a united and wholehearted glory against the German!')

The poetic I appears once more in the guise of a warrior, exhorting comrades to do battle for the good of the cause. This is one of the early manifestations of a virulent anti-Germanism which was to last throughout Khlebnikov's life. The poem is almost certainly a response to specific events of the time. The threat of the great powers of Germany, Austria and Turkey to the small Slav peoples of the Balkans, the struggles of these peoples for independence and the ensuing Balkan wars helped arouse in Khlebnikov the pro-Slav and anti-western militancy that is evident in many writings of the period.

It should be underlined that it is not only Khlebnikov's creative writings which reflect the influence of such concerns. These preoccupations were, after all, ideological as well as aesthetic. The little known articles which Khlebnikov wrote in 1913 for the newspaper *Slavyanin* are also expressions of his militant pan-Slav sympathies. 'Who are the Ugro-Russians?' ('Kto takiye ugro-rossy?') was an attempt to acquaint the Russian people with the plight of a small group of Slavs, which was in danger of being swallowed up by the great powers of central Europe. The article 'Western Friend' ('Zapadnyy drug') was a strong attack on Germany and on its contempt for the peoples of Slavdom.[8]

Khlebnikov's anti-western stance is even manifest in the crusading work he undertook to publicize the poetry of a thirteen-year old girl, three poems by whom were published on Khlebnikov's insistence in 1913 in *Trap for Judges* II. One of these poems, entitled 'I want to die' ('Ya khochu umeret''), proclaimed the young girl's reluctance to study French or German:

Frantsuzskiy ne budu
Uchit′ nikogda!
V nemetskuyu knigu
Ne budu smotret′.
Skoreye, skoreye
Khochu umeret′!

(I shall never learn French! I shall never look at a German book. Rather, rather, I want to die!)[9]

In describing how 'fine' these lines were, Khlebnikov's aesthetic judgement was being guided by ideological concerns. Khlebnikov wrote of this poem: 'here is heard the cold flight of truth: the motherland is stronger than death' (NP 340).

Pan-Slav sentiments form the keynote of one of Khlebnikov's earliest published works, the 1908 'Proclamation of Slav Students', which was carried anonymously by the St Petersburg newspaper *Vecher*, and even posted in the corridor of the University of St Petersburg which Khlebnikov was then attending.[10] This proclamation was, on Khlebnikov's own admission (NP 353), a response to the annexation by Austria in October 1908 of Bosnia and Hercegovina and is a prime example of the bellicose nature of Khlebnikov's pan-Slav sympathies.

Like the poem 'Battlesong', it is a paean to the unity of the Slav race and an exhortation to Slavs to rise up and avenge the flouted rights of their fellows:

> Our lips are full of vengeance, vengeance drips from the horses' bits, let us then carry our festival of vengeance, like fine wares, to the place where there is a demand for it – the banks of the Spree. Russian steeds know how to trample the streets of Berlin with their hoofs.
>
> (SS III 405)

Vengeance provides a motivation for the conflict, a justification and legitimacy for the act of war that is urged. Khlebnikov sees what is happening as a 'struggle between the whole of Germandom (*germanstvo*) and Slavdom' (SS III 405) and the text of the proclamation moves towards its conclusion with his belligerent sentiments in full flight:

> War for the unity of the Slavs, from wherever it has come, from Poznań or from Bosnia, I welcome you! Come! . . . Holy and necessary, coming and near, war for the flouted rights of the Slavs, I welcome you! Down with the Habsburgs! Curb the Hohenzollerns! (SS III 405–6)

Khlebnikov is quite clearly writing as a proponent of war and retribution and has found a motivation to write in his desire to convince others of the rightness of his cause.

This glorification of war is also seen by Khlebnikov as having certain popular aesthetic foundations. He provides a justification for his own positive evaluation of the warrior figure by asserting that war and military enterprise are themes glorified in Russia's folk epos. This is one of the views expressed in the 1912 *Teacher and Pupil* dialogue, where this warrior-like aspect of popular art is compared with the unwarlike attitude of contemporary writers:

I. Glorifies the military feat and war.
II. Reproaches the military feat, and understands war as pointless slaughter.

	I	II
Tolstoy A. N.		+
Merezhkovsky		+
Kuprin		+
Andreyev		+
Veresayev		+
Folk song	+	

(SP v 181)

It is of some note that in this early period Khlebnikov is equating the glorification of war with his praise for the life-affirming nature of folk art (SP v 180–1). Khlebnikov does not perceive war in terms of the horrors of carnage and death it involved. His vision of combat is in many ways romantic, influenced by popular and epic accounts of heroic feats in battle. At this point war for him was not 'pointless', but a legitimate means to a desired end.

The 'proclamation' was published in the same month as his first neologistic creative prose. It demonstrates a different, but equally important aspect of Khlebnikov's writing. It is a non-fictional, publicistic work by a writer clearly involved in contemporary affairs. However, in spite of the fact that this appeal is non-fictional in form, it is not without literary merit and bears many of the hallmarks of Khlebnikov's creative writing. The prose is rhetorical and there is extensive use of imagery. Furthermore, the call for the Slavs to unite echoes the appeal for unity contained in that foundation stone of Russian literature, the *Lay of Igor's Campaign*. As Khlebnikov wrote in another of his works which had war as a major concern ('War in a Mousetrap'):

My sozdadim slovo Polku Igorevi
Ili zhe chto-nibud′ na nego pokhozheye. (SP II 244)

(We shall create a *Lay of Igor's Campaign* or something which is similar to it.)

His 'proclamation', like the *Lay of Igor's Campaign*, is an appeal for unity against an external aggressor. The early manifestation of Khlebnikov's warrior *persona* embraces both aesthetic and ideological concerns.

III

It was during the pre-war period when his pan-Slav sympathies were prominent that Khlebnikov first came into contact with the writers who were soon to hail him as the genius of Futurism. While his pan-Slav preoccupations were not to be taken up wholeheartedly by his fellow Hylaeans, his militant temperament was well incorporated in the attitudes adopted by the incipient Futurist movement. From the outset, with its strident and insulting manifestoes and its public displays of contempt for the established literary luminaries, the new movement signalled a revolt against the literary status quo.

Militancy was the order of the day. As David Burliuk wrote later, this was an 'implacable war for the new in art' (NP 421). Without having the oratorical presence of some of his Hylaean comrades, Khlebnikov was nonetheless a party to this war on the literary establishment and his participation in it is yet another aspect of the belligerent nature of his art. As well as being a fighter for the cause of Slav unity, Khlebnikov was a fighter for the cause of Futurism, or, as he would have put it, *budetlyanstvo*.

It is worth noting in this context that, despite the few details known about Khlebnikov's break with the establishment's 'Academy of Verse' in early 1910, his final departure may have been rather stormy. Nikolay Khardzhiev cites an unpublished jotting by Khlebnikov to the effect that he was 'expelled' (*izgnan*) by this illustrious body and points to Khlebnikov's satires of those associated with it as confirmation that his exit was rather 'belligerent'.[11] If this was indeed so, it would not be out of character. Certainly, in his satirical works Khlebnikov was penning caricatures of his literary peers before the Futurist manifestoes, which also bore his name, began to subject the same writers to even further ridicule.

Khlebnikov was also quite capable of writing his own declarations on behalf of the Futurist 'collective', announcing the arrival of the 'new breed of people: the brave Futurists (*budetlyane*)' to replace what he contemptuously calls the 'Bryu-Bal-Merezh entity' (a reference to the Symbolist writers, Bryusov, Balmont and Merezhkovsky) (SP v 193).[12] Khlebnikov's notebooks contain a similar statement, comparing the Futurists' warrior-like eminence to the rather lowly status of their literary antagonists:

> They are divided into warriors and puppies; the warriors – that is us, and the puppies are those who feed on our leftovers; of the most notable puppies one should mention . . . the puppy Kuprin, and puppy [Sologub]. (SP v 328)

Khlebnikov's attacks on the literary establishment were also marked by an important fusion of both his pan-Slav and his Futurist militancy. Ideological and aesthetic concerns merge in his depiction of Symbolist writers begging 'for mercy before the awaited victor, foreseeing the rout from the east' (SP v 193).

One should recall that Khlebnikov saw many of the established contemporary writers as propagating an alien culture. As a pan-Slav militant he opposed the oppression by western powers of Slavs outside Russia; as a writer his critical gaze turned inwards to Russia itself where he espied a comparable western domination in the field of his own national culture. It is in Khlebnikov's attack against such mores that the warrior *persona* also reveals himself as a potential revolutionary:

> O, vy, chto russkiye imenem,
> No vidom zamorskiye shchogoli,
> Zavetom 'svoyo na ne russkoye vymenim'
> Vy vidy otechestva trogali.
> Kak pirshestv zabytaya svecha,
> Ya lezveye poyu mecha,
> I vot, uzhasnaya obrázina
> Pustyn′ moguchego posla,
> Ya prikhozhu k vam ten′yu Razina
> Na zov [shirokogo] vesla.
> Ot resnits upala ten′,
> A v ruke visit kisten′. (NP 208)

(Oh, you, Russian in name, but in appearance fops from over the sea, by your behest 'let's swop ours for things not Russian' you have disturbed the appearance of our fatherland. Like the forgotten candle of feasts, I sing of the blade of the sword, and there before you, the awful countenance of the deserts' mighty envoy, I come to you as Razin's shadow to the call of the [wide] oar. The shadow has fallen from the eyes' lashes, and the hand wields a cudgel.)

This early (probably 1911) reference to Razin is eloquent testimony to Khlebnikov's sympathies for popular revolt.

On another level, Khlebnikov saw the literary struggle he was waging in terms of a conflict between the generations. In a short article, written in the autumn of 1912, in which he is again comparing the 'decadent world view of the Symbolists' with 'the life-affirming themes of folk poetry' (NP 460), he accuses what he calls the 'older generation' (the writers Artsybashev, Andreyev and Sologub are mentioned) of giving the young a poisoned cup from which to drink. And he adds later in the article:

> We have stretched out our sword to strike down this criminal cup.
> It is an uprising of youth.
> We are its shield and its leader against the elders. (NP 335)

Revolutionary implications are again apparent. They become even more noticeable when the idea receives further development in Khlebnikov's 1916 *Trumpet of the Martians* manifesto. Here Khlebnikov condemns those whose lives are governed by 'the laws of families and the laws of commerce' and calls for a sword to be forged from the 'pure iron of young men' (SP v 152). The anti-bourgeois elements of this declaration are reinforced in his attack on the exploitation by 'acquirers' (*priobretateli*) of 'inventors' (*izobretateli*) (SP v 153). Khlebnikov clearly considered himself among the 'combat detachment' of the latter (SP v 153).

The declaration also shows how, as a part of this struggle, the dimension of time was now taking over from the dimension of space. The 'people of the past' believed that the 'sails of the state can only be constructed for the axes (*osi*) of space' (SP v 151), but 'we', Khlebnikov continues, 'dressed in a coat of victories alone, are beginning to construct a union of youth with a sail around the axis of time' (SP v 151).

As the concept of the warring generations implies, the battlefield on which Khlebnikov is to wage combat moves out of the realms of space and into the realms of the fourth dimension – time. Khlebnikov proposed: 'to introduce everywhere, instead of the concept of space, the concept of time, for example, war between the generations of the globe, war of the trenches of time' (SP v 159). It was in the *Trumpet of the Martians* manifesto that Khlebnikov even went so far as to call for the establishment of an 'independent state of time' (SP v 153).

Khlebnikov did not only regard himself as a 'military commander' (*voyevoda*) (NP 370) in the literary conflict. He was also a 'warrior of the future' (NP 364). While for most the name of Futurism was merely a label to attach to an artistic movement, for Khlebnikov the concept of the future and the dimension of time had considerably greater ramifications. This was the measure of Khlebnikov's *budetlyanstvo*.

Ironically, it was Khlebnikov's belligerency which also contributed to decline and dissension within the Futurist ranks. The occasion was the visit to Russia by the Italian Futurist Marinetti. Khlebnikov was furious at the prostration by some of his countrymen 'at the feet of Marinetti'; he saw them as 'betraying Russian art's first step on the road to freedom and honour and placing the noble neck of Asia under the yoke of Europe' (SP v 250).

The clash over Marinetti prompted Khlebnikov to speak of breaking with Hylaea ('from now on I have nothing in common with the members of "Hylaea" ' – NP 369).[13] The same anti-western, pan-Slav militancy with which Khlebnikov had aided the Futurist movement's onslaught on the literary establishment was now directed at the movement itself. Khlebnikov's anti-European aesthetic sentiments and his espousal of the cause of the independence of Russian art, in the final analysis, proved stronger than any loyalty to Hylaean unity.

IV

The disastrous defeat of the Russian Baltic fleet by the Japanese navy at Tsushima in May 1905 marked a watershed not only in the life of Russia, but also of Khlebnikov. This was the event, he was to note over 15 years later, which became the point of departure for his persistent attempts to discover the 'laws of time'. He recorded the fact in the first section of his 'Boards of Fate':

> The first decision to seek out the laws of time occurred on the day after Tsushima, when news of the battle of Tsushima reached Yaroslavl region, where I was living at that time in the village of Burmakino . . .
> I wanted to find a justification for the deaths.[14] (SS III 472)

The battle was thus perceived by him not so much with reference to the world of space and the loss or gain of national or Slav territory as with its significance in the fourth dimension. It was in a study of the 'laws of time' not of space that Khlebnikov hoped to discover a reason for the deaths which the battle had caused.

One might have expected feelings of national pride to surface, similar to those evoked by the 'German' oppression of the Slavs. But there was an important distinction. This conflict was taking place not in the west, but in the east and, measured by Khlebnikov's aesthetic and ideological yardstick, the east was generally seen in a positive light. Indeed, Japan figures prominently in Khlebnikov's attempts to achieve some form of Asian unity. In

1916, for example, two Japanese youths called, through the press, for links with their Russian counterparts (SP v 348). Khlebnikov took it upon himself to answer this appeal from 'distant friends' (SP v 154), even setting out the agenda for an 'Asian congress' (SP v 156–7). 'I can more readily understand a Japanese youth speaking old Japanese than some of my fellow countrymen speaking modern Russian', he told them (SP v 155).[15] Such considerations will have muted the expression of chauvinistic sentiments.

Khlebnikov devoted two poems specifically to the Tsushima battle. Both seem to have been written some years afterwards. This distancing in time from the event will have contributed to the muting of any nationalist sentiments. It is also, however, a measure of the battle's significance for Khlebnikov that he felt a need to return to it in his art several years after it actually occurred. 'Monument' ('Pamyatnik'), the first to be published, was printed in the *Slap* collection of 1912 and was written, according to the editors of the NP, in 1910 (NP 16). The contrast with 'Battlesong' could hardly be greater. The poem is narrative and descriptive rather than lyrical or exhortatory, and there is no overt presence on the part of the poetic I. Rather than an immediate appeal to turn back the wave of the enemy, this reflective portrayal describes the battle in almost non-partisan terms:

Von lad′ya i drugaya:
Yapontsy i Rus′.
Znamen′ye bitvy: grozya i rugaya,
Oni podnimayut boya brus.
Togda leteli drug k drugu lodki,
Pushki blesteli kak luchiny.
Im ne byl strashen golod glotki
Bezdnoy razvernutoy puchiny.
Ryov voln byl dal′she, glushe,
Reveli, leteli nad morem olushi,
Gruzno osveshchaya tem′ i belyye,
Kak by voproshaya; vy zdes′ chtó delaya? (SP II 85)

(There one boat and another: the Japanese and Russia. The sign of battle: threats and curses, the beam of combat raised. Then the boats flew at each other, cannon sparkled like splints. The hunger of the deep's gullet, like a gaping abyss, held no terrors for them. The roar of the waves was more distant, hollow, above the sea fulmars screeched and flew, and white, heavily illuminating the dark, as though questioning: just what is it that you are doing here?)

This is no eulogy to nationalist concerns. Furthermore, the human element is played down at the expense of the environment and the material elements of the battle: sea, birds, boat and cannon.

Even the actual victory of the Japanese is depicted by Khlebnikov in a somewhat detached manner:

> S korotkim upornym smeshkom:
> 'Vozvratis′, k chernozemnomu beregu chali,
> Khochesh′ li more pereyti peshkom?'
> Yapontsy russkomu krichali.
> I voiny, kazalos′, shli ko dnu,
> Smert′ prinesla s soboy dukhi 'smorodina'.
> No oni pomnili yeyo odnu –
> Dalyokuyu russkuyu rodinu! (SP II 86)

(With a short stubborn laugh, the Japanese called to the Russian: 'Go home, back to the mooring of the black earth's shore, do you want to cross the sea on foot?' And the sailors seemed to go down to the bottom, death brought with it the scent of 'smorodina'. But they recalled one thing alone – the distant Russian motherland!)[16]

There is a certain legitimacy in the portrayal of the Japanese dominance at sea. The Japanese seem at home among the waves; the Russians do not. Khlebnikov is hinting here at a conflict of forces which runs deeper than a simple clash between two warring nations.[17]

Confirmation for such a view can be found in the late 1914 treatise *Battles 1915–1917: A New Teaching about War*, which, as the title suggests, demonstrated that questions of war and the activity of warriors had by this time become more than just a theme for poetic inspiration or publicistic exhortation. This is a numerological study which continues that 'first decision to seek out the laws of time' taken after the Tsushima naval battle. Notably, the question of the Russo-Japanese war formed an important part of the work.

The treatise was, as Khlebnikov termed it, a 'cuneiform about destinies', which had the declared aim of demonstrating that 'battles at sea occur every 317 years or its multiples – 317.1, 2, 3, 4, 5, 6, and also of demonstrating the shifts of supremacy at sea of different peoples at times which are multiples of 317' (SS III 413). The subject of supremacy at sea provides Khlebnikov with a good link to the Russo-Japanese war. In brief, he develops the theory that the events which took place in this war, and in the siege of Port Arthur in particular, were a reduced (measured in days instead of years) but reverse repetition of the events which occurred in the Russian military conquest of Siberia that began in the sixteenth century. Khlebnikov explains:

> The days of the Russian failures in the war of 1904 are a response to those years of the centuries when the Russians reached the rivers of Siberia.
>
> The years of the Volga, the Ob, the Yenisey, the Lena and the Amur provide a long list of the battles with an unsuccessful outcome for the besieged.
>
> On the other hand, the years of the Russian campaigns against the peninsulas of Siberia coincided with days which were unsuccessful for the Japanese. (SS III 425–6)

According to Khlebnikov, the number and the dates of the Russian defeats in the Russo-Japanese war were governed by the number and dates of crossings of rivers in the Siberian conquest; the Russian victories on land (peninsulas) in the Siberian conquest determined the defeats for Japan in the war.

This led Khlebnikov to formulate the following conclusion: 'if the war was a struggle between sea and dry land, then it is not surprising that rivers, which enter the sphere of the sea (threads of the sea), and peninsulas – parts of land, exerted a different influence on the scales of victory . . . ' (SS III 426). It is, at the very least, a curious theory of historical causality, though a guide towards Khlebnikov's reasoning can be seen in the fact that he cites the role of rivers in Homer's *Iliad* as a model for his thought.[18] It is a theory which, however, has some ramifications for Khlebnikov's poetic work. This notion of the Russo-Japanese war as a clash between the forces of land and sea is reflected poetically in 'Monument'.

In addition, *Battles* also showed that 'supremacy at sea' followed a determinable pattern: the wave westwards of the Japanese in the war was a reaction, determined by the 'laws of time', to the start of the Russian wave eastwards across the Siberian rivers over three centuries earlier. Should one not expect at some later date another 'shift' in this supremacy as Russia exacted a legitimate retribution? It is probably this that Khlebnikov had in mind when he referred in 'Monument' to 'the coming victory of the Russian' (SP II 87).[19]

The poem is, therefore, to be seen not so much in the light of a militant nationalist response of a warrior of space, but of the developing concerns of a warrior of time; it is a reflection of Khlebnikov's desire 'to find a justification for the deaths'.

The other poem dealing with the battle of Tsushima, which also demonstrates a rather complex blend of concerns, is 'Things were too blue' ('Byli veshchi slishkom sini'). It was first published over a year later than 'Monument' in Khlebnikov's *Creations* (*Tvoreniya*) collection in 1914, but, according to the editors of the NP (NP 17), it was written at about the same time (1910). It begins as follows:

Byli veshchi slishkom sini,
Byli volny – khladnyy grob.
My pod khokhot nebesini
Pili chashu smutnykh mrob.
Ya v volne uvidel brata,
On s volnoyu sporil khlyabey
I tuda, gde net obrata,
Bronenosets shol 'Oslyabya'.
Nad volnoy kachnulis' truby,
Dym razorvan byl v kol'tso,
Ya uvidel blizko guby,
Brata mutnoye litso.
Nad puchinoy yemlya ugol,
Tolp bezumnykh polon bok,
I po volnam kos i smugol
Shol yaponskoy roty bog. (SP II 31)

(Things were too blue, the waves were a cold coffin. Beneath the laughter of heaven blue we drank from the cup of troubled doombrew. In the wave I saw my brother, arguing with the wave's deep, and to the place where there is no return went the battleship 'Oslyabya'. Above the waves the funnels rocked, smoke was torn into a ring, I saw lips nearby, the troubled face of my brother. Seizing a corner above the deep, a side full of mad crowds, through the waves, slant-eyed and swarthy came the god of the Japanese company.)

The poem is less detached and more lyrical than its companion 'Monument'. The presence of the poetic I as witness to the disaster makes the event more immediate and personal. However, like 'Monument' and in line with the ideas voiced in *Battles*, the poem stresses as a major concern the struggle not so much with the Japanese foe as with the sea itself. The sea is later even described in the poem as 'sated with human foam', as though it were some kind of monster which had consumed the unhappy Russian sailors. Direct responsibility for the deaths does not seem to be entirely in Japanese hands.

Nevertheless, unlike in 'Monument', there are rhetorical

elements in the poem, and nationalist sentiment is not entirely absent. The poem concludes with a warning to the 'swarthy faces of the Japanese' to 'grow pale', which echoes an earlier exclamation: 'Listen, listen, children, let alarm fill the brown faces' (SP II 32–3). But the pledge which follows this threat to the Japanese is highly equivocal:

My klyatvu dayom:
Vnov′ orosit′ svoyey i vashey
Kroviyu – sey siyayushchiy
Bespredel′nyy vodoyom.
Razdayotsya Rusi k moryu gnev,
Ne khochesh′ byt′ s Rossiyey, s ney?
Tak, chashey puchiny zazvenev,
Krovyami obshchimi krasney! (SP II 32)

(We pledge: to irrigate again with our and your blood this shining boundless reservoir. The anger of Russia against the sea rings out, do you not want to be with Russia, with her? So, having rung out like the cup of the deep, grow red with our common blood!)

The anger of Russia, echoing the ideas of *Battles*, is directed not against Japan, but the sea.

The underlying conflict with the sea is also evident elsewhere in the poem when it declares that 'at Tsushima the throat of the seas was bound with a necklace of Russian lives' (SP II 32). Furthermore, as Barbara Lönnqvist has pointed out, the word necklace (*monisto*) can refer to the 'strings of years' which Khlebnikov used to calculate his 'laws of time'.[20] It is perhaps not surprising, therefore, that 'Things were too blue' also refers to the 'triumphant law' (*likuyushchiy zakon*) (SP II 32) which hovers above the defeated Russians. In Khlebnikov's view it is the 'law of time' which triumphs, not the Japanese; and it is in this context that the poem foretells Russia's coming revenge:

Chto Rusi rok v gryadushchem chertit,
Ne uzhasnulsya, kto glyadel.
Yeyo vzdymayetsya glava
Skvoz′ oblakov-vremena,
Kogda istlevshiye slova
Stali vragov yeyo imena. (SP II 32)

(He who has seen what fate maps out for Russia in the future has not been struck with horror. Russia's head arises through the times of clouds, when the names of its enemies have become words decayed.)

The outcome of battles between the warring nations seems to be out of the hands of men and in the hands of fate.

That higher forces than men are at work in Khlebnikov's portrayal of the battle can be seen elsewhere in the poem. After the opening depiction of the conflict and the presentation of the enemy forces as the 'god of the Japanese company', the poem's poetic I continues:

> I togda moi ne mogut boleye molchat′ usta!
> Perun tolknul razgnevanno Khrista.
> I, mlat skhvativ, stal mech kovat′ iz rud,
> Dav klyatvu pokazat′ vselennoy,
> Chtó znachit russkikh sud! (SP II 31)[21]

(And then my lips can stay silent no longer! Perun angrily pushed Christ aside, and, seizing up a hammer, began to forge a sword from ore, pledging to show the universe just what the judgement of the Russians means!)

Russia's pagan god of thunder, Perun, who had been ousted after Russia's conversion to Christianity, now pushes aside the figure of Christ in order to exact revenge for the Russian defeat. Khlebnikov's poem favours a national, Slav, god over an imported and foreign religion.

Notably, another poem, 'To Perun' ('Perunu'), published in 1914, gives voice to a similar notion, again connecting the Russian defeat at Tsushima specifically with the renunciation of Russia's warrior-god of thunder.

> Ne predopredelil li ty Tsusimy
> Rodu nizvergshikh tya lyudey?
> Ne znal li ty, chto nekogda vosstanem,
> Kak nekaya vselennoy ten′,
> Kogda gonimy byt′ ustanem
> I obretyom v vremenakh ren′,
> Sil sinikh snem. (SP II 198)

(Did you not predetermine Tsushima for the breed of people who overthrew you? Did you not know that one day we would rise up, like some shadow of the universe, when we were tired of being pursued and would find a shoal in the passage of time, a gathering of blue forces.)

The deposing of Perun had somehow preordained the forthcoming disaster at Tsushima. In addition, a further prediction ensues here, a prediction of rebellion (*nekogda vosstanem*); and the 'laws of time' and even the forces of the sea seem to be at work again (*I obretyom v vremenakh ren',/Sil sinikh snem*).

In Khlebnikov's poetic reflections upon the defeat of the Russians at Tsushima militant nationalism is tempered by an increasing awareness of the workings of other forces and by a desire to determine the nature of these forces. The Russo-Japanese war prompted in Khlebnikov not only a literary, but also a 'scientific' response; to establish by means of mathematical calculations the 'laws' of time and of fate which lay behind the defeats and victories of different peoples at different times; to examine the past with regard to the present and the future; to engage in prophecy as well as literature and to begin the lengthy assault on the 'tower of time'.

However, the Tsushima poems still do not portray any evidence of opposition to war. Khlebnikov's early work on time is merely trying to establish how war is regulated, and, in spite of the sea that sates its appetite on the bodies of Russian sailors, the call is still for war and for Perun to wield his sword to show the universe just what the 'judgement of the Russians means'.

V

The question of historical parallels in Khlebnikov's work (such as the linking of Perun's overthrow with the Tsushima battle) has also been raised by Henryk Baran. In an analysis, mainly of the short poem 'Bekh', Baran showed how Khlebnikov could present in his work a battle in the past in order for it to be seen in the light of the present and the future.[22] The battle which 'Bekh' deals with is one which involved the Russians and the Tatars. The poem takes its name from a herb which, according to legend, grew from the bones of the warriors killed in the battle, and which had the magical property of being able to articulate its own name. As Khlebnikov puts it in the last four lines of the poem:

> I kosti besheno krichali: 'bekh',
> Odety zelen'yu iz prosa,
> I kosti zvonko vyli: 'Da!
> My budem pomnit' boy vsegda.'[23]

(And the bones furiously cried out: 'bekh', dressed in the green of millet, and the bones ringingly howled: 'Yes! We shall remember the battle forever.')

The historical parallel, which, according to Baran, the poem presents, is the past threat to national identity from the Tatar hordes and the war which 'Khlebnikov anticipates . . . between the Russian and the German Empires'.[24] Khlebnikov's poetic accounts of past conflict seem to be written with an eye for the lessons of history.

Such accounts should also be seen in the light of Khlebnikov's desire to expand the frontiers of Russian literature. For Khlebnikov these frontiers stretched, after all, not only spatially, but also temporally. Baran is quite right to speak in this context of 'the theme of the preservation of memories of the past'.[25] The bones of the dead warriors in 'Bekh' cry out for such a commemoration. Curiously, there is another poem written during this period ('Bekh' dates from about 1913 – NP 406) in which the bones of a dead warrior also serve as a plea for remembrance.

It is not clear precisely when 'The Pecheneg Cup' ('Kubok pechenezhskiy') was written, though some indication might be found in the title under which the poem was first published in 1916 – 'Written before the War' ('Napisannoye do voyny').[26] The poem deals with the defeat and death of the Russian warrior-prince Svyatoslav at the hands of the Pechenegs. Like other such historically orientated texts, this poem should also be seen in the light of Khlebnikov's pronounced aesthetic task to write of 'Russia in the past', particularly as Khlebnikov actually mentions 'the Svyatoslavs' in this connection (SP v 298).

The similarity with 'Bekh' lies in the fact that the poem tells how the skull of the defeated Svyatoslav was fashioned into a drinking cup by the Pechenegs. As the Pecheneg craftsman reshaping the skull relates in the poem:

> Znamenityy sok Dunaya,
> Nalivaya v glub′ glavy,
> Stanu pit′ ya, vspominaya
> Svetlykh klich: 'Idu na vy!' (SP II 223)

(Pouring the famed juice of the Danube into the depth of the head, I shall drink and remember the cry of the bright ones: 'I come at you!')

Like the bones of 'Bekh', the skull of Svyatoslav is also associated with a distinctive utterance. On this occasion it is the famous battle cry of Svyatoslav, the memory of whom the skull cup has now preserved.

It is difficult to say whether Khlebnikov intended his portrayal of this conflict to be seen as an historical parallel with his own time. If so, then it may be as a warning, since it is not a Russian victory but a defeat which the poem depicts, and it is just such a warning that one commentator has identified in 'Bekh'.[27]

Yet even in defeat, the memory which Khlebnikov preserves of Svyatoslav in the poem is by no means negative. The depiction of the battle shows a great regard for the courage of this Russian prince, who sets his enemies 'trembling' with fear and rises like a 'cliff' before them (SP II 223). It is a depiction which continues to reflect Khlebnikov's positive aesthetic view of the Russian warrior.

It would appear that the elements of fate manifest in the Tsushima poems are not present in the portrayal of this conflict. One might voice, however, two reservations. Firstly, Svyatoslav is killed by the 'snakelike flight of a lash' (SP II 223), and, as Barbara Lönnqvist has shown, it was in the image of a snakelike movement that Khlebnikov portrayed the workings of his own 'laws of time'.[28] Moreover, Khlebnikov referred to his battle against fate as against a 'serpent' (SP V 315–16). It is therefore as though Svyatoslav has been cut down not by man but by fate. Secondly, the poem makes much of the 'internal declension' interplay between sword (*mech*) and ball (*myach*). These are developed in the poem (and elsewhere in Khlebnikov's work) into symbols for war and peace. As such, they demonstrate that although the poem tells the tale of a single battle, it has as a backdrop concerns which are much broader. Elements of fate might therefore be not entirely absent.

They are certainly not absent from another work of this period. 'Children of the Otter' actually includes reference to numbers which feature in Khlebnikov's attempts at mathematical prediction (SP II 165). In addition, this early 'supertale', which also has mention of the skull-cup of Svyatoslav (SP II 176), contains the following passage:

My zhrebiya voyn budem iskat',
Zhrebiya voyn zemle neizvestnogo,
I krov'yu voyny stanem pleskat'
V liki svoda nebesnogo.
I my zhivyom verny razmeram,
I sami voyny sut' lady,
Idyot chislo na smenu veram
I derzhit kormchego trudy. (SP II 163)

(We shall seek out the lot of wars, the lot of wars unknown to the earth, and we shall splash the faces of the firmament with the blood of war. And we live true to measure, and wars themselves are harmonies, number comes to replace faiths and takes upon itself the labours of the helmsmen.)

This is clearly a poetic expression of Khlebnikov's developing numerological theories and it demonstrates further that by the time war broke out with Germany in August 1914, despite his positive aesthetic appraisal of the Slav warrior, his view of conflict in the third dimension already reflected a desire to find a 'justification for the deaths'.

This does not mean, however, that Khlebnikov did not at first welcome the war. Indeed, there is evidence to suggest that Khlebnikov's initial response to the outbreak of war was positive and patriotic. The rough and incomplete short poem 'Tverskoy', dated by Khardzhiev as being written at the end of 1914 (NP 448), talks, for example, of hostility towards the west and of 'hastening there on a campaign' (NP 262). The tone of the work is certainly not one of protest or of pacifism. The same can be said of the references in the 'autobiographical tale' (SP v 346) 'Ka^2':

In the first days of the war I remember the black air of rapid twilights on the corner of the Sadovaya and the Russians going off to the west.
– We'll all die, someone said in a hollow voice, looking at me.
– To die is not enough, victory must be won, – I remarked sternly. Thus the first week began. (SP v 129)

Such patriotic sentiments are in tune with Khlebnikov's earlier pan-Slav hostility to the 'German' aggression against the Slavs. It was in 1913, for example, only a year before the hostilities of war began, that Khlebnikov published the anti-German article 'Western Friend' in the newspaper *Slavyanin*. Moreover, as if to emphasize his continuing pro-Slav and anti-European attitudes, at the beginning of 1914, he republished in his belligerently entitled *Roar! Gauntlets* collection the 1908 pan-Slav 'proclamation' welcoming the 'coming . . . war for the flouted rights of the Slavs' and calling for Russian horses to trample the streets of Berlin. On the outbreak of war this assumed great topicality. Its prophetic nature was even proclaimed by Mayakovsky in November 1914 in order to back up his own initial patriotic response to the war. Mayakovsky wrote:

What is this? A portrait of Russia written yesterday evening by someone who has already filled his lungs with vengeance and war? No, this is an

illumination by the prophet and artist Velimir Khlebnikov. A prediction made six years ago . . .
A squad of poets with such a warrior is already justified in claiming primacy in the kingdom of song.[29]

Khlebnikov's militancy thus found itself taken up briefly once again in the service of the Futurist cause. Nor too was Kruchonykh averse to publicizing Khlebnikov's belligerency. He wrote in the preface to Khlebnikov's *Battles*: 'V. Khlebnikov is an extremely belligerent man and was born as such.'

However, despite the evidence of an initial patriotic response, the anti-German exhortatory verse which one might expect Khlebnikov to have written is notable only by its absence. The increasing preoccupation with the external forces which Khlebnikov believed were at work in the history of conflict was obviously making some mark. Some of the poems which relate to the early period of the war seem to exemplify this. Two might be noted in particular: 'Death in a Lake' ('Smert' v ozere') and 'Funeral' ('Trizna').

In 'Death in a Lake' (SP II 224–5), although the warring parties in the battle depicted are actually named as the 'Germans' and a 'Russian regiment', the time and nature of the conflict are left unspecific. Nor is it clearly apparent who the victor is, though there is some indication that, once again, a Russian defeat is being portrayed. The poem, for example, speaks of the death of those who are on the River Vistula, but are 'singing of the Don' (SP II 224). Lines in the poem which describe how the Germans were filled with 'horror' at the sight of the 'awesome (*strashnyy*) Russian regiment' (SP II 225) may have prompted one Soviet critic to refer to a resurgence in Khlebnikov's 'patriotic sentiments',[30] but it is probably the sight of slaughtered Russians which prompts this German horror, rather than any fear of Russian military prowess. Khlebnikov's editor Stepanov labelled the poem not patriotic, but 'anti-militarist'.[31]

What the poem does, in fact, depict is summed up in its title – 'Death in a Lake':

V rukakh ruzh'ya, a okolo pushki.
Mimo lits tuchi serykh ulitok,
Pyostrykh ryb i krasivykh rakushek.
I vypi protyazhno ukhali,
Motsarta propeli lyagvy . . . (SP II 224–5)

(Rifles in their hands and cannons round about. Past the faces clouds of grey snails, of variegated fish and beautiful shells. And the bitterns boomed protractedly, the frogs sang Mozart . . .)

Khlebnikov presents us with a scene of soldiers' bodies floating in a lake. The main hero of this poem is not the valiant forces of Slavdom struggling against the German Empire. It is death: 'Eto smert′ i druzhina idyot na polyud′ye,/I za neyu khlynuli valy' (This is death and its retainers off for the tribute, and the waves gushed after it) (SP II 224). The watery fate which the soldiers have encountered is portrayed in the poem as the passage of death, personified as a charioteer, whipping up 'a troika of cold horses' to the accompaniment of 'piercing' cries (SP II 224).

The emphasis on water and death recalls the Tsushima poems.[32] External forces are at work again, epitomized, perhaps, in the sinister laughter of a bird of evil portent, the 'thoughtful eagle-owl', which, in the poem's closing lines, surveys the field of battle (SP II 225).[33]

The poem 'Funeral' also directs its attention not at victory or exhortation, but at death. It is, moreover, the death of Russian soldiers that the poem laments:

U kholmov, u sta ozyor,
Mnogo palo tekh, kto zhili.
Na surovyy, dubovyy kostyor
My russov tela polozhili.
I ot strogikh myortvykh tel
Don voskhodit i Irtysh.
Sizyy dym, klubyas′, letel.
My stoim, khranili tish′. (SP II 229)

(By the hills, by the hundred lakes, many fell of those who lived. On to a grim fire of oak we placed the bodies of the Russians. And from the stern bodies of the dead rise the Don and the Irtysh. Bluish smoke curled up in flight. We stand, observed a silence.)

The funeral of the fallen Russians is portrayed sympathetically, but the poem lacks any overt indications of blame or hostility for those who killed them. The enemy is not even mentioned.[34] The poem does, however, have a reference to fate:

Lyudi my il′ kop′ya roka
Vse v odnoy i toy ruke?
Net, nits vemy; net uroka,
A okopy vdaleke. (SP II 229)

(Are we people or the lances of fate all in one and the same hand? No, we know nothing; there is no lesson, and the trenches are in the distance.)

Khlebnikov's, as yet rather uncommitted, response to the question does not detract from the significance of its being posed. Deaths in battle cause him to reflect not on vengeance in the hands of humans, but of humans in the hands of fate.[35]

It is a question which reflects poetically the notions which had begun to preoccupy Khlebnikov mathematically soon after the outbreak of the war and which found expression in the *Battles* treatise, his 'cuneiform about destinies'. Khlebnikov had become convinced that the determining factors for battles throughout history lay in certain 'laws of time' which were mathematically calculable. Once such 'laws' had been discovered, the knowledge could be used to determine the dates and outcome of future battles. Thus, as well as plotting what he saw as the 'predictable' course of the Russo-Japanese war, Khlebnikov was engaged in an exercise of prophecy. As the full title of the *Battles* pamphlet indicates (*Battles 1915–1917: A New Teaching about War*), the years of its concern are alleged to lie in the future. Hence, in his preface to the pamphlet, Kruchonykh not only endowed Khlebnikov with the epithet 'belligerent', but also wrote:

> Whoever has read his 'Battlesong of the Slavs', his appeal to 'follow the sun against the German (*nem'*)', 'Night in Galicia' etc . . . knows that the great war of 1914 and the conquest of Galicia were already sung of by Khlebnikov back in 1908!

The pan-Slav exhortation to struggle against the Germans and a poem dealing with Galicia are now stated to have been prophetic indications of the First World War. Khlebnikov's literary work is placed in the context of prophecy and the *Battles* pamphlet is a theoretical exposition of this. However, while the 'Battlesong' was a committed poetic act expressing hostility against the Germans, *Battles* is a non-partisan, as Khlebnikov termed it, 'semi-scientific' study (NP 370). This attitude is reflected in his letters to Matyushin in December 1914 (NP 372–7), which deal with the work on *Battles*. They reveal an overriding preoccupation with little else but the value of his own calculations and predictions. Questions of victory and defeat do not even merit mention. It is this numerological 'uncommitted' approach which can now find its way into verse.

In *Battles* Khlebnikov declared that it was possible to determine the course of a war by a study of the preceding centuries (SS III 427), and he tried to plot the occurrence of battles in the First World War (and beyond) by analogy with battles in the past, using the measure of 317 years as his guide. For example, he wrote that the year of 1915 should turn out to have been 'a year of decline for the islanders at sea' (SS III 417). Similar ominous developments for the naval fortunes of Britain are reflected in the following poem, which reads in part:

1187
Zvezda voskhodit Saladina,
I s krov'yu pal Iyerusalim.
I vot sozvuchnaya godina
V te dni zazhgla nad Chili dym.
Lish' tol'ko voysku Saladina
Iyerusalima klyuch vruchili,
Smenilo more gospodina
U beregov dalyokikh Chili.
I vidyat Monmut i Otranto,
Kak gibnet gordost' Al'biona.
Nad ney provodit krugi Dante
Ruka kholodnogo tevtona.
I etot den', prichast'yu veren,
Slomil britanskiye suda.
Kak budto znak iz myortvykh zeren,
O, tyomno-krasnaya voda! (SP II 231–2)

(1187 – the star of Saladin rises, and Jerusalem fell with blood. And then a year in harmony kindled smoke above Chile during those days. As soon as the troops of Saladin received the key of Jerusalem, the sea changed its master off the far-off shores of Chile. And Monmouth and Otranto see how the pride of Albion perishes. Above it the hand of the cold Teuton draws the circles of Dante. And this day, true to the sacrament, wrecked the British ships. As though a sign from dead grain, oh, dark-red waters!)[36]

These lines (which are from a poem that Khlebnikov entitled 'Story of a Mistake' – 'Rasskaz ob oshibke' – after some unfulfilled predictions) strive to link the twelfth-century battles of the crusades with the battles of the First World War. Like the poems on Tsushima, which also reflected Khlebnikov's work on time and fate, this poem has as a central concern the historical legitimacy of supremacy at sea ('the sea changed its master'); the chief arbiter in the battle is not the combatants themselves but the appointed 'day' on which the events take place.

Khlebnikov continued these concerns in his further pamphlet *Time a Measure of the World*, which was published in 1916. 'It would be a first step,' he wrote here, 'if, on the as yet clean canvas of the concept of time, one could just manage to sketch a few features, marking with angles and points the nose, the ears and the eyes of the face of Time' (SS III 437). The artist of 'space' was turning into the artist of time. As he wrote home in August 1915 – a year after the war had started – 'the study of war has turned into a study of the conditions of similarity between two points in time' (SP V 304). To be forewarned was to be forearmed. The poet-warrior was acquiring the guise of the poet-prophet and beginning to direct his militancy at the 'tower of time'.

VI

Spending the winter and spring of 1914–15 in the south of Russia at Astrakhan, Khlebnikov will have been largely sheltered from the impact of the war. He was engaged during this period with war in the abstract, with his calculations on battles and time. However, his return to the north, to Moscow and Petrograd, in the summer of 1915, will certainly have brought him into closer contact with the reality of war and some of its more unpleasant aspects.

We can gauge something of his attitude upon his return north from some autobiographical writings (including 'Ka^2') which date from about January 1916. Khlebnikov talks here of the 'proximity . . . of the voices of war' (SP IV 70), he refers to the flood of refugees which was causing 'alarm' (SP V 125, SP IV 72); and he is greatly preoccupied with the question of death.

Providing us, perhaps, with some indication of the creative impulse behind 'Death in a Lake', he alludes to the war as a 'swim in the stream of death' (SP V 125), out of whose waters people will emerge 'differently', 'shamefully putting on their clothes'. He writes at one point:

> And I saw him – him, the youth of the terrestrial globe: he was hastily emerging from the water and putting on a crimson cloak, split in two by a black stripe the colour of dried blood. All around the grass was too green, and the refugee ran, cast off by the bowstring of war deep into an alien land.[37] (SP IV 73)

Khlebnikov felt at this time that he had been introduced to the 'god of death' (SP V 131). The war was clearly disturbing for him. He put it bluntly: 'the whip of war is offensive to me' ('mne protiven bich voyny') (SP v 133).

By the end of 1915 Khlebnikov was showing not only a lack of enthusiasm for the war, but also a distinct hostility to it. This is reflected in his poetic work. The December 1915 miscellany *Took* contained a poem by Khlebnikov written about a month before,[38] which opens as follows:

> Gde volk voskliknul krov'yu:
> 'Ei! Ya yunoshi telo yem'.
> Tam skazhet mat': 'dala synov ya'. –
> My, startsy, rassudim, chto delayem.
> Pravda, chto yunoshi stali deshevle?
> Deshevle zemli, bochki vody i telegi ugley?
> Ty, zhenshchina v belom, kosyashchaya stebli,
> Myshtsami smuglaya, v rabote nagley!
> 'Myortvyye yunoshi! Myortvyye yunoshi!'
> Po ploshchadyam pleshchetsya ston gorodov. (SP II 247)

(Where the wolf exclaimed in blood: 'Hey! I am eating the body of a young man'. There the mother will say: 'I gave my sons'. – We, elders, let us consider what we are doing. Is it true that young men have become cheaper? Cheaper than land, than a barrel of water and a cart of coal? You, woman in white, scything the stalks, swarthy in muscles, be more shameless in your work! 'Dead youths! Dead youths!' The groan of cities laps through the squares.)

The war had devalued human life in Russia to such an extent that it had become 'cheaper' than coal or water, and Khlebnikov is using this poem to express his sorrow and his anger. His militant *persona* had resurfaced, and it had found a new antagonist in the shape of war itself, which, in the guise of a wolf,[39] was devouring the bodies of the young men of Russia. It was now not so much war which provided the aesthetic attraction for the poet as the struggle against it.

This was, however, a response to war which had ideological as well as aesthetic implications. The poem's suggestion of the complicity of the older generation in furthering the horrors of war is also to be seen in the context of Khlebnikov's Futurist militancy and his war between the generations. The events of the war reinforced an ideological and aesthetic opposition not towards the German foe, but towards the Russian 'elders'. The poem has certain revolutionary connotations.[40]

It is also important to note that although Khlebnikov is opposed here to a particular war, this opposition was, in effect, an opposition to warfare in general. Moreover, it began to express itself in such a belligerent manner that it took on the aspect of warfare itself. Khlebnikov could now issue exhortations to make war against war. Another poem (first published in 1916)[41] included the lines:

Velichavo idyomte k Voyne Velikanshe,
Chto volosy cheshet svoi ot trup'ya.
Voskliknemte smelo, smelo kak ran'she:
Mamont naglyy, zhdi kop'ya! (SP II 249)

(Let us approach with majesty the Giantess War, that combs the corpses from her hair. Let us exclaim boldly, as boldly as before: brazen mammoth, await the spear!)

Further evidence of Khlebnikov's growing distaste for war at this time can be found elsewhere in *Took*. His aphoristic 'Proposals', which the miscellany also contained, called, for example, for isolating war to a 'special desert island' where all who wanted could fight each other out of harm's way; he also put forward a proposal to neutralize the effects of war by the introduction of 'sleep bullets' (SP V 159). His espousal of the folk song which glorified the feats of war had clearly undergone some revision. Notions of the glories of warriorhood underwent even further revision when, to Khlebnikov's horror, the war intervened in his own personal life and in April 1916 he suddenly found himself drafted into the 93rd reserve infantry regiment of the tsarist armed forces in Tsaritsyn.

Khlebnikov's response to the regimentation of military service has been well-documented. He tried urgently to achieve a discharge or a transfer and, as Vladimir Markov has noted, 'he began to mail desperate pleas for help to his friends'.[42] 'The king is in a dungeon, the king is languishing', he wrote to Petrovsky, 'in infantry regiment 93 I have died like children die' (NP 410). In a short poem written in May 1916 Khlebnikov uses the same words:

Gde, kak volosy devitsyny,
Pleshchut reki, tam v Tsaritsyne,
Dlya nevedomoy sud'by, dlya nevedomogo boya,
Nagibalisya duby nam nenuzhnoy tetivoyu
V peshiy polk 93–iy
Ya pogib, kak gibnut deti. (NP 169)

(Where, like the hair of a maiden, the rivers lap, there in Tsaritsyn, for an unknown fate, for an unknown battle, the oaks bowed down like a bowstring we did not need, in infantry regiment 93 I have died, like children die.)[43]

In spite of his calculations on destiny and war, he does not now appear willing to make predictions about his own 'unknown fate', and his search for a way out of military service led him quickly into hospitals for psychiatric checks in an attempt to have himself declared mentally unfit.

The irony of this former belligerent pan-Slav warrior suffering horrors in a reserve infantry regiment has not been lost on some commentators.[44] However, Khlebnikov himself could also extract irony from the situation. In one of his letters to Nikolay Kulbin (who, as a senior member of the staff at the military medical academy, was in a position to help him) Khlebnikov wrote in bewilderment: 'in peacetime we were called plain mad, mentally ill; thanks to that we were banned from any sort of service; but now in time of war, when every move must be especially responsible, I am made a fully-fledged citizen' (SP v 311). 'Do what is necessary to prevent a poet and a thinker from being turned into a soldier', he begs in this letter, concluding it with a plea to Kulbin to 'send a diagnosis' (SP v 310–11).

Letters extant from this period give some idea of the anguish and humiliation which Khlebnikov suffered. He writes to his mother: 'many times I ask the question: will or will not this Arakcheyev-like regime (*Arakcheyevshchina*) be the death of a poet, more – a king of poets? (SP v 306). Khlebnikov is here comparing his own military service to the harsh military colonies set up by Arakcheyev – a favourite of Aleksandr I – in the early nineteenth century. Another letter to Kulbin expressed similar sentiments:

Again the hell of the transformation of a poet into an animal devoid of reason, with whom they talk in the language of stable-hands, and, as an act of kindness, with the help of a knee, pull your belt across your stomach so tight that it takes your breath away, where a blow on the chin has been forcing me and my comrades to hold our heads higher and look happier, where I am becoming a meeting point for rays of hate because I am [different] not the crowd and not the herd, where there is one answer to all questions, that I am still alive, whereas whole generations have been wiped out in the war. But does one evil justify another evil and their chains? . . .

As a soldier, I am absolutely nothing. The other side of the military fence I am something . . . And what am I to do with their oath, I, who have already sworn an oath to Poetry? (SP v 309)

The strict regimentation of military life not only clashed with poetic notions of warriorhood, but was also clearly a great physical and mental strain for Khlebnikov. At the end of an evening's training, he told Kulbin, he had been driven 'crazy' and he could not even remember which was his right and which his left leg (SP v 309). He was subjected to the humiliation of being addressed not as 'he', but as 'it' and of being regarded as 'physically underdeveloped' (SP v 310).

But it was not simply the mental and physical abuse which Khlebnikov found abhorrent. Nor was it the material deprivations he suffered as a soldier (he could, and did, suffer much worse with considerable equanimity). The aspect which made Khlebnikov 'the most pathetic'[45] of the Futurist war victims was the deprivation of his liberty as a poet. He was accustomed to wandering and creating at will; now he was physically and mentally constrained. The snares of this tsarist military encampment were causing, as Khlebnikov put it, the murder of his 'rhythm' (SP v 309). His vocation as a poet and his liberty to pursue this vocation was a factor which overrode for him all other concerns. Inside the military camp he had been transformed from something (*nechto*) into nothing (*nichto*). In the prison-like barracks of his regiment, it was not so much the man that was being destroyed, as the poet:

A poet has his own complex rhythm, that is why military service is especially difficult . . . So, defeated by war, I shall have to break my rhythm . . . and fall silent as a poet. This is no joke at all for me, and I shall continue to shout to a stranger on the ship to throw me a life-belt. Thanks to the monotonous and severe abuse, the feeling for language is dying in me. (SP v 309–10)

And he added in this letter:

I am a dervish, a yogi, a Martian, anything you like, but not a private in an infantry reserve regiment. (SP v 310)

The war which was defeating Khlebnikov was not the external aggression of German militarism, but the internal Arakcheyev-like military regime of his own country. He was, as he put it in one poem, the captive of 'wicked elders' (SP II 246).

This poem, and many others which contained his response to the 'mammoth' war, were later (apparently about 1919) brought together by Khlebnikov into the cycle or 'supertale' which he aptly entitled 'War in a Mousetrap'. This title was possibly partly inspired by a 1915 art exhibition, which included among its exhibits 'a mousetrap with a real mouse fixed to a canvas' (as Khlebnikov himself described it – SP v 128).[46] The implications are, however, fairly self-evident. Instead of mankind being caught in the 'trap' of war, Khlebnikov envisages the trapping of war itself. Nor does Khlebnikov restrict himself here to an image of war ensnared. One poem in the cycle also calls for the 'universe' to be muzzled so that it can no longer bite the young men of Russia (SP II 251). And in another poem the image of a mousetrap for war is transformed into the image of a trap for fate itself:

Vchera ya molvil: gullya, gullya!
I voyny prileteli i klevali
Iz ruk moikh zerno.
I nado mnoy sklonilsya deder,
Obvityy per'yami grobov,
I s myshelovkoyu u beder,
I mysh'yu sudeb mezh zubov.
Kriva izvilistaya trost'
I zly sineyushchiye ziny.
No belaya, kak lebed', kost'
Glazami zetit iz korziny.
Ya molvil: 'Gore! myshelov!
Zachem sud'bu ustami derzhish'?'
No on otvetil: 'Sud'bolov
Ya – i voley chisel – lomoderzhets.' (SP II 254)

(Yesterday I uttered: gullya, gullya! And wars flew down and pecked grain from my hands. And a devil bent over, girded in feathers of coffins, and with a mousetrap at his hips and the mouse of fates between his teeth. Crooked the twisting cane and evil the eyes growing blue, but white, as a swan, the bone peers from a basket with its eyes. I spoke: 'Woe! Mousetrapper! Why do you hold fate in your mouth?' But he replied: 'I am a fatetrapper, and by the will of numbers, a smashocrat.')

The poetic hero has war feeding tamely from his hands, but above him hovers a monster of all monsters, not just fate, but a 'fatetrapper', by whom fate can be gripped like a mouse between the teeth. Yet, however awesome this figure might be, the reference to the 'will of numbers' makes it clear that this 'fatetrapper' is a projection of Khlebnikov's own poetic I, reflecting the author's own aspiration to establish control over fate by mathematical calculations. War was directed not by man, but by fate, and its control called for a 'fatetrapper'.

We do not have to look far in Khlebnikov's works to find similar references. In April 1917 Khlebnikov and Petnikov planned a talk based in part on the following points:

> 1. We are swarthy hunters, who have hung on our belt a mousetrap, in which Fate fearfully trembles with black eyes.
> Definition of Fate as a mouse.
> 2. Our answer to wars – the mousetrap. The rays of my name.
> (SP V 258–9)

Khlebnikov expressed similar ideas in his 'Conversation' ('Razgovor'), which he wrote during the same month (SS III 524).[47] One of the participants in this dialogue, referring to his collocutor's (and Khlebnikov's) numerological teachings, notes:

> I see that 317 years is the true wave of the ray of time and that it is as if you carry a mousetrap at your belt in which fate is sitting. Allow me to call you fatetrapper, as people call green-eyed black cats mousetrappers. Out of your teaching comes a united mankind, not split up into states and peoples.
> (SS III 458)

It is of some note that in his preface to Khlebnikov's *Battles*, published only about four months after the war began, Kruchonykh was already linking Khlebnikov's mathematical calculations on time with his campaign against war: '... only we, now Futurists (*budetlyane*), now Asiatics', Kruchonykh wrote, 'risk taking in our hands the lever of the *numbers of history* and turning them like the handle of a coffee-grinder.' And he concludes: 'but now brave Khlebnikov has issued a challenge to war itself – man the barricades!'

This dual notion of the Futurist (*budetlyanin*) as scholar or prophet in charge of fate ('the numbers of history') and as warrior manning the barricades against war echoed Khlebnikov's own development of the theme. In 1916 Khlebnikov wrote the following programmatic statement. I quote it in full:

> One could swim in the amount of tears which have been shed by the best thinkers over the fact that the destinies of mankind have still not been measured. The task of measuring destinies coincides with the task of skilfully throwing a noose on the fat leg of fate. This is the urgent task which the Futurist (*budetlyanin*)[48] has set himself. Not to know this and to

excuse himself by ignorance is something which the Futurist cannot do and has no right to do. When this has been achieved, he will enjoy the sorry spectacle of destiny, caught in a mousetrap, fearfully eyeing people. Destiny will sharpen its teeth against the mousetrap, the phantom of escape will rise before it. But the Futurist will tell it sternly: 'Nothing of the sort', and thoughtfully bending over it, will study it, puffing out clouds of smoke.

The following lines correspond to that moment when the rider puts his foot in the stirrup. Fate, saddled and bridled, beware!

The Futurist has taken the reins in his iron hand. He has pulled at your horse's mouth with the bit! Another blow from the wind and a new wild gallop of pursuit will begin for the riders of fate. Let the Blue Don teach them the intoxication of the gallop! (SP V 144)

The task of the Khlebnikovian Futurist is both to capture and to study destiny; to tame the wild horse of fate and to ride it. Images of warrior and prophet begin to merge together.

The impact of the war on Khlebnikov then was not to eradicate his militancy but to reshape it. And to reshape it not so much for further battles among the 'states of space', but for the grander campaigns against time and fate. Although the war meant that the 'old clothes of mankind' were floating in the 'waters of death', Khlebnikov now felt capable of assuming the role of the 'tailor' of humanity, who was hastily spinning and weaving 'new clothes' for mankind to put on (SP IV 71).[49]

The 'War in a Mousetrap' cycle ends with the following short poem:

Veter – peniye
Kogo i o chom?
Neterpeniye
Mecha stat′ myachom.
Ya umer, ya umer
I khlynula krov′
Po latam shirokim potokom.
Ochnulsya ya inache, vnov′,
Okinuv vas voina okom. (SP II 258)

(Wind – singing, whose and of what? Longing of sword to be ball. I have died, I have died and the blood has gushed over my armour in a broad torrent. I came to as another, anew, casting the eye of a warrior over you.)

The poem gives voice to the 'longing' of war to become peace (of sword to become ball) and although this is followed by death, the death is immediately transformed into resurrection. As Henryk

Baran has pointed out, 'the lyrical "I" perishes in the cosmic struggle, but returns to life'.[50] This warrior figure of 'War in a Mousetrap' is not defeated, but rather reforged for the sterner battles ahead.

VII

The political and social liberation of the Russian people signalled by the collapse of autocracy and the February revolution of 1917 more or less coincided with Khlebnikov's own personal liberation from the army. Once free on furlough, he soon joined in the general fray, publishing in April 1917 his 'Proclamation of the Chairmen of the Terrestrial Globe'. Not surprisingly perhaps, given his recent experiences, this attack on the 'states of space' and 'poetic' seizure of power by Khlebnikov's own world 'rulers' also constituted what Nikolay Khardzhiev has rightly called 'an anti-militarist manifesto'.[51] Khlebnikov's 'proclamation' was a rejection of the 'commercial enterprises of War & co.' and of the monster 'states of space' which were 'crunching' the people between the jaws of war (SP III 19–21). Khlebnikov's revolutionary militancy can be immediately associated with his opposition to war.

Naturally, the pro-war policies pursued by the provisional government did not endear it to Khlebnikov. He did, however, find an opposition to war on the part of the Bolsheviks, and this will have been of considerable importance in attracting his support for them. He was later to write, for example, of the 'wild ravings' of the provisional government about 'war until victory', comparing it with the subsequent twist of fate which brought to power the 'government of Lenin' (SS III 396). Such sentiments are also very much in evidence in his memoir on the events of October 1917, 'October on the Neva' ('Oktyabr′ na Neve'), which was written in 1918 to mark the Bolshevik revolution's first anniversary.

This memoir speaks of a decision by Khlebnikov's 'chairmen' to blind the single eye of the 'monster war'[52] and it also demonstrates Khlebnikov's contempt for the provisional government leader, Kerensky. Indeed, according to the memoir, Khlebnikov was calling for the removal of Kerensky some days before the Bolshevik revolution put him to flight. Khlebnikov tells us that on 22 October, a 'session' of the 'Government of the Terrestrial Globe' decreed: '(1) to consider the provisional government provisionally non-existent and the insect-in-chief Aleksandr Feodorovich Kerensky under strict arrest.'[53] Khlebnikov's dislike of Kerensky's pro-war policies will certainly have been strengthened by the fact that he was still in some danger of being called up into the army. At one point, Khlebnikov apparently even planned to flog an effigy of Kerensky in a central Petrograd park.[54]

When the Bolshevik takeover came, with its policy of ending the war, there can be little doubt that Khlebnikov welcomed it. There can be little doubt also, however, that like many writers of the time, Khlebnikov did not fully share the Bolsheviks' perspective and viewed the revolution in his own, rather idiosyncratic, way. Khlebnikov saw the revolution not as a progressive act by a proletarian vanguard of workers, but as a popular uprising of the masses against oppression; as an act of vengeance. This wave of popular retribution could, moreover, in his opinion, be measured in terms of his calculations on time and destiny. The events of the revolution and the subsequent events of the civil war were to feature prominently in the compilation of his 'Boards of Fate'. Khlebnikov also saw the revolution in terms of a potential takeover by his own prospective world government and the subsequent establishment of a utopian 'state of time'. In associating the revolution with a coming utopia, Khlebnikov was by no means unique. Here one can compare him with Mayakovsky and the Futurist desire to leap from an unacceptable present into a harmonious future. Khlebnikov provides us with glimpses of this prospective harmony in various prose sketches and in the long poem *Goodworld*.

As well as an upsurge in utopian writings, Khlebnikov's support for the revolution also meant a resurgence of the militant exhortatory form. It was between the two revolutions of February and October, for example, that Khlebnikov wrote his short poem proclaiming freedom and the sovereignty of the people. It begins:

Svoboda prikhodit nagaya,
Brosaya na serdtse tsvety,
I my, s neyu v nogu shagaya,
Beseduyem s nebom na ty.
My, voiny, strogo udarim
Rukoy po surovym shchitam:
– Da budet narod gosudarem,
Vsegda, navsegda, zdes' i tam! (SP II 253)

(Freedom comes naked, casting flowers on the heart, and we, marching in time with her stride, talk to the heavens on familiar terms. We, warriors, shall strike severely with fists on stern shields: – may the people be sovereign for always, for ever, there and here!)

Such exhortations continued throughout the years of revolt and this rhetorical and exhortatory style can also be found in the several longer poems which the revolution inspired Khlebnikov to write. 'Washerwoman' and *The Present Time* (*Nastoyashcheye*) with its 'voices from the street' stand out in particular, but exhortatory verse can also be found among the utopian visions of *Goodworld*, where the cosmic proportions of Khlebnikov's pro-revolutionary militancy also became evident.[55]

Khlebnikov's support for the October revolution helped him to gain employment with a number of Bolshevik propaganda organizations and publications, where he was able to find a welcome outlet for his work. Take, for example, his short poem 'Liberty for All', published in the army newspaper *Krasnyy voin.* It reads in part:

Vikhrem bessmertnym, vikhrem yedinym
Vse za svobodoy – tuda!
Lyudi s krylom lebedinym
Znamya pronosyat truda.
Vsekh silachey togo mira
Smelo zovyom my na boy . . .[56]

(Like a whirlwind immortal, a whirlwind united, everyone follow freedom – there we go! People with the wing of a swan bear the banner of labour. All the champions from the other world we boldly summon to battle . . .)

It was poems such as this which enabled Khlebnikov to establish some revolutionary credentials. His work as a propagandist for the Bolsheviks did not always, however, make for an easy alliance. He was, as one of the editors of *Krasnyy voin* put it, 'not a newspaper man' and his work could at times prove too complex to be of use for propaganda purposes.[57] Nevertheless, his pro-revolutionary 'agitational' works were frequently printed in the Bolshevik press (including a poem in *Izvestiya* not long before his death).[58] In Baku in October 1920 he is even reported to have lectured on the 'History of the Socialist Movement' for the Volga and Caspian fleet.[59]

Khlebnikov's willingness to associate himself with the Bolshevik armed forces during this period contrasts considerably with his desperate attempts to avoid military service in the tsarist army.

While the need to find some means of staying alive and procuring food and shelter during the chaos of revolution and civil war certainly had some bearing on this, his support for the revolution and its aims, at least as he understood them, was also an important factor.

However, despite his revolutionary militancy, of overriding significance was the fact that he was able to find work with the Bolshevik armed forces not so much as a soldier, but as a poet. When Khlebnikov travelled with the revolutionary expeditionary forces to Iran, his military duties were apparently non-existent. As one of the propaganda workers who accompanied him on the expedition later recalled: 'Khlebnikov had no duties at all. Consequently, although he was counted as serving (*chislilsya na sluzhbe*), he had all of his time to himself' (IS 58). This is confirmed in other memoirs of this time, which paint a portrait of Khlebnikov wandering the countryside freely, spending his time visiting opium dens and writing poetry.[60] Not only did the revolutionary forces recognize him as a writer and publish some of his works, but they accorded him a freedom of movement and operation that was vital for his spiritual well-being. Hence, in spite of his previous offensive against the 'monster war', Khlebnikov was now quite happy to participate as a volunteer in the military campaign of a 'liberating' army.

There was a certain 'internationalist' aspect about the Red Army's Persian campaign which also cannot but have attracted Khlebnikov. The possibility of the revolution hastening the arrival of a universal brotherhood had found in Khlebnikov a ready response, though his eyes turned instinctively not westwards towards the industrial proletariat of Europe, but eastwards to the people of Asia. Khlebnikov had been hoping to visit Iran for some time and the possibility of a trip to that country will have been particularly welcome. The development of his pan-Slavism into a kind of pan-Asianism had been given a considerable stimulus by the revolution (he was already compiling his pan-Asian manifestoes in 1918).

Yet by the time he had joined the Red Army in Iran, Khlebnikov had experienced not only revolution, but also civil war, and while his support for the revolution remained relatively undaunted, his anxieties at the horror of war had soon reasserted themselves. This was particularly so during the difficult year (1919–20) he had spent in the thick of the civil war in Kharkov, where he must have been witness to some of the violent reprisals meted out as the city changed hands.

Khlebnikov's works reflect the violence of the events. One poem, for example, depicts the execution of a defiant young woman by those fighting for 'freedom and the throne' (SP III 57). But Khlebnikov did not restrict himself to portraying the bloodshed caused by the Whites. Elsewhere he portrays with some distress the piles of corpses left in the wake of the Reds' ruthless advance ('they do not take prisoners') (SP III 49):

V snegu na bol'shake
Lezhat bortsy nenuzhnymi polenami,
Do potolka lezhat ubityye, kak doski,
V pokoyakh prezhnego uchilishcha.
Gde sumasshedshiy dom?
V stenakh, ili za stenami? (SP III 49)

(In the snow on the highway fighters lie like unwanted logs, up to the ceiling the murdered lie, stacked like boards, in the rooms of the old college. Where is the madhouse? Within these walls, or outside them?)

Khlebnikov, who spent some months in a Kharkov psychiatric hospital trying to avoid conscription, surveys the scene of conflict and wonders where the insanity really lies.

During his unhappy time in Kharkov, the reprisals exacted by the Bolsheviks became for Khlebnikov a subject of some concern. One unpublished poem, entitled 'Chairman of the *Cheka*' ('Predsedatel' Cheki'), describes in part the unsavoury occurrences at the local headquarters of the Bolsheviks' 'Extraordinary Commission for Combating Counter-Revolution and Sabotage' (known as the *Chrezvychaynaya komissiya* or more simply the *Cheka*). This was an establishment, Khlebnikov tells us, of torture and of death:

Dom Cheki stoyal na vysokom utyose iz gliny
Na beregu glubokogo ovraga
I zadnimi oknami povernut k obryvu.
Ottuda ne donosilos' stonov.
Myortvykh vybrasyvali iz okon v obryv.
Kitaytsy u gotovykh mogil khoronili ikh.
Yamy s nechistotami byli neredko grobom,
Gvozd' pod nogtem – ukrasheniyem muzhchin.[61]

(The House of the *Cheka* stood on a high outcrop of clay on the edge of a deep ravine, with its rear windows facing a precipitous slope. From there the groans did not carry. The dead were thrown out of the windows over the edge. Chinamen buried them in ready-made graves. Cesspits often served as a coffin, a nail under the finger-nail as jewellery for the men.)

The experience of such events probably accounts for Khlebnikov's state of mind in Kharkov in 1920 when he was reported to have told Petrovsky that the revolution was 'depressing' him at that time.[62] Further evidence of this 'depression' can be seen in another unpublished poem, 'In the sea of pestilence!' ('V more mora!'), which almost certainly dates from the same period as 'Chairman of the *Cheka*'. This poem plays on the sound of the name *Chrezvychaynaya komissiya*, which, when reduced to *Chrezvychayka*, allows the Russian word for seagull (*chayka*) to emerge. The potential of this play on words was seized upon by Khlebnikov, who promptly transformed the Bolshevik *Cheka* into a bird whose natural environment was the 'sea of death' and of torture. The poem begins:

V more mora! V more mora!
Tochno chayka!
Chrezvychayka
To v podvale, v cherdake-to,
To v gostinoy, to v khalupe,
Zakovala, zakovala
Gory trupov
Tochno chayka!
Chrezvychayka
To opustit lapy alyye,
V more smerti okunyotsya,
Stona smerti zacherpnyot,
To v prostyni zemlyanyye
Obov'yot tela ustalyye,
Trupy myortvykh zavernyot,
I podushkoy chornoy gliny
Uspokoit mertvetsov,
I pod nogti blednosiniye
Gvozdi dlinnyye vob'yot.[63]

(In a sea of pestilence! In a sea of pestilence! Like a seagull, the *Chrezvychayka*, now in a basement, now in an attic, now in a sitting room, now in a cottage, has put in chains mountains of corpses. Like a seagull! The *Chrezvychayka* will now lower its scarlet feet, will plunge into the sea of death, will scoop up the groan of death, will now bind in earthen sheets the tired bodies, will wrap up the corpses of the dead and will calm the dead with a pillow of black clay and will drive long nails under pale blue finger-nails.)

This portrayal of terror in a revolutionary civil war then continues with the following memorable lines:

More plachet. More voyet.
My proshli morya i stepi.
Gody, gody
My mechtali o svobode.
I svidetel′ nashi deti!
Razve eti
Smert′ i tsepi
Pobeditelya venok?[64]

(The sea cries. The sea howls. We have passed through seas and steppes. For years, for years, we have dreamed of freedom. And our children bear us witness! Can this death and these chains really be the victor's laurels?)

The 'Chairman of the *Cheka*' poem tells of a *Cheka* officer in Kharkov who had himself been sentenced to death, because he had failed to order any executions. As Ronald Vroon has pointed out, it is a work which contains distinct echoes of another Khlebnikov poem, 'Rejection' (SP III 297), where the lyrical I spurns the idea of being a ruler and proclaims that it is 'much more pleasant to look at the stars than to sign a death warrant', and 'more pleasant to listen to the voices of flowers' than 'to see guns killing those' who are in turn threatening death.[65] Imminent extinction is also a concern of the lyrical hero in 'Stone Woman' ('Kamennaya baba'):

I ya posledniy zhivopisets
Zemli neslykhannogo strakha.
Ya kazhdyy den′ zhdu vystrela v sebya. (SP III 33)

(And I am the last painter in a world of unprecedented terror. Every day I expect a bullet in me.)

However, as we have seen elsewhere, Khlebnikov believed that forces beyond man were at work in these conflicts between nations and classes. As 'Stone Woman' also points out, when in Khlebnikov's poetic world rivers run red with blood, it is because 'sobbing numbers have passed above the poor world' (SP III 34). Part of the strength of Khlebnikov's outstanding long poem of the revolutionary period, 'Night Search', is that it reflects the full complexity of his attitude towards the revolutionary conflict. Violence is met with violence, while in the background, as a kind of grand arbiter, lurks the 'iron grid' of fate.[66]

Some of the tensions evident in Khlebnikov's attitude towards the revolutionary war surface in his portrayal of Stepan Razin, the seventeenth-century peasant rebel leader. Razin was a figure of immense importance for Khlebnikov and named or unnamed he haunts many of his works. Khlebnikov was so drawn to this figure that he even saw parallels between his own life and Razin's, not least, for example, in their associations with the River Volga and the city of Astrakhan (where Khlebnikov lived for much of his life and which Razin occupied during his rebellion). Nor was the fact lost on Khlebnikov that Razin too had crossed the Caspian Sea to visit Iran. Khlebnikov was quite aware that in his own trip to Iran he was following in Razin's footsteps. Khlebnikov also detected some affinity in their shared espousal of revolt and missions of liberation, invoking the image of Razin as a revolutionary warrior hero. Indeed, perhaps not surprisingly, during the years of revolution the image of Razin enjoyed a particular vogue, and many writers invoked his name. As Kornely Zelinsky pointed out:

> In those years Stepan Razin was virtually the most popular of historical heroes. Khlebnikov, Kamensky, the *Proletkul't* writers – all began to sing of Stepan Razin.[67]

However, although the close identification with the rebel hero can lead to the appearance in Khlebnikov's works of a veritable double (Khlebnikov actually uses the phrase 'Razin double' – SP IV 147), the portrayal can also have the qualities of an inverted double, an 'antipode'.[68]

One poem where a certain tension comes to light is 'Shimmering rain drips from the oars' ('Kapayet s vyosel siyayushchiy dozhd''), which was included by Khlebnikov in his 'War in a Mousetrap'. The poem can be considered as part of the 'Razin constellation'[69] since, although Razin is not named directly, certain allusions indicate his presence. The poem begins:

> Kapayet s vyosel siyayushchiy dozhd'
> Sinim plovtsov velichaya.
> Besplotnym venkom ty uvenchan, o vozhd'!
>
> To vidim i verim, chuya i chaya.
>
> Kakoy on? On rusyy: tochno zori;
>   Kak kolos speloy rzhi.
>   A vzory – l'dy i more,
>   Gde plavayut morzhi.[70]

(Shimmering rain drips from the oars, acclaiming the mariners in blue. A spectral laurel wreathes your brow, oh leader! This we see and believe, sensing in suspense. What is he like? Golden brown, like the dawn. Like an ear of ripe rye. And his gaze – ice and sea, where the walruses swim.)

The reference to 'mariners' with their 'leader' recalls Razin and his rebels as they plied the Volga and the Caspian. Elsewhere, Khlebnikov actually uses the epithet 'mariner' (*plovets*) to apply to Razin (SP I 247). The description of the poetic hero's gaze as 'ice and sea' almost certainly relates to Razin's pilgrimage as a youth to the Solovki monastery on the White Sea – also portrayed by Khlebnikov in another important Razin text, 'Razin: Two Trinities' ('Razin: dve troitsy') (SP IV 146–51).[71] Moreover, the reference to *zori* (the glow of dawns) brings to mind the singular form of this plural noun, *zarya*, used frequently by Khlebnikov in anagrams or palindromes of Razin's name (*Ya Razin*) to link his own *persona* with that of Razin's. If one adds to this the image of the 'ear of rye' (that is, 'bread' – *khleb*), which has elsewhere been associated with the *persona* of Khlebnikov,[72] then one has in this poem, as Stepanov has pointed out, a fusion of the figure of Razin and of the author himself.[73]

However, the poem also includes the following lines:

No stoit, derzha kormilo
I ne druzhit s kistenyom . . .[74]

(But he stands, hand on the helm and is no friend of the cudgel . . .)

This seems a rather contradictory image in a poem which has as its hero a representation of Khlebnikov's warrior *persona*. The hero, although depicted in control of the vessel's helm, contrary to the image in 'Song for Me' ('Pesn′ mne') ('and the hand wields a cudgel'), has abandoned the symbol of warriorhood, his weapon. Significantly, another version of the poem reinforces this image:

No stoit, derzha pravilo,
Ne gorditsya kistenyom. (SP II 250)

(But he stands, hand on the rudder, no pride in the cudgel . . .)

Instruments of navigation have replaced the weapons of war. It is an important development. A different type of poetic *persona* with a different implement in his grasp appears to be encroaching on the figure of the warrior.

It is with this in mind that one should also view a hybrid Khlebnikov/Razin presentation in *Goodworld*. Here, although the warrior figure passes through the land igniting the fire of revolt, in his hands is not a weapon, but 'a series of numbers, like a staff' (SP I 199). The warrior has forsaken his weapon for an implement made up from Khlebnikov's own calculations, the means by which Khlebnikov hoped to wage his struggle against war and fate. It seems the warrior's cudgel has been abandoned for the prophet's staff. It is an image on a par with the guiding role of the helm in 'Shimmering rain . . .'.[75]

The Razin figure is not the only presentation of the warrior *persona* in Khlebnikov's verse to show such a development. The following short poem is also of considerable interest in this process of 'disarming' the warrior in Khlebnikov's work:

O yedinitsa!
Podslushay govor zvyozd.
I krikni moy zavet.
Vot moya okhota, lapu polozhiv.
Ona prekrasna – moya dich'!
Vse brosyatsya otnyat' tvoyu dobychu.
I to zhe skazhut – moy zavet.
I ty Atilla bez mecha,
Vsekh pobediv,
Ikh sdelal dannikami zvyozd
I zavoyeval dlya neba
Velikiy rychagami ya. (SP V 85)

(Oh unit! Listen in to the talk of the stars. And shout my behest. This is my hunt, paw in place. It is fine – my game! Everyone will rush to take your catch away. And they will say the same thing – my behest. And you, Atilla without a sword, having vanquished all, I, great in levers, have made them pay tribute to the stars and have conquered them for the sky.)

This complex short poem with its shifting narrative stances is an invocation to the mathematical unit – *yedinitsa*. With its mix of familiar images of the stars, the hunt, and its reference to the 'behest' of the authorial *persona*, it is clear that this 'unit', like the 'staff of numbers' in *Goodworld*, is related to Khlebnikov's own mathematical struggle with the forces of fate. It is this 'unit' which enables the poetic I to be 'great in levers'. The notion of the 'lever' or 'handle' for the control of fate occurs elsewhere in Khlebnikov's work (see, for example, SP III 98–9) and is an extension of the 'rudder' and 'staff' images. If the poetic hero is 'great in levers', then he will not be needing his weapon; this short poem, consequently, addresses the 'unit' as 'Atilla without a sword'. Once more it is the presentation of a warrior without his weapon, but not without his power. It is a parallel image to Razin without his club. The poetic *persona* is transmuting from warrior to prophet.

A similar portrayal can be seen in another hybrid Khlebnikov/ Razin presentation in 'Gul-Mullah's Trumpet':

> I v zvyozdnoy okhote
> Ya zvyozdnyy skakun,
> Ya Razin naprotiv,
> Ya Razin navyvorot.
> Plyl ya na 'Kurske' sud'be poperyok.
> On grabil i zhog, a ya slova bozhok.
> Parokhod-vetrosek
> Shol cherez zaliva rot.
> Razin devu
> V vode utopil.
> Chto sdelayu ya? Naoborot? Spasu!
> Uvidim. Vremya ne lyubit udil.
> I do pory ne otkroyet svoy rot. (SP I 234–5)

(And in the star hunt I am a star steed, I am Razin in reverse, I am Razin inside out. I sailed on the 'Kursk' against the flow of fate. He plundered and burned, but I am an idol of the word. A steamer-windcutter crossed the mouth of the bay. Razin drowned a maiden in the water. What shall I do? The opposite? I shall save her! We shall see. Time does not like to take the bit. And till the moment comes will not open its mouth.)

Recalling the verbal form of the palindrome, which formed the basis of another work on Razin, the poetic hero describes himself as 'Razin in reverse', as 'Razin inside out'. He is sailing against the current of fate. Razin plundered and burned, but he is 'an idol of the word'. According to popular belief, Razin drowned his Persian princess. Khlebnikov's poetic *persona*, however, will do the opposite, he will rescue her.[76] Furthermore, not only is this portrayal removed from the earth to the heavens ('And in the star hunt'), but Khlebnikov also immediately invokes the already familiar image of taming the wild horse of time. The actions of this 'Razin in reverse' are associated with battles not in the third dimension, but in the fourth. The image of the revolutionary warrior merges with the image of Khlebnikov's own prophet-like *persona*.

Thus, although Khlebnikov is still able to portray himself in terms of a poet-warrior in the military campaign in Iran ('and I shall begin to write new songs . . . A gun and my manuscripts by my side'

– SP I 244), he was also precisely that 'dervish' whose lot he had preferred to that of the soldier several years before. It was in Iran that the poet-warrior was christened the 'priest of flowers' (SP I 245) and where the 'streaming golden south spread out before the feet of the Mohammed of the north like the best silk' (SP V 319). Khlebnikov the warrior was also the 'Mohammed of the north', the prophet. As he wrote to his sister Vera soon after his arrival in Enzeli: 'I told the Persians that I am a Russian prophet' (SP V 321).

VIII

The theme of prophecy is as prevalent in Khlebnikov's work as the theme of war and the figure of the prophet or sage makes numerous appearances, ranging from some of the earliest prose to the final verse. Like the warrior or rebel, Khlebnikov's portrayal of the prophet figure has positive aesthetic connotations. It was also a figure which was not restricted to a purely literary role. The prophet figure was, of course, closely associated with Khlebnikov's own *persona*.

It is clear from Khlebnikov's writings that he was personally concerned with the possibilities of prophecy from an early age. In the 1904 self-styled epitaph, which was itself prophetic, Khlebnikov had already written that he 'dreamed of being a prophet' (NP 318). By the middle of the following year he had taken his post-Tsushima pledge to discover the 'laws of time' and it was not too long before he actually began to make some predictions. He soon had a 'shining success' (SP II 10), which earned him considerable renown. In his 1912 pamphlet *Teacher and Pupil* Khlebnikov asked: 'should one not expect the fall of a state in 1917?' (SP V 179). One should, indeed: 1917 was, of course, the date of the Russian revolution.

As we have seen, Khlebnikov continued his calculations on time and made many predictions in various pamphlets, articles, and even in his private correspondence. In a December 1916 letter, for example, he predicted with some foresight that the war with Germany would end in a year and a half, but only to be followed by an 'internal war' (SP V 312). As Khlebnikov himself was ready to acknowledge, however, his predictions were not always a success (hence his 'Story of a Mistake').[77]

It is worth noting that Khlebnikov's calculations cover an extremely broad range of phenomena: the nature and time not only of historical events, but of thoughts and feelings, of the origin of creative works, of births and deaths; the location of cities, the movements of planets, the frequency of heartbeats, the vibration of sound waves, and so on and so forth. The range is staggering. As he himself put it:

> If the pure laws of time exist, then they must govern everything that has its course in time, irrespective of whether it is the soul of Gogol, Pushkin's 'Yevgeny Onegin', the heavenly bodies of the solar world, the shifts of the earth's crust and the terrible change from the kingdom of serpents to the kingdom of people, the change from the Devonian age to the age marked by the interference of man in the life and construction of the terrestrial globe. (SS III 479)

Khlebnikov felt that some unifying form of measure could be found for all things.

For much of his life it was the number 317 which predominated in his search for the 'laws of time'. It was this figure which he reached from his formula 365 ± 48, a formula by means of which, he was already claiming in 1914, he had 'given people ways of foreseeing the future' (NP 352). By the end of 1920, however, he had revised his theories substantially. This revision occurred when he claimed to have finally discovered the 'laws of time' which he had been seeking. He records his achievement in his 'Boards of Fate':

> The pure laws of time were found by me in 1920 when I was living in Baku, in the country of fire, in the tall building of the naval hostel . . . on 17th November precisely. (SS III 471)

Khlebnikov immediately linked his 'discovery' with the potential for prophecy. 'I wished to find the key for the clock of mankind, to be mankind's clockmaker and mark out the principles for foreseeing the future', he writes (SS III 471). If the principles which these 'laws' encapsulated were correct, Khlebnikov wrote elsewhere, then they provided 'in embryo the long desired foresight of the future. The clock of mankind has been discovered.'[78]

These principles were quite simple. Khlebnikov himself explained:

> I understood that time was built on the steps of two and three, the smallest even and odd numbers.
>
> I understood that the repeated multiplication of two and three by themselves is the true nature of time . . . (SS III 473)

He described the important difference between the numbers two and three, his new key units of time, in a letter to Pyotr Miturich:

> My basic law of time: a negative shift in time occurs every 3^n days and a positive shift every 2^n days; events, the spirit of the time goes into reverse every 3^n days and intensifies its numbers every 2^n days; between the Moscow uprising of 22nd December 1905 and 13th March 1917 there were 2^{12} days; between the conquest of Siberia in 1581 and Russia's reverse at Mukden on 25th February 1905 there were $3^{10}+3^{10}$ days. (SP v 324)

In short then, the figure two was associated with the reinforcement of an event by a similar occurrence (the February revolution reinforces the 1905 Moscow uprising); and the figure three with the negation or the reversal of an event (Russia's defeat at Mukden in 1905 in the war with Japan reversed the 1581 success in the conquest of Siberia). It was the events governed by the figure three which Khlebnikov came to regard in terms of his 'law of the seesaw'. As he wrote in his 'Boards of Fate': 'we often feel, in taking one or another step along the road of fate, that we are now, the whole people, all descending some sort of ravine, going down, or are now flying upwards, as though on a seesaw, and some sort of hand is bearing us upwards without effort' (SS III 504). In general terms, however, Khlebnikov began to associate two with 'youth', 'growth' and 'life', whereas three signified 'decline' and 'retribution'; three was an 'evil' number, the 'wheel of death', the 'wing of death'.[79]

The efforts to plot a chart of the passage of time were undertaken by Khlebnikov in all seriousness. As his contemporary Spassky noted: 'he believed in the reality of his predictions'.[80] We also have manifold evidence of this from Khlebnikov himself. So concerned was he to demonstrate the validity of his prophecy, that when he had once publicly predicted the correct date of a 'new Soviet government' he seems to have persuaded no fewer than three Bolshevik officials to sign a document testifying to his success (SS III 531). This 'testimony' was subsequently published in a Moscow magazine in 1922. Some of his prophecies were given in his verse. Take, for example, the following, which was unfulfilled at the time, but which may be considered by some still to have a certain relevance:

> Klyanemsya volosami Gurriet el′ Ayn,[81]
> Klyanemsya zolotymi ustami Zaratustry –
> Persiya budet sovetskoy stranoy.
> Tak govorit prorok! (SP v 85)

(Let us swear by the hair of Qurrat al-Ain, let us swear by the golden lips of Zarathustra – Persia will be a Soviet country. Thus speaks the prophet.)

Khlebnikov's great preoccupation with the mathematical calculations which formed the basis for his predictions has led many to perceive in him a dichotomy between the man of science and the man of literature. Vladimir Markov observed, for example, with some justification, that 'mathematics always fought with language for Khlebnikov's affection, and it was certainly his greater ambition to "discover the laws of time" than to leave his name in the history of poetry'.[82] However, like many of the 'oppositions'[83] present in Khlebnikov's works, the conflict which seems to exist between the number and the word, between science and poetry, is not without a certain resolution. Indeed, although it might be argued that Khlebnikov's mathematical analyses of history should be separated from his artistic work,[84] one of the most important elements of Khlebnikov's writings is, on the contrary, the integration of scientific and poetic interests.

There are several factors which might be considered here. Firstly, even Khlebnikov's early aesthetic programme detailed tasks which had extra-literary implications. The wish to chronicle in his works 'Russia in the past' (SP v 298) is already evidence of the historical interests which were to preoccupy him in his calculations on time. Khlebnikov never intended his artistic works to be divorced from his social, ideological, or scientific concerns, and he frequently used his creative works precisely as platforms for such concerns. Secondly, as we have seen, Khlebnikov came to see himself not only as an 'artist of word', but also as an 'artist of number'. Science itself was for him an art. 'A poet must study mathematics. Poetry and mathematics are from the same source' – are words attributed to Khlebnikov by one memoirist.[85] Thirdly, the very concept of prophecy itself, which stimulated many of his mathematical writings, shares an intimate relationship with poetry. The roots of prophetic utterances lie also at the basis of poetry's origins.[86] The mathematical calculations on which Khlebnikov was engaged were part and parcel of a prophetic vision of universal harmony, which was, for Khlebnikov, as aesthetically based as it was scientifically founded.

The result was, as Tzvetan Todorov has pointed out, that 'the opposition between literature and non-literature does not seem to have any meaning'[87] for Khlebnikov. Literature and non-literature, art and science, are not divided by the customary boundaries. Thus, while a certain tension between the poet and the scientist may be felt, Khlebnikov's concept of literature was something which allowed for the expression of these dual concerns and which strove towards their reconciliation. Khlebnikov's 'scientific' work was also creative.

Given this, it is not surprising to encounter a peculiar mix of literature and science. On the one hand, lines of verse preface his 'Boards of Fate', and his 'laws of time' are conveyed not only mathematically, but also metaphorically. On the other hand, calculations and equations frequently crop up in ostensibly literary works or are translated into distinctly 'poetic' language:

Cherez dva raza v desyatoy stepeni tri
Posle vzyat'ya Iskera,[88]
Posle surovykh ochey Yermaka,
Otrazhonnykh v sibirskoy reke,
Nastupayet den' bitvy Mukdena,
Gde mnogo zemle otdali udali.
Eto vsegda tak: posle tryokh v stepeni ennoy
Nastupil otritsatel'nyy sdvig. (SP III 350)

(In two times three to the power of ten after the taking of Isker, after the stern eyes of Yermak, reflected in the Siberian river, comes the day of the battle of Mukden, where much boldness was given up to the earth. It is always thus: after three to the power of n the negative shift has come.)

The mathematical predictions of the scientist and the prophetic visions of the artist merge to form a single framework for both the literary and the non-literary.

The concepts of prophecy and poetry merged to such an extent for Khlebnikov that he even came to see creative works which had no overt prophetic content in terms of prophecy. No doubt spurred on by the utterances of Kruchonykh (who, it will be recalled, saw some of Khlebnikov's early poetry as presaging the battles of the First World War), Khlebnikov began to develop something of an aesthetic theory based around the alleged prophetic nature of his work. In the 1919 introduction to his abortive collected works he wrote:

Minor works (*melkiye veshchi*) are significant when they start the future, in the same way as a falling star leaves behind itself a fiery trail; they must have sufficient speed to break through the present . . . we know that a work is good if, like a stone from the future, it sets the present alight.

In 'Grasshopper', 'Bobeobi' and 'Oh, laugh' were knots (*uzly*) of the future – a small outlet for the god of fire and his happy spray. When I noticed how old lines suddenly faded when the content hidden in them became the present day, I understood that the home of creation is the future. It is from there that blows the wind of the gods of the word.

(SP II 8)

The hidden content which Khlebnikov perceived in the word, he now also perceived in his works, and they revealed for him the real 'Futurist' nature of creation.[89]

The belief in the intrinsically prophetic nature of artistic work is also evident in Khlebnikov's view of the folk tale or fairy tale (*skazka*). Khlebnikov believed that the poetic fancy of the folk tale contained within itself the prophecy of a scientific fact. For example, the reality of air travel had been predicted by the story of the flying carpet. The folk tale prophesied what science was to achieve:

For a thousand years, for tens of centuries, the future was smouldering in the world of the folk tale and suddenly it became the today of life. The foresight of folk tales is like a stick giving support to the blind man of mankind. (SP V 196)

Khlebnikov acts as code-breaker, interpreting the prophetic 'allusions' (*namyoki*) (SP V 196) contained in these texts. Elsewhere, discussing the same subject, he asks rhetorically: 'So, should the artist follow on the heels of science, of everyday life, of events? Where has he place for foresight, for prophecy . . . ?' (SP V 275).[90]

One of the important consequences of Khlebnikov's theories on the 'laws of time' was the question mark which they placed against the free will of man. The predictability of events implies a certain determinism and the implacability with which Khlebnikov's 'seesaw' of fate rises and falls, bringing with it the 'wheel of death', does not augur well for man's freedom of action. Khlebnikov's mathematical tables on the movements of peoples and the battles of history are compiled as testimony to the immutable nature of the 'laws' involved. All mankind is subject to these 'laws of time'; they govern its wars, its religious beliefs, even its prophets:

We people are like waves thrown against each other by the iron law which relates time and place; the age-old contract between time and space makes itself felt in our wars, prophets and faiths ... It is pleasant to feel oneself a thing. (SS III 500)

Man's actions, unbeknown to him, are dictated by some higher order. The retribution exacted by man upon his fellows in wars and revolutions occurs not as the manifestation of his own will, but at the behest of the 'laws' of fate which govern his actions in time and space. Khlebnikov explains:

I did not invent these laws; I simply took the living values (*velichiny*) of time, striving to strip myself clean of existing teachings, and examined the law according to which these values change one into another and constructed equations, relying on experience. (SS III 474)

Whether Khlebnikov invented these 'laws' or discovered them is, of course, a moot point. After the battle of Tsushima he pledged to find the 'laws of time'; some fifteen years later this is precisely what he has claimed to have done. Khlebnikov seems to have started from the premise that the 'laws' exist and then set out to prove them. The conclusion seems to have been posited before the search began. As Tzvetan Todorov points out:

The important thing, then, is not time or space but, as Khlebnikov puts it, 'proportion, order, and harmony'. His first goal is to denounce 'so-called chance', to show that there is nothing fortuitous, that the arbitrary is merely a relationship not yet understood.[91]

However, there is evidence that Khlebnikov was not entirely happy with the determinist theory which he had constructed. A fear that he might have imprisoned himself in a net of numbers of his own making is, for example, expressed in the following lines:

Yesli kto setku iz chisel
Nabrosil na mir,
Razve on um nash vozvysil?
Net, stal nash um yeshcho boleye sir! (SP III 357)

(If someone has thrown a net of numbers on the world, has he really elevated our mind? No, our mind has become more orphan than before!)

The significance which Khlebnikov attributed to these lines can be judged from the fact that although they first appeared in a poem dating from 1912 (NP 25), they are quoted above from the 'supertale' *Zangezi*, written almost ten years later.

Further evidence of a concern for man's free will can be seen in the critical remarks voiced in 'Children of the Otter' about Marx and Darwin, who have seized 'tender minds' in the 'claws' of their determinism (SP II 172).[92]

Thus, while one work may proclaim how pleasant it is 'to feel oneself a thing', another work can portray the inexorable nature of the 'laws' in a less favourable light. Noting how 'number' and 'triangle' were shepherding people into the 'iron mousetrap' of war (SP IV 144–5), Khlebnikov wrote:

> I whispered curses to the cold triangles and arcs, feasting above people . . . I saw distinctly the cold 'tatar yoke' of the hordes of triangles, of the vortices of the circle, which was advancing upon us, the people, like evening upon day . . . (SP IV 144)

Khlebnikov seems far from being a willing victim in a predetermined slaughter. As he wrote elsewhere: 'I am not the mouse, but the mousetrap' (SP I 176).

His siege of the 'tower of time' was not prompted by a desire to enslave man in determinist chains. On the contrary, one of the main impulses behind his striving to discover the 'laws of time' was an impulse towards freedom and free will. 'Liberty for All' was, we should recall, the title of one poem;[93] and in one jotting he wrote: 'Is this a surrender to fate? . . . Far from it. We shall sound out the opposition.'[94]

In his 'laws of time' Khlebnikov wished to put at man's disposal the knowledge which would enable him to become the master of his own destiny. He believed it was not events which governed time, but time which governed events.[95] His 'Boards of Fate' opens with the following passage:

> The fate of the Volga gives lessons for fatecraft.
>
> The day the Volga channel was sounded became the day of its subjugation, of its conquest by the force of sail and oar, the surrender of the Volga to man. The sounding of fate and the study of its dangerous places should make the navigation of fate as easy and as tranquil an affair as sailing the Volga became easy and safe once hundreds of buoys with their red and green lights had marked the dangerous spots, the rocks, the shallows and the sandbanks of the river bed. In the same way can the splits and shifts in time be studied.
>
> One can take similar soundings for the flow of time too, establishing the laws for tomorrow, studying the channel of future times, proceeding from the lessons of past centuries and arming reason in the ways of measuring fate with new mind's eyes to see into the distance of future events.

It has long since become a commonplace that knowledge is a form of power and that to foresee events means to control them. (SS III 471)

The powers of prediction which Khlebnikov's 'laws of time' provided did not place man at the mercy of events, but events at the mercy of man.

In writings which were probably to form further parts for the 'Boards of Fate', Khlebnikov likens the powers of foresight in his 'laws of time' to a gift of eyes for a blind man so that he can see the pitfalls which lie ahead. 'I thought that it would not be useless to find something approximating to galoshes for the puddles of fate', he also writes.[96]

This is why, in spite of the apparently immutable nature of Khlebnikov's 'laws', Nikolay Aseyev could talk of his predictions as a barometer capable of forewarning mankind and directing its progress, and Vladimir Markov can write that Khlebnikov had 'the truly Futurist dream of a free man, a man who will know the laws of existence and will be able to regulate his life'.[97] As Khlebnikov himself explained, once the 'huge rays of human fate' had been studied, 'one may think that the centuries-long oscillations of our giant ray will be just as obedient to the scientist as the infinitely small waves of a ray of light. Then people will at the same time be both the nation which inhabits the ray's wave and the scientist directing the course of these rays, changing their path at will' (SP V 239–40). It is a vision of man as an arbiter of his own destiny.[98]

Ultimately, then, in Khlebnikov's view, the potential existed for the chains of determinism to be transformed into a universal harmony where 'the equation of human happiness was resolved' (SP IV 298) and the 'dungeon of time' in which man found himself would not be such an unpleasant place to inhabit:

Neolegislation (*zakononovshestvo*): they cannot be violated, cannot be disobeyed: they can be seen or not seen . . .

We are uncovering, we are laying bare, the joyful dungeon in which man lives, out of which he cannot go; everyone alive is an inhabitant of this dungeon of time; life is the living quarters.

Long live the deck of the terrestrial globe![99]

In Khlebnikov's siege of the 'tower of time' the two images which predominated were those of warrior/hunter and of prophet/scientist.[100] This familiar combination of images can also be seen in Khlebnikov's announcement of his victory in the struggle. He writes in his 'Boards of Fate':

Having discovered the significance of even and odd in time, I had the sensation that in my hands was a mousetrap, in which ancient destiny trembled like a small frightened beast. (SS III 473)

The scientist who has discovered the significance of 'even and odd' is equated with the hunter who has fate trembling in his trap. The prophet figure performs a mental act which echoes the physical act of the warrior.

The shifting of conflict from the level of physical violence to the level of the intellect developed into a concept of considerable importance for Khlebnikov. We have already noted the 'disarming' of Razin and 'Atilla without a sword'. Other instances of such a process can also be cited. 'Storming of the Universe', for example, may feature a cosmic rebellion, but the locality of the action is, in fact, a 'skull' and the power is controlled by 'the levers of the brain' (SP III 97). Towards the end of the poem this 'intellectualization' of the conflict receives direct expression when the hero finally saves his beleaguered people not by force of arms but 'by mind and thought alone' ('umom i tol'ko mysl'yu' – SP III 99).

The warrior and prophet combination is evident too in the letter which Khlebnikov wrote to his sister from Baku in January 1921.[101] 'This year will be the year of the great and final fight with the serpent', he writes (SP V 315). And he continues:

Over this time I have fashioned a lance for the struggle against it – this is foresight into the future: I have equations of stars, equations of voice, equations of thought, and equations of birth and death. (SP V 316)

The weapon with which the poet is fighting his 'serpent' is forged from the equations of his own prophecies. The transformation of poet as warrior into poet as prophet was thus rendering conflict on the physical plane redundant. The intellectual crusade against fate and against time was bringing success against another major adversary – war. Fate in a mousetrap was also 'war in a mousetrap'; the discovery of the 'laws of time' would also eradicate the need for war. One 'proclamation', dated 1919–21, reads in part:

Who will be able to violate our laws?
They are made not from the stone of desire and passions, but from the stone of time.
People! Say all together: No one!
Erect, stern in their outlines, they have no need of support from the sharp cane of war, which wounds whoever relies upon it. (SP V 165)

The 'Boards of Fate' was a fitting place for a similar proclamation. This exposition of Khlebnikov's 'laws of time' opens with a poem which begins in the following manner:

Yesli ya obrashchu chelovechestvo v chasy
I pokazhu kak strelka stoletiya dvizhetsya,
Neuzheli iz nashey vremyon polosy
Ne vyletit voyna, kak nenuzhnaya izhitsa? (SS III 469)

(If I turn mankind into a clock and show how the hand of the century moves, will not war fly off from our band of times, like a useless *izhitsa*?)

It is Khlebnikov's discovery of the 'clock of mankind' which will make the elimination of war possible. War is to be transformed into a 'useless *izhitsa*' (*izhitsa* being a letter which disappeared in the post-revolutionary alphabet reform of 1918).

A further metamorphosis of war into written sign occurs in the mathematical equations by means of which Khlebnikov presented his 'laws of time'. He describes the process as follows:

It is strange to think that in their countless *coups d'état*, nations have just been following several rules of algebra. Mankind, in its bloody wars, in its handwriting of the sword of wars, has simply been following along like a pupil, folding back the corners of the page of the book of numbers ... Majestic war, which is carrying off so many lives, often simply means a change in the sign of an equation. We must learn to read the signs inscribed on the pages of the past in order to free ourselves from the fatal line between the past and the future ...[102]

Once mankind realises that his 'bloody wars' can be reduced to algebraical formulas, Khlebnikov believes, he will be able to free himself from the 'fatal line' which marks his present.

This potentially liberating transformation of war into sign can even take the form of musical notation. In 'Our Foundation' the victory of the Futurist over conflict is likened to the sound of music from a balalaika:

Before you is the Futurist (*budetlyanin*) with his 'balalaika'. Upon it, chained to the strings, trembles the spectre of mankind. But the Futurist plays: and it seems to him that it is possible to replace the hostility of countries (*vrazhdu stran*) by the fortune-telling of strings (*vorozhboy strun*). (SP V 239)

International hostilities are transformed on the Futurist balalaika into prophetic sound. This reference to 'fortune-telling' brings to mind the magical element which is also associated with the act of prophecy. The Futurist performer acts as a magician, charming away the conflict between nations, 'resolving by the playing of strings, that which is resolved by gunfire' (SP v 313).[103]

An important example of this magical element is also evident in 'Storming of the Universe', where Khlebnikov again writes of his post-Tsushima pledge to discover the 'laws of time':

Ya dal obeshchaniye,
Ya natsarapal na siney kore
Bolotnoy beryozy
Vzyatyye iz letopisi
Imena sudov,
Na golubovatoy kore
Nachertil tela i truby, volny, –
Kudesnik ya khitr, –
I vvel v boy dalyokoye more
I rodnuyu beryozu i bolottse.
Chto sil′neye: prostodushnaya beryoza,
Ili yarost′ zheleznogo morya? (SP III 94)

(And I gave a pledge, I carved on the blue bark of a marsh birch the names of ships taken from the chronicle, on the light blue bark I marked the bodies, the funnels, the waves, – I am a cunning sorcerer, – and I engaged in battle the distant sea and the native birch tree and the marsh. Which is stronger: the simple-hearted birch, or the fury of the iron sea?)

Once again human conflict is represented by Khlebnikov in terms of signs. This time it is not an algebraical or musical presentation, but one composed of words and pictures. When Khlebnikov received the news about the battle of Tsushima he claimed to have inscribed his pledge to find the 'laws of time' on a birch tree (SP II 10). The above passage elaborates: ships' names and the images of ships are carved into the bark as the poet re-enacts the battle between the land and sea. Khlebnikov the 'cunning sorcerer' is at work. Like an ancient magician he fights his battles not on a physical level with a weapon in his hand but on the level of incantation or sorcery. It is war by proxy. Like primitive man with his cave paintings, he etches the target of his spell representationally, in visual form, to enable him to effect his magic against it. This is the level at which Khlebnikov can defeat both war and fate.

Weapons have been cast aside in favour of implements with which to create signs. As an extension of this, the field of battle for

Khlebnikov's siege of the 'tower of time' becomes not a scene of physical conflict but a desk at which Khlebnikov the writer sits and compiles his calculations which will put fate in a mousetrap and eliminate the need for war:

> People have been calculating time by the blood of war, by the sword. It follows that wars will cease when people learn to calculate time in ink. War has turned the universe into an inkwell filled with blood in which it has wished to drown the pitiful, absurd writer. But the writer wishes to drown war in his own inkwell, to drown war. A clash of faiths – the sound of wills. Who will win? (SP v 266)

War and the 'pitiful, absurd writer' challenge each other for control of the universe, each trying to drown the other in an 'inkwell'. 'Who will win?' Khlebnikov asks. We can find his answer in unpublished writings probably intended for his 'Boards of Fate':

> One day I was sitting thoughtfully pen in hand. The pen hung idly in the air. Suddenly in flew war and like a happy fly landed in the inkwell. Dying, it crawled some way across the book and these are the traces of the steps it made as it crawled in a sticky lump, all covered in ink. Such is the fate of war. War will drown in the writer's inkwell.[104]

War is transmuted into sign again and writes its own epitaph as it crawls dying across the writer's book.

In pursuing his siege of the 'tower of time', Khlebnikov aimed not only to snare fate in a mousetrap, but also to bring his war against war to a successful conclusion.

5
The single book

I

One of the fundamental elements in Khlebnikov's vision of the lost idyll of primitive times is the presence of a universal language. A state of harmony where universal communication meant universal understanding, where 'words destroyed enmity and made the future transparent and calm' (SP v 216). Such a universal communication lies at the heart of Khlebnikov's visions of a futuristic utopia too. Here, the fruits of science and the arts receive instant transmission in the huge 'shadebooks' and 'radio reading rooms' which adorn the future world's settlements (SP IV 287–95).

Given this, it is somewhat ironic that the dissemination of Khlebnikov's own work has been far from ideal. Not only was the transmission of his work far from instantaneous and universal, but it was also far from accurate. One critic has even suggested that no single other Russian poet has been presented to the reader in such distorted texts.[1]

The distortion which Khlebnikov suffered at the hands of some of his early Futurist editors was certainly considerable. The reproduction of his work abounded in inaccuracies and inconsistencies. As Mayakovsky himself admitted: 'frequently, the end of one piece was stuck on to the beginning of another'.[2] Unfortunately some of these distortions also found their way into the five-volume edition edited by Stepanov, who was himself not beyond reproach in his editorial work.

Clearly one of the problems (though this can by no means justify all the distortions) was the rather chaotic state of Khlebnikov's manuscripts. His handwriting is frequently illegible, corrections and additions can be made somewhat haphazardly, and unfinished works and jottings for new works can appear together on the same page, so that, as Khardzhiev and Trenin have pointed out, 'on many occasions it is difficult even to decide to which work . . . one or another text belongs'.[3] Benedikt Livshits summed up as follows some of the problems that he and Nikolay Burliuk encountered when trying to make some sense of Khlebnikov's manuscripts:

> ... jottings of a most varied nature spread out in all directions, one overlapping another in the minutest of hands. There were columns of some sorts of words mixed up with the dates of historical events and mathematical formulas, rough copies of letters, proper names, columns of numbers. In this sheer flood of inscription elements of organized speech could only be grasped with difficulty.
>
> To put this chaos into something resembling a system was a completely hopeless task. We had to immerse ourselves in it blindly and extract at random now one thing, now another ...
>
> Of course, we were not handwriting experts, moreover, the text itself, which abounded in neologisms, made our work extremely difficult, but I can say with a clear conscience that we made every effort not to distort a single word of Khlebnikov, since we fully recognized the whole gravity of the responsibility which we had taken upon ourselves.[4]

In the light of such problems the attitude of Khlebnikov himself towards his manuscripts becomes of some interest. What then was this attitude?

The testimony of Khlebnikov's contemporaries is virtually unanimous: that he was careless with his manuscripts to a degree of neglect. 'He loses everything', David Burliuk wrote to Levky Zheverzheyev in 1913;[5] and Mayakovsky too noted Khlebnikov's tendency to fill a pillowcase full of manuscripts and then lose it.[6] Consequently, Khlebnikov's Futurist colleagues stress not so much their distortion of his manuscripts as the important role they played in rescuing his works from oblivion and immortalizing at least some of them in print.

Nikolay Aseyev, for example, allotted David Burliuk a particular part in this task. For Aseyev, far from being a chief distorter of Khlebnikov's texts, Burliuk was their saviour. Aseyev commented, during Khlebnikov's lifetime:

> ... to list the works of Khlebnikov is a futile task. The majority of them do not get into print because of the negligence of their author who has no concern for their fate and thanks to the criminal indifference of his contemporaries, of whom only D. D. Burliuk had the ability to discern the future pride of Russian art and to publish his works ...[7]

Nor was Burliuk hesitant in publicizing his own role. He describes how on one occasion he salvaged from the floor a scrap of paper which turned out to be what he calls the '*chef d'œuvre* of the new Russian literature'. It was Khlebnikov's 'Incantation by Laughter'.[8] There is certainly no question about Burliuk's high regard for Khlebnikov. 'Khlebnikov is above criticism', Burliuk wrote in the letter to Zheverzheyev. And he added: 'Khlebnikov needs to be taken care of. His work must be gathered together. His manuscripts must be preserved.'[9]

Despite this, however, there was the one occasion at least (that we know of) when Khlebnikov expressed disquiet over the way Burliuk exercised this care. Nikolay and David Burliuk were criticized by Khlebnikov for publishing without his permission, and for distorting, works which were not intended for publication. In addition, Khlebnikov accused them of acquiring his 'old waste paper' by 'cunning' (SP v 257). Khlebnikov was far from consistent in his outrage at being treated in such a manner (his work was subsequently distorted, apparently, without such complaint), but this certainly shows that he was not *entirely* oblivious to the fate of his manuscripts. Indeed, his correspondence shows that on two occasions in 1909 and 1915 he specifically asked Kamensky to return his unpublished autographs to him. 'These manuscripts are dear to me', he writes in the first of these letters (NP 355, 380).

Furthermore, towards the end of his life he became particularly concerned at the fate of some of his autographs. At the end of 1921, far from being negligent, he was pondering the idea of entrusting Tatlin with the construction of 'a chapel for manuscripts', 'an iron skull . . . preserving our deeds and thoughts to prevent the mice of time from gnawing at them'.[10] Nor were the 'mice of time' his only antagonists at that point. It was also at this time that Khlebnikov again came into conflict with some of his fellow Futurists over the mistreatment of his manuscripts, with his accusations of theft and plagiarism. Clearly, the notion that Khlebnikov was continually negligent over the fate of his autographs is simply not true.

Khlebnikov's concern that his fellow Futurists could be less than scrupulous in their dealings with his manuscripts is bound up with his whole relationship with the Futurist movement. While his work may have been in some degree distorted in the endeavours to 'slap the face of public taste', he was at least receiving the benefits of being proclaimed a genius and of seeing his work published, which, even given the distortions, was of considerable importance to him. After the reluctance of the literary establishment to put his works into print, the Futurists provided a crucial outlet for him. Vahan Barooshian has gone as far as to suggest that 'Khlebnikov apparently allied himself with the Futurists because he essentially wanted to publish his works'.[11]

Certainly, whatever his attitude towards his manuscripts, Khlebnikov had a positive attitude towards publication. Although he may have opposed the publication of individual items or have been dissatisfied with the printed outcome of certain works, he was never opposed to publication in principle. His letters abound with references to the publication of his works or the journals and collections which carried (or were to carry) them. In addition, it is possible to trace persistent attempts by Khlebnikov to secure the publication of collected editions. 'Go ahead and publish!' he appealed to Matyushin in 1911 during one such attempt; 'send me a telegram with the mysterious word – yes!' (NP 359–60). These sentiments are still being repeated nearly 10 years later in a letter to Osip Brik about yet another abortive attempt to publish a collected works. Khlebnikov writes: 'the main secret, shining like the north star, is – have my works been published or not? I greatly fear that they have not!' (NP 384).

It was the failure of this edition to materialize which prompted some of the suspicions and ill feeling evident in the last months of his life. For Khlebnikov, his literary colleagues were now failing in a function for which he had previously been able to rely on them – the publication of his works. Moreover, he was particularly keen at this point to publicize his success in discovering the 'laws' of time. Given, however, that it was proving difficult at this juncture even to secure the publication of his poetry, his urgent desire to publish his calculations on time was clearly not likely to have met with much sympathy.[12]

The aftermath of the friction between Khlebnikov and his fellow Futurists is reflected in Stepanov's comments in the first volume of the SP. Stepanov saw Khlebnikov as being 'obscured by the forests of Futurism' (SP I 34). Moreover, Stepanov, as distinct from Khlebnikov's fellow Futurists, insisted that Khlebnikov 'treated his manuscripts with great care' (SP I 15) and had 'a far from indifferent or negligent attitude' towards his works (SP I 35). In addition, Stepanov makes the valid point that Khlebnikov constantly carried his manuscripts around with him. 'They were his sole baggage', he says (SP I 15). If we recall that Khlebnikov spent most of his life travelling across Russia without any specific 'fixed abode', then what can at first sight seem indifference or neglect can at second sight seem relative care. His manuscripts were his only possessions, his constant companions. What for Khlebnikov's Futurist colleagues was a case of manuscripts being abandoned, for Stepanov could be the sensible precaution of their being deposited for safe-keeping.

The evidence concerning Khlebnikov's attitude towards his manuscripts can be conflicting and somewhat confusing. Part of an answer to the problem may lie in the specific nature of the manuscripts themselves (note, for example, his reference to 'old waste paper' SP v 257), or in Khlebnikov's own changing attitudes. Part may also lie, however, in what Aleksandr Parnis has called Khlebnikov's 'ideal of the wandering minstrel' (*ideal brodyachego pevtsa*).[13]

In line with many of those who knew him, Anfimov, the Kharkov psychiatrist who examined Khlebnikov in 1919, testified that he 'was constantly losing his manuscripts'.[14] Anfimov also pointed out, however, that Khlebnikov devoted his whole being to a Bohemian literary existence and it was his literary credo that 'poets should wander and sing'.[15] Anfimov is citing here the 'Declaration of Creators' ('Deklaratsiya tvortsov'.) which Dmitry Petrovsky says he composed jointly with Khlebnikov in 1918.[16] This declaration, which called for poets to be exempt from laws and given free travel, was even apparently put before, and rejected by, the Bolshevik Commissar for Enlightenment, Lunacharsky.[17]

It seems as though Khlebnikov's attitude towards the production of his creative work may have been somewhat at variance with the demands of his time. If his approach to his writing was based on the concept of the 'wandering minstrel', the pre-literate bard, then the significance of the literary manuscript could be greatly undermined. For the wandering bard of old, the text was not on paper but in the mind. Moreover, there would not necessarily be a definitive and unalterable text, but a work which was in a constant state of flux. Khlebnikov, however, was writing in a literate epoch where the medium was the written and the printed word. The contradictions which resulted may go some way to explaining his apparently conflicting attitude towards the well-being of his manuscripts. Was this, perhaps, the reflection of a bardic mentality in an age of literacy?

Khlebnikov was certainly well aware that, in the early twentieth century, for his work to be preserved it was necessary to publish. Yet his very creative method seems somehow to have militated against the production of a final, static, printed text.

One of the most fundamental aspects of this method is Khlebnikov's constant reworking of texts which had already been written. This has been noted by virtually all who have examined his manuscripts[18] and it was this to which Stepanov referred when he spoke of Khlebnikov's 'far from indifferent . . . attitude' towards his works (SP I 35). Yet it was precisely this reworking of autographs which for Khlebnikov's Futurist editors was not so much an expression of literary care as an act of literary vandalism. The problem was (and it must have contributed towards the distortion of his texts) that Khlebnikov's editors could not allow him to read his proofs, because he would immediately rewrite the work in question. Numerous contemporaries have testified to this fact. 'He never corrected, but rewrote from scratch, letting any "new ideas" take him where they would', Petrovsky wrote. 'He could not be allowed near the proofs – he would cross out everything, all of it, providing a completely new text', Mayakovsky noted. David Burliuk too made the point that Khlebnikov was 'incapable of correcting proofs – he writes a new version over the top. He has to be removed from the process of printing completely.'[19]

Khlebnikov's early editors sought to 'protect' the manuscripts from Khlebnikov himself. Their attitude towards his autographs was thus formulated not only with regard to the threat to their physical existence (posed by Khlebnikov's alleged lack of care) but also to the 'threat' to their literary existence (posed by Khlebnikov's creative method). Khlebnikov would commit his works to paper, but then constantly rework them. This is clearly a mode of creation which is at variance with the fixed literary entity which characterizes the world of print.

Khlebnikov's constant reworking of texts is one of the elements which led many to form an opinion about the fragmentary and unfinished nature of his work. Mayakovsky was one of the most forthright when he wrote (somewhat unjustly) that the 'completeness' of Khlebnikov's printed work was a 'fiction', 'an appearance', which was most often the result of 'the hands of his friends'.[20] The question of the fragmentary nature of Khlebnikov's work is complex, but one of the main consequences of his reworking of written texts was not so much the production of a series of incompleted fragments, as of a series of completed variants each of which could form an independent definitive version. Khlebnikov's editors are thus often presented with the problem not of publishing unfinished works (though these, of course, do exist) but of choosing between different finished versions of the same work.

It even seems to be the case that Khlebnikov would write new variants of old works from memory (IS 477–8). However, this is not the precise memory of the fixed lines of what David Burliuk called the 'typewriter poet',[21] but the flexible re-creation of a work, perhaps more typical of the pre-literate bard. A work already written could be rewritten in a different version which did not so much replace the preceding one as take its place independently alongside it.[22] It was in connection with this manifestation of multiple variants that the editors of the NP, Khardzhiev and Grits, came to the following important conclusion:

> Khlebnikov frequently reworked his verse, not only to give it a more 'finished' or 'complete' version, but also because he felt that each of his verbal constructs was not a thing, but a process. (NP 12)

And they also point out:

> The concept of the canonical text is inapplicable to many of Khlebnikov's works. (NP 12)

This serves to emphasize the mobility and fluidity which marks Khlebnikov's method of creation. Ultimately then, a work could be both finished and unfinished, both complete and fragmentary. On the one hand it could be constantly rewritten by the author in different versions, but on the other hand each different version was a completed work in its own right.

However much the Futurist editors may have despaired of this aspect of Khlebnikov's creative method, it is in many ways an embodiment of some of the principles of Futurist aesthetics. The Cubist movement in painting dispersed previously static forms and rendered them into a state of flux and fragmentation. The texts of the accompanying Futurist poetic movement reflected this tendency. Moreover, this emphasis on mobility and fluidity is also evident in the early Futurist manifestoes of which Khlebnikov himself was a co-signatory. The *Word as Such* talks of Futurism's fragmentation of words in its attempts to destroy the 'former congealed language'.[23] 'Letter as Such' ('Bukva kak takovaya') speaks in favour of hand-written, not printed, texts and similarly attacks the 'still born' word of established literature (SP v 248).[24]

It is in the context of this method of creation that one might also view the occasions when Khlebnikov requested others to add their own touches to his work. Mayakovsky wrote, for example, of how Khlebnikov, when presenting something for publication would add: 'if something is not right – then change it'.[25] Creation was a process, not a singular act, and it was a process which, for Khlebnikov, was not necessarily exclusive to a single author. One notable aspect of Khlebnikov's work was his creative partnership with Kruchonykh. Since they co-authored several works, it should not be particularly unusual for Khlebnikov to tell Kruchonykh that he may make alterations to a text which he is sending him (SP v 298).[26] Khlebnikov not only reworked his creative output himself, he also allowed others to do so. What for some had been seen as a lack of care in the literary treatment of his manuscripts might be seen by others as a conscious and specific stance on the nature of the creative process.

II

It is the dynamic nature of Khlebnikov's creative process which has contributed to the perception of his poetry as a 'single unceasing poem',[27] or as a 'huge fresco in an active and incessant state of re-creation'.[28] The point is that, as well as individual works being rewritten and thus relating to each other as individual variants, one of the key elements of Khlebnikov's work is the presence of groups of texts which are not so much variants of the same work as variations on the same theme. The aesthetic principle which seems to guide this is that although individual works may be seen on one level as self-contained entities, since the creative process which generates them is dynamic, on another level they also move outwards, relating to other works, which can in turn be related to others, and so on. It is a creative process which finds its critical response in the 'open approach' discussed earlier.[29] Ronald Vroon put it succinctly when he noted of one poem that it tended to confirm that

> ... the poet's entire *œuvre* is an integral complex, that any one work implicates and is implicated by many others. When considered in isolation,

some pieces will appear fragmentary or compositionally disarrayed, but when they are brought together with other pieces, they form a coherent whole.[30]

Bearing this in mind, it is not surprising that Khlebnikov's works can be frequently approached in cycles or 'constellations'. It is as though he gravitated towards this form by virtue of a natural attraction. Moreover, it seems to have been an attraction which he came to recognize.[31]

It would be untrue to suggest that Khlebnikov was totally averse to using traditional genre indicators; or for that matter was averse to experimenting with some unusual genres.[32] However, he seems at the same time to have been striving to escape such confines and to develop a new genre which was more compatible with his creative outlook. The direction he took was towards the composite form of the 'supertale' or 'transtale' (*sverkhpovest'/zapovest'*), a development which constituted a recognition of the cycle as a compositional element.[33] Here Khlebnikov could combine various texts, sometimes with a mixture of forms (verse, prose, drama), within a single framework. Each text could preserve its identity as an individual work but could at the same time interact with the other texts to produce a complex network of relationships. Khlebnikov seems to have been contemplating this type of form as early as 1909. A letter written in August of that year to Kamensky showed that he was considering a 'complex work "Across Times" ("Poperyok vremyon") in which the rules of logic of time and space would be broken as many times as a drunkard raises a glass to his lips in one hour'. Khlebnikov also wrote that each chapter should be a distinct entity (*dolzhna ne pokhodit na druguyu*), and that he wished to use all his 'colours and discoveries' (NP 358).

The reference to breaking the 'rules of time and space' suggests that Khlebnikov saw such a formal development in terms of his own work on time and the need to overcome temporal barriers. Certainly this is achieved in 'Children of the Otter' where such figures as distant in time (and space) as Hannibal, Razin and Copernicus are brought together on 'Khlebnikov island'. Questions of time and the 'laws' which Khlebnikov saw as governing it are also an important feature of *Zangezi*, the culmination point of Khlebnikov's 'supertale'.

Since comments on form by Khlebnikov are comparatively rare, the introduction which he wrote for *Zangezi*, explaining some of the compositional principles involved, is of considerable interest. He wrote in part:

> The supertale or transtale is made up of independent fragments (*otryvki*), each with its own particular god, its own particular faith and its own particular statutes . . . It is like a sculpture made from different coloured blocks of different stone, the body – from white stone, the cloak and clothes – from blue, the eyes – from black . . . A story is architecture from words. Architecture from 'stories' is a supertale. (SP III 317)

It is a form which reflects the nature of Khlebnikov's creative method, uniting the concepts of fragment (*otryvok*) and whole. The independent blocks make up a single 'sculpture'.

Although every fragmentary work of Khlebnikov cannot be viewed as being so due to a specific authorial intention, it is clear from the above that the concept of the fragment did enter into Khlebnikov's formal considerations. This view receives some confirmation in Stepanov's observation in the SP that Khlebnikov evidently planned at one point a large undertaking with the title 'A Twentieth Century Osiris' ('Oziris XX veka').[34] Khlebnikov saw this work being written 'as "Ka" was written', 'using the method of letters', 'the method of fragments' (*metod otryvkov*), 'descriptions of things', 'sorting out the trunk' (SP IV 331). The reference here in this context to 'Ka' and the earlier quoted reference to breaking the rules of logic in time and space makes one wonder whether this tale (whose hero spans centuries and continents) should not also be considered in terms of the 'supertale'.

In line with Khlebnikov's general approach to form, the parameters of this new Khlebnikovian genre show some flexibility. 'Children of the Otter', written in 1911–13 and generally considered the first 'supertale', and *Zangezi*, the last, have a unifying element in their protagonists, who are present in many of the 'independent fragments', which have been written or rewritten with an overall framework in mind. Moreover, both include a mixture of prose and drama as well as verse. But 'War in a Mousetrap' and 'Azy iz uzy' ('A's Unbound') are much more akin to a cycle of independent poems with a unifying theme. The flexibility is such that one might even regard other works, such as the long poems 'Washerwoman' and *The Present Time* in the context of the 'supertale'.[35] They are certainly examples of composite texts.

It is within the context of the 'supertale' too, as well as in the context of Khlebnikov's constant reworking, and apparent recomposing from memory that one can place the curious phenomenon in his work known by the Russian term *zagotovka* (meaning something which is procured for later use). In terms of Khlebnikov's poetry, it means that independent fragments or lines from one work can suddenly turn up in another. One example is the lines describing the 'net of numbers' which appear in both 'Hearts more transparent than a vessel' ('Serdtsa prozrachney, chem sosud') (NP 25) and *Zangezi* (SP III 357). Other instances could be cited.[36] It is also worth noting that individual works used in a 'supertale' could coexist as independent pieces or could be subsequently 'isolated' and used again as individual texts.[37] This seems like the notion of the *zagotovka* on a grand scale.

Given the general dynamic element of his art and the fact that he saw the creative act as something of a process, it is understandable that Khlebnikov's view of the static and lifeless nature of the book could be less than sympathetic. An opposition to the traditional printed text was one of the general aesthetic principles of the Hylaean Futurists. When the Hylaean poets were making their first appearances on the literary scene, Russia's established poets were publishing their works in luxurious journals such as *Zolotoye runo* (*Golden Fleece*), *Vesy* (*Scales*) and, of course, *Apollon*. The Hylaeans rebelled against this good taste in the area of formal presentation. One of their hallmarks came to be the production of books which were deliberately shoddy in appearance. The sumptuous nature of the Symbolist editions was rejected in favour of a purposefully non-luxurious presentation. The first *Trap for Judges* of 1910, for example, was 'printed entirely on the reverse side of patterned wallpaper, with the title label glued to the wallpaper cover'.[38] Printed texts and lavish illustrations were countered by the reproduction of hand-written texts and, 'to the uninitiated, scribbles'; 'the hand-made look was clearly intended, not to rival the fastidious elegance of Symbolist publications, but in deliberate antithesis'.[39]

This disrespect for the well-polished published text reached an exaggerated pitch of destructiveness. The *Word as Such* manifesto of Kruchonykh and Khlebnikov proclaimed that readers should be instructed to tear up their books after they had been read: 'speech-creators (*rechetvortsy*) should write on their books: *tear up after reading*!'[40] An action which Khlebnikov apparently carried out in practice, since, according to David Burliuk, 'he had a "bad habit" of tearing out the pages he had read'.[41]

For Khlebnikov, however, this pronounced anti-aestheticism was more than a purely negative phenomenon. It was with this bookish inertness of the literary establishment that he juxtaposed the living art of folklore forms. This is one of the many thrusts in the argument of the early pamphlet *Teacher and Pupil*, in which Khlebnikov posed the question: 'why are the Russian book and the Russian song in different camps?' (SP v 182). This rather unsympathetic attitude towards the book can also be detected elsewhere in the dialogue between the teacher and his pupil. The pupil points out that he has been considering 'the action of the future on the past'. And he continues: 'but is it possible to think of such things with such a pile of books as old mankind possesses . . . Where are the great destroyers of books?' (SP v 174).

The anti-aestheticism of the Hylaean Futurists reflected an attempt to revitalize artistic perception; to renew an image and resurrect a word which had become fossilized. The experiments in word creation strove to produce 'new living words'.[42] This concern is reflected in Khlebnikov's 'Our Foundation' which contends:

> Word creation is the enemy of the bookish petrifaction of language, and, guided by the fact that language is still being created in the countryside, near the rivers and forests . . . it conveys this right to the life of letters. A new word must not only be named but also directed toward the thing being named. Word creation does not violate the laws of language.
>
> (SP v 233–4)

The book is associated with the petrifaction of language, whereas word creation stems from the natural language creation activities of life itself.

The opposition between life and the book is brought out clearly in images elsewhere in Khlebnikov's works. *Zoo* (*Zverinets*) contains the following memorable comparison: 'Zoo, zoo, where the glance of an animal means more than the piles of books which have been read' (NP 286). The poem, 'Song for Me', incorporates a similar suggestion: 'In the age of books I exclaimed: "We only believe animals!"' (NP 205). Another manifestation of this juxtaposition between book and life occurs in the long poem 'Siniye okovy' ('Blue Fetters'), where the book is presented periphrastically in terms of the death of the trees which are chopped down to make paper. The poem calls for 'living people instead of the white page'; and Khlebnikov also talks of the 'living word' and the 'alphabet of events' (SP I 292).

Khlebnikov's opposition to the book, particularly learned volumes, could also involve a lack of sympathy for their authors. Since one such 'scribe' to bear the brunt of criticism was none other than Karl Marx, it is an aspect of his work which has not endeared him to some Soviet critics. In 'Children of the Otter', where the theories of Marx and Darwin are subjected to some critical remarks, Khlebnikov even has his character, the Carthaginian leader Hannibal, threaten Marx with physical violence. Having found refuge with Scipio on 'Khlebnikov island', Hannibal notes Marx's 'gloomy' teachings and suggests:

Davay voz'myom zhe po bulyzhniku
Grozit' uslugoy tyomnoy knizhniku? (SP II 173)

(Shall we then take a cobblestone each and threaten the scribe with some dark deed?)

Boris Yakovlev, who published the fierce attack on Khlebnikov in *Novyy mir* (*New World*) in 1948, was quite naturally able to make use of such a fact to help demonstrate Khlebnikov's disrepute.[43]

Yakovlev was also able to cite another incidence of Khlebnikov's disregard for Marxist literature:

In the 'comic poem' 'Malusha's Granddaughter' ('Vnuchka Malushi') Khlebnikov calls for a 'joyous fire' to be made from the books which are tormenting young people like 'fierce chains of penance', – thus does he characterize Marxist literature.[44]

The Marxist literature which Khlebnikov consigns to the flames in this work is that by Kautsky and Bebel. However, Yakovlev gives a rather distorted picture. The whole of Khlebnikov's relevant passage reads:

Chelpanov, Chizh, Klyuchevsky,
Kautsky, Bebel', Gabrichevsky,
Zernov, Passek – vse gorite!
Ogney slovami – govorite! (SP II 75–6)

(Chelpanov, Chizh, Klyuchevsky, Kautsky, Bebel, Gabrichevsky, Zernov, Passek – all burn away! In words of fire – have your say!)

The other authors whose works are burnt are thus not at all the writers of Marxist literature: they include a psychologist, a psychiatrist, a historian, a medical bacteriologist and so on.[45]

The fact that Kautsky and Bebel were socialist writers is of less significance than the attack against books in general and textbooks in particular. As Markov writes of the poem: 'its theme is a strongly satirical contrast of modern education and its dry, bookish study of natural sciences, with pagan freedom and closeness to nature'.[46] Once again the characteristics of the book are compared unfavourably with the value of the natural world. One can also detect here the notion of book-burning as an anti-authoritarian gesture. The books being destroyed are symbols of authority. In Khlebnikov's 1917 anti-militarist 'Proclamation', one might note, he listed publishers on a par with the hated 'states of space' and the 'commercial enterprises of War and Co.' (SP III 21).

The ritual burning of books developed into something of a particular theme for Khlebnikov. One important example occurs in 'Conversation Between Two' ('Razgovor dvukh osob'), a sequel to the *Teacher and Pupil* dialogue, first published in 1913. Here a brief attack on the works of another German philosopher for whom Khlebnikov had scant regard, Immanuel Kant, turns into a call for the burning of books in general:

> I long for a great bonfire of books. Yellow sparks, rapid fire, translucent ash which disintegrates when touched or even breathed upon, ash on which it is still possible to make out individual lines, words of boasting or arrogance, – all this is transformed into a black, beautiful flower, illuminated by fire from within, grown from the book of people, as the flowers of nature grow from the book of the earth ... (SP V 183)

In this ritual-like conflagration the book undergoes a metamorphosis into a flower, a metamorphosis which demonstrates progression from an artificial creation by mankind to a natural creation by the earth. Through the medium of fire the printed book is transformed into something wholesome. It can now be compared to a very different book: a flower has grown from the 'book of men' just as a flower grows from the 'book of the earth'.

It is appropriate that Khlebnikov's opposition to the book should find expression in this 'conversation', a type of Socratic dialogue, since in Khlebnikov's 'Boards of Fate' we can find the following:

> Take the following series:
>
> There is Socrates, familiar to all, prophet of conversation (*ustnaya beseda*), born in 468 BC.
>
> In 365.5 after him came Tsong-Kha-pa – the great teacher of the Mongols, born in 1357.

> This was a preacher of good for the remote steppes of the continent, an enemy of books, who proceeded along the path of conversation with his pupils; he founded the teaching of the lamas.
> This was the Socrates of the desert Asia. (SS III 491–2)

Socrates is the prophet of conversation, his Asian counterpart, Tsong-Kha-pa, was a 'preacher of good', a practitioner of conversation with his pupils, and, most important, 'an enemy of books'. Khlebnikov links ethical considerations with an opposition to the printed text and an espousal of the oral tradition of literature. Khlebnikov's penchant for the dialogue form almost certainly relates to such attitudes. Although it was conveyed to the reader in print, the dialogue seems to have been regarded by him as essentially oral and as an antithesis to the books which he wished to see reduced to ashes.

Another important episode of book-burning occurs in the short prose piece which begins 'No one will deny ...' ('Nikto ne budet otritsat′ ...') and which depicts in part the burning of Flaubert's *La Tentation de Saint Antoine*. Khlebnikov describes the incident in the following manner:

> ... at night the city was fine. Dead silence as in the Moslem settlements, deserted streets and the bright black glow of the sky. I was without light after the filament of incandescence had danced its dance of death and was quietly dying before my eyes. I thought up a new form of illumination: I took Flaubert's *The Temptation of St Antony* and read it all, setting fire to one page and reading another by its light; a multitude of names, a multitude of gods flashed across my consciousness, hardly disturbing it, touching some chords, leaving others in peace, and then all these faiths, cults and teachings of the terrestrial globe turned into black rustling ash. Having done this, I realized that I had had to act in that way. I was submerged in the acrid, white smoke ... above the sacrifice. Names, religions burned like dry brushwood. Magi, priests, prophets, possessed ... all were bound together like brushwood in the hands of the cruel priest. (SP IV 115–16)

There are several aspects worth noting here. The first is that the book-burning is presented directly as a ritual sacrificial act with Khlebnikov's *persona* as the officiating 'cruel priest'. It is a ritual which seems to reflect the religious nature of the text in question. Secondly, within this sacrificial burning the diverse elements of the book achieve a certain unity, all the various gods and prophets are bound together as 'brushwood' and transformed into the same 'black ash'. As Khlebnikov also writes here, the founders of the three great religions, Christ, Mohammed and the Buddha 'trembled in the fire' together (SP IV 116). Thirdly, the portrayal of the book demonstrates a certain ambivalence. Although the book is again subject to destruction by a Khlebnikovian poetic I (with clear autobiographical implications),[47] it is not only read by the sacrificer, but also its very sacrifice is the method by which it achieves self-fulfilment. It is read by the light of its own burning pages. The book seems to have evoked some attraction as well as suffering destruction. Khlebnikov continues:

Acrid smoke hung around me. It became easy and free . . .
I had tried for a long time not to notice this book, but, full of mysterious sound, it had modestly worked its way on to the table, and, to my horror, hidden by other things, had not got down from there for a long time. Only having turned it into ash and having suddenly attained inner freedom, did I understand that this had been some sort of enemy of mine.

(SP IV 116–17)

In spite of being 'full of mysterious sound', the destruction of the book provides relief and 'inner freedom'; and Khlebnikov comes to realize that the book had been 'some sort of enemy'. Its destruction is not, however, without a certain synthesis. Similar to the burning of the work by Kant, the burning of Flaubert's book produces not just ashes, but a flower, in this case a 'black rose' (SP IV 116).

Khlebnikov's position as regards the book must have presented him with somewhat of a dilemma. On the one hand, he was keenly aware of the need to publish books to preserve his heritage. Yet, on the other, the book was 'some sort of enemy' for him, his very creative method and aesthetic principles seemed to work against the production of such an entity. The transformation of the book of man into the flower and the 'book of the earth' reflects his search for a new type of book, for a way out of this dilemma.

It is in the context of such transformations that one should view the whole series of metaphors in Khlebnikov's works in which, to use Henryk Baran's words, 'nature, or some aspect of it, is presented as a book, or as some aspect of the processes associated with the creation and use of written texts'.[48] Examples of such comparisons abound in Khlebnikov's work. Baran, for instance, has quite correctly noted[49] such lines as: 'the proverbs and patter of spring crawled across winter's books' (SP III 31); 'and I wanted to walk along the Nevsky and begin the book of the sun and its spring days' (SP III 100). Another example can be found in 'Razin: Two Trinities', where the claw marks of a bear are 'printed' in the marsh, 'published by the river in a luxury edition with wide margins' (SP IV 150).

Nor is the text of nature in Khlebnikov's poetic world exclusively printed or written, there can also be a strong oral presence in the imagery. In 'Hearts more transparent than a vessel', for instance, a stream is described as singing 'in a word of varied metre' (NP 25). Similarly, 'Stone Woman' (SP III 32–5), in spite of the 'charmed silence' which it claims to portray, is a veritable cacophony of sounds and oral discourse. The bark of a willow tree mutters folk tales 'like people'. The rustling leaves of a poplar are depicted in terms of conversation, and mountains display the 'firm curves of the sound of centuries' (and into this scene is introduced the 'dumb' poet). The stone effigies are seen here as 'folk tales of stone board'. It is little surprise then that in this poem one of these stone figures is incanted to life by the Khlebnikovian butterfly.

The 'stone' text too features in 'Hearts more transparent than a vessel', where the 'stone bed' of the stream is a 'book' for eyes to see and understand (NP 26). There is also reference to a 'stone diary' (NP 25), a combination of the elements of stone and time which also features in 'Cold water stream' ('Ruchey s kholodnoyu vodoy'). This poem describes a rocky gorge as a 'stone book' upon which is written the 'stone news' of the last hundred thousand years (SP III 136). 'Stone books' also figure in the 'supertale' *Zangezi* (SP III 318). The bedrock of the earth provides the medium whereby the text of nature can take its shape. Natural elements assume the roles of literary artefacts. This was a conscious aesthetic stance by Khlebnikov. As he once wrote in a letter to Kruchonykh: 'my opinion about verses can be reduced to a recollection of the affinity between verse and the elements' (NP 367).[50]

Not surprisingly, the sky and stars also find representation in Khlebnikov's nature/book metaphors, particularly as the book of destiny, 'the book of constellations, where everything is already reckoned' (SP III 263). This familiar poetic theme of reading fate in the stars had, of course, an enhanced significance for Khlebnikov, who was himself compiling his own 'Boards of Fate'.

On occasion Khlebnikov's nature/book metaphors relate not in general to the natural world, but more specifically to countries and continents. He described Russia, for example, as a 'common book'

(SP I 142); elsewhere, in one striking image, he wrote: 'I thought of Russia with its succession of tundra, taiga and steppe as like a single divinely-sounding verse' (SP II 78). The image of the book or text as a country or continent can progress to the stage where the comparison is with the whole world. In one of his notebooks he talked of the 'manuscript of the world' (SP V 266); and one of the points prepared by Khlebnikov and Petnikov for a lecture in 1917 concluded with the notable phrase: 'the world as a poem' (SP V 259). The nature/book metaphor is elevated to the status of an aesthetic principle. Khlebnikov's search for an adequate literary form leads him to the very structure of the world in which he lives. It is in many ways a reflection of the tendencies in the Khlebnikovian 'supertale', where there is a striving to move away from the static book and to re-create in a composite form both the temporal dynamism and the spatial diversity of a single living world.[51]

Frequently the image of the writer in Khlebnikov's works undergoes a related development. If the world is his text then the author can turn into a 'world writer' with the elements of nature as his implements. His pen becomes an uprooted pine, his inkwell – the sea (SP V 155).[52] The *persona* of the writer, too, becomes represented in terms of nature. We can find, for example, a poetic I whose flowing hair is equated to the world's major rivers (SP V 25), whose body is representative of Russia and even the whole world (SP IV 35). Perhaps the most renowned such exposition of the poetic I is his depiction in 'Poet', as 'an entire landscape of mountains, ravines, waterfalls and glaciers across which gallops a herd of deer', as bearing within himself 'the whole universe'.[53]

With the world itself providing a model for both poet and poetry it is understandable that Khlebnikov can propose as the poetic heroes of a single work no less than the whole of mankind. In a letter to Mayakovsky, upstaging Mayakovsky's own '150,000,000', Khlebnikov wrote:

> I am thinking of writing a thing in which the whole of mankind's three thousand million would participate and for whom playing in it would be obligatory. (SP V 317)

The 'texts' of the book and the world become indistinguishable.

Such a tendency receives development elsewhere in his work,

particularly in his 'Boards of Fate'. At one point he talks of the earth as 'a book with the vociferous title of "man"' (SS III 479). He also voices the following opinion:

> In the usual verbal exposition mankind is likened to a white mass, to heaps of damp, freshly set sheets of print, not yet assembled into a book. The slightest wind will scatter them. But there is a way of setting (*sverstat'*) these separate white sheets into a stern book, by using the method of measuring the births of people whose fate shares the same curve on the graph.
>
> Such births, like stiff wire, make a good binding for the pages of the future book which are in danger of being dispersed. (SS III 491)

Khlebnikov is referring here to the 'laws of time' which, he felt, governed the births and deaths of people whose fates were somehow associated. It is following upon this passage that he notes the 'law' which linked the births of Socrates and 'teacher of the Mongols' Tsong-Kha-pa. Khlebnikov's concept of the book, therefore, ultimately bears a specific relationship not only to the earth and its inhabitants but also to the 'laws' of time and fate which he perceived as governing them. These 'laws' would provide the means whereby the disparate pages of mankind could be bound together as a single whole. This was the 'future book' which Khlebnikov the writer was endeavouring to create.

The ideas also receive emphasis in unpublished writings probably also intended for the 'Boards of Fate'. Talking of the 'proto-people' (*pervolyudi*) of the different nations of the world (such as 'Adam for the Jews'), Khlebnikov continues:

> The column of the years of their births is a pillar, upon which the book of the unity of mankind lies open for all – if you would only learn to read it, if you want, turn its pages.
>
> Here is the column of births, the pillar for the book of the unity of peoples.[54]

It had long been Khlebnikov's desire to read this 'book' of fate. The 'pupil' in the 1912 *Teacher and Pupil* dialogue, for example, had already expressed a desire 'to read the characters etched by fate upon the scroll of human deeds' (SP V 174). What Khlebnikov is now saying, however, is that he has not only discovered how to read this 'book', but also how to make its text accessible to others. Khlebnikov maintains that his 'book' of fate is open to all who learn to read it. Moreover, this text provides not only a 'future book', but also a future harmony. Khlebnikov's 'book' is also his vision of the 'unity of mankind'.

This ambitious attempt to reveal the harmonious workings of the world was, however, not unique. Other texts shared similar aspirations. Khlebnikov's 'Boards of Fate' reflects concerns which can also be found in the great religious works of man, such as the Bible, the Koran and the Vedas. In compiling his 'Boards of Fate' Khlebnikov was well aware of these illustrious predecessors.

Khlebnikov was not particularly a 'religious' man in the accepted sense of the word. He was, as Ronald Vroon has correctly pointed out, not a mystic but a visionary.[55] If he inclined towards any religions, they were the religions of the east, Hinduism, Islam, or Buddhism, with its belief in reincarnation. In his self-presentations as a prophet the creed which he was propagating was, however, in his view, based on a rational and scientific interpretation of the processes of time and fate. But, even so, the sphere of his concerns took him into the areas of faiths and religions. Tzvetan Todorov went as far as to remark:

> On the horizon of this superrationalist system appears – however vaguely – the shadow of a theology. If the events of this world obey a regular rhythm, it is because the principle of this rhythm comes from somewhere else.[56]

Khlebnikov is concerned with 'feeding' not only man's reason, but also his spirit. He described one of his early works (probably *Teacher and Pupil*) as 'a magical table-cloth laid with a feast for the spiritual mouths of the whole of mankind' (SP v 293).

If the notion of the 'book of the unity of mankind' seems to reflect in some way the aspirations of man's religious texts, then Khlebnikov's concept of the book also recalls these religious texts in another important way. It is an intrinsic element of the religious book that it presents itself in the terms of a 'book of nature', more particularly as the 'book of the earth' or the 'book of life'. This is as true for the Bible as it is for the Koran.[57] And Khlebnikov's notion of 'the world as a poem', of life as a 'scroll of human deeds' is a reflection and an emulation of this.

Notably, as though in recognition of this fact, Khlebnikov introduces the religious book into his own 'book of nature' metaphors. For example, he told Vyacheslav Ivanov after a visit to the zoo that he had been struck by 'some sort of link between the camel and Buddhism and the tiger and Islam'; 'in the calm face of the camel I read the opened Buddhist book', he wrote (NP 356).[58] In one poem he described a poplar tree as 'a happy theologian of the spring's Koran' (SP III 30).[59] But Khlebnikov's preoccupation with the religious texts goes well beyond the poetic metaphor. References or allusions to religious texts also feature in his polemical and theoretical writings. He viewed, for example, his literary attempts to expand the bounds of Russian literature as attempts to fill in the missing chapters of the 'Russian Bible' (NP 341). An allusion to biblical texts might also be seen in his wish to title a section of a planned collected works the 'Book of Testaments' ('Kniga zavetov') (NP 6). Khlebnikov even regarded the Koran as 'a collection of verse' and Mohammed as a 'great poet' (SP V 241). Similar tendencies are revealed in the conclusion to an early article, where he refers to his own verse as 'allusions and Korans' (*namyoki i korany*) (SP V 195).

A reference to the Koran also featured prominently in a lecture he gave in Baku in December 1920, which he entitled 'The Koran of Numbers' (SP V 316). This lecture not only contained a successful prophecy concerning Soviet power (SS III 531) but was also apparently a fully fledged exposition of his 'laws of time' (NP 385, 485). During the lecture Khlebnikov claimed to have told Moslems that he was a 'continuation of the prophecy of Mohammed who had become dumb and replaced word with number'. He told the 'Marxists' that he was 'Marx squared' (SP V 316). The lecture was evidently not a great success.

The notion of Khlebnikov equating his own work on time with the Koran also finds expression in unpublished writings. He prefaced one notebook containing calculations associated with his 'laws of time' with the jotting 'my Koran'.[60] Echoing the thoughts of his 1920 lecture, he writes elsewhere: 'the Koran has already been written once in words. It has to be written in number.'[61] He seems to have looked upon the equation governing his 'laws of time' as being of sufficient merit to act as a worthy substitute for man's renowned religious teachings:

> That which was talked of in the old dogmas, which was threatened, in the name of retribution, becomes the simple and cruel force of this equation; in its dry language is enclosed: 'Vengeance is mine and I will repay' and the formidable, unforgiving Jehova of the ancients.

The law of Moses and the whole Koran is perhaps confined within the iron force of this equation.

But how much ink is saved! How the inkwell can rest! (SS III 474–5)

For Khlebnikov, the measure of mathematics has come to replace the faith of religion. In 'Children of the Otter' (written 1911–13) Khlebnikov had declared that number was coming as 'a substitute for faiths'; some ten years later, after the alleged discovery of the 'laws of time', he announced the usurpation: 'measure has replaced faith'.[62] Khlebnikov writes in his 'Boards of Fate':

So, the face of time was painted in words on the old canvases of the Koran, the Vedas, the Gospels and other teachings. Here in the pure laws of time that same great face is being sketched by the brush of number and thus another approach has been used to the business of our predecessors. It is not the word which is being applied to the canvas, but the precise number, like an artist's brush-stroke painting the face of time.

Thus, a certain shift has taken place in the ancient occupation of the dauber of time.

Having rejected the jumble of words, the dauber of time holds in his hands a precise measure. (SS III 472–3)

Khlebnikov felt that the doctrines of world religions were tumbling before his mathematical onslaught. Number, his 'precise measure' of time, was making redundant the words of the Koran, the Vedas and the Gospels. 'The ancients peopled heaven with gods', Khlebnikov writes. 'The ancients said that gods control events', but 'it is clear ... that the gods of the ancients are the indices of the mathematical power (*pokazateli stepeni*)' (SS III 494).

This conferment of the status of deity upon number is fully evident in Khlebnikov's 'mystery tale' 'The Scythian's Skullcap', where the god of time is given the name *Chislobog* (Number-god). Although this deity is somewhat elusive, he turns out to be none other than the poetic I's double – his 'old friend from the mirror' (SP IV 84). Since Khlebnikov's writings aspired to replace the religious texts of old, it is perhaps not surprising that this god of time should prove to be a representation of the poet's own *persona*.

It is an elevated presentation of the poetic I – as 'creator' – which also appears in the poem 'Single Book'. As the title indicates, the poem serves as something of a culmination of many of Khlebnikov's ideas on the book, and the literary entity which it depicts bears a marked resemblance not only to his 'book of the unity of mankind', but also to the 'book of the earth'. Its pages are 'the great seas, which flutter like the wings of a blue butterfly' and the silk thread of its bookmark is 'the great rivers in a blue flow' (SP v 24). The whole of mankind is its reader and Khlebnikov is its author. However, it is not simply another book of nature. It opens in the following manner:

Ya videl, chto chornyye Vedy,
Koran i Yevangeliye,
I v sholkovykh doskakh
Knigi mongolov
Iz prakha stepey,
Iz kizyaka blagovonnogo,
Kak eto delayut
Kalmychki zaryoy,
Slozhili kostyor
I sami legli na nego –
Belyye vdovy v oblako dyma skryvalis′,
Chtoby uskorit′ prikhod
Knigi yedinoy . . . (SP v 24)

(I have seen the black Vedas, the Koran and the Gospels, and in their silken boards the books of the Mongols from the dust of the steppes, from the sweet-scented dung, as made by the Kalmyk women at dawn, form a fire and lie down upon it themselves – white widows hidden in a cloud of smoke, to speed up the coming of the single book . . .)

This poem is also yet another expression of the ritual burning of books which can be found elsewhere in Khlebnikov. This time, however, the books consigned to the flames are not those of Flaubert or of Kant, or the writings of scholars or Marxists, they are precisely those religious texts which Khlebnikov's 'Boards of Fate' had come to replace[63] and it is the arrival of Khlebnikov's own 'single book' that their ritual burning is called upon to hasten.

Khlebnikov wished to encompass in his 'single book' not only the 'book of the earth', but also the illustrious texts which strove to interpret the destiny of that earth.[64] It was a 'single book' which was both representation of and interpretation of a single world.

Postscript

When Khlebnikov voiced his notion of besieging the three towers, it was by no means an isolated reference in his work to architectural forms. As well as the battlements of towers and walls which he constructed from numbers and the Futurist household built aloft on piles, Khlebnikov constructed in his poetic world various edifices, ranging from a town from the 'logs of sound' to 'palace-pages' and 'palace-books', and to a town of 'glass pages' which opened and closed like a flower with the coming and the passing of day (SP III 63–5, V 86–91).

It is difficult to determine what prompted Khlebnikov's interest in architectural forms. Perhaps there was no specific impetus beyond his general interest in all the man-made and natural phenomena which he encountered in his short life. Certainly his knowledge of most things was encyclopaedic and his ability to assimilate and process this knowledge poetically is at times little short of astounding. Vladimir Markov is not exaggerating when he writes that Khlebnikov's 'poetic imagination is . . . almost inhuman; the reader is often unable to keep pace with it and gives up, exhausted'.[1]

Architecture attracted his attention at an early age. A letter written home during his first visit to Moscow (probably at the age of 18) already calls, for example, for the compulsory teaching of architecture in the seminaries so that the clergy would learn how to look after the 'monuments of old' (SP V 282–3). Were he to return to Moscow today, he would doubtless be similarly disappointed at the way the secular post-revolutionary authorities have treated some of the city's architectural monuments. He would, however, not be entirely unsympathetic to Moscow's modern look, since, as Konstantin Kedrov has pointed out, some of the city's new structures are virtual embodiments of his own ideas.[2] Architecture was yet another area in which Khlebnikov attempted prophetic utterances. Khlebnikov was not only interested in becoming a 'speech-creator', but also a 'street-creator' (SP IV 275). His Futurism stretched well beyond the parochial concerns of some of his literary colleagues.

Khlebnikov first set out his vision of the city of the future in the article 'We and Houses' ('My i doma'), written about 1915, but not published until several years after his death (SP IV 275–86). He even jotted down some sketches of his future apartment blocks.[3] Needless to say, towers feature prominently among the projected structures, with dwellings hoisted aloft in such as the 'house-poplar', towering above the dirt and dust of the streets. As well as laying siege to towers, Khlebnikov was also striving to construct them. His 'chairmen of the terrestrial globe' were 'worker-architects', his 'supertale' was 'architecture from "stories"', his story 'architecture from words', his letters were a 'structure on piles', his mathematical formulas 'a street of towers'.[4] Time continually acquires material qualities in his works and Khlebnikov the 'architect' shapes its structure, 'planing the centuries into carpenters' boards (SP V 90).

It is the shaping of time which forms the theme of one of Khlebnikov's last poems, where, in a familiar form of self-projection, he adopts for a poetic hero the architect of St Petersburg's Kazan Cathedral, Andrey Voronikhin. This serf from Siberia, who rose to the rank of academician, was able, in Khlebnikov's eyes, to erect 'century upon century', and to gain his freedom from serfdom by a 'vision of time in stone', by constructing 'a tower from time' (SP V 103–4). It was just such a construction of liberation that Khlebnikov himself was engaged upon:

> Tak dushu svobo<dy>
> Dayot dym vremeni, dym nezhnykh chisel vremeni.
> Vershina bashni – eto mysli,
> A osnovan'ye – volya . . . (SP V 105)

(Thus does the smoke of time, the smoke of the tender numbers of time, give the soul of freedom. The summit of the tower is thought, and the foundation is will . . .)

The early post-revolutionary period was, of course, a time when grand architectural schemes were being contemplated, not least perhaps by Vladimir Tatlin, for whom Khlebnikov had a high regard. Tatlin's own tower, the Monument to the Third International, was displayed in model form in 1920, something of which

Khlebnikov cannot have been unaware. Indeed, the regard was mutual, Khlebnikov and Tatlin were particularly close at times, and it is now widely suspected that Khlebnikov was a considerable influence on the latter's constructions.[5]

But Tatlin was by no means the only important figure to come under Khlebnikov's influence. Vladimir Mayakovsky, who, after all, recognized Khlebnikov as his 'teacher', continued to populate the poetic continent discovered by his 'Khlebnikov-Columbus' long after Khlebnikov's death.[6] Naturally, one might expect Mayakovsky, one of the original Cubo-Futurists, to be sensitive to Khlebnikov's example, but this example was also felt by more poetically distant talents such as Osip Mandelstam.

When Mandelstam was arrested at Samatikha in 1938 and dispatched towards his tragic destiny, Khlebnikov was one of the few authors whose books he had with him. And although Nadezhda Mandelstam can point to essential differences in the nature of their work, some of the parallels are equally striking (Mandelstam too was, for example, greatly preoccupied with architectural form). These two poets may have built different edifices, but they shared many of the materials used for construction.[7]

A poet of a later generation, Nikolay Zabolotsky, drew extensively from Khlebnikov's visionary works.[8] Khlebnikov's prose was seen as an example for all to follow by a very different writer, Yury Olesha.[9] The extent of Khlebnikov's influence was so broad that in the late 1940s the Soviet literary establishment felt it necessary to counter the threat with the article by Yakovlev, denouncing him as a 'poet for aesthetes', condemning his example, and urging its eradication.[10] This has clearly been a vain struggle.

The broadness and vitality of Khlebnikov's influence stems from his very diversity as a literary phenomenon. Epic poems, lyric verse, dramatic works, dialogues, prose sketches, manifestoes, theoretical writings, numerological treatises, mathematical calculations, ornithological observations, utopian visions – all merge together in his 'single book'. As Osip Mandelstam (yet again) perceptively remarked, Khlebnikov's works are like 'a huge all-Russian book of prayers and icons (*trebnik-obraznik*) from which all who wish may be able to draw for century upon century to come'.[11]

It has been rightly pointed out by several critics that rather than with the nineteenth century into which he was born, Khlebnikov's literary affinities lay with the preceding, eighteenth century. One can point, for example, to the narrative, didactic, ode-like quality of much of his verse.[12] Shklovsky called him the 'Lomonosov of modern Russian literature'.[13] It is in many ways a fitting comparison, since Lomonosov too was a man of many parts, with writings which were not only literary, but also scientific, covering subjects as diverse as astronomy and metallurgy. Moreover, Lomonosov reflected the philosophic outlook of the eighteenth century, the notion of order in the universe and of the ability of reason to penetrate the secrets of nature, which is, of course, reminiscent of Khlebnikov's own notion of universal order, embodied in his 'laws of time'.

Some of the philosophic ideas of the seventeenth and eighteenth centuries were of a particular relevance for Khlebnikov's thought. This was an age marked by projects for new universal languages, ranging from the philosophic language of Bishop John Wilkins, to the notions advanced by the philosopher and mathematician Leibniz who 'looked forward to the day when controversies would be resolved by the mere invitation to sit down and calculate'.[14] A proposal which Khlebnikov himself, naturally enough, quoted with some favour (SS III 446–7)

However, if one is looking for models for Khlebnikov's own attitude towards literature and life, one can go back much further than recent centuries, to ancient times and to the ancient sage, to figures such as Pythagoras, who regarded all natural phenomena as a legitimate area of enquiry. Khlebnikov himself explicitly recognized his links with Pythagoras[15] and his preoccupation with number was distinctly Pythagorean, as were some of his ideas of reincarnation.

It was in his ideas of reincarnation, governed by the 'laws' of birth, that Khlebnikov ultimately saw the possibility of victory over death. 'We are standing at the threshold of a world when we shall know the day and hour when we shall be reborn, when we shall look upon death as a temporary dip in the waves of non-existence,' he wrote in 'Our Foundation' (SP V 241). Khlebnikov had a keen sense of tragedy and disaster and the struggle against death is reflected in much of his writing. Yet throughout his works laughter rides with grief on the 'seesaw' of fate, and backed by his numerological 'laws' for the control of destiny he is finally able to conjure up utopian visions free from conflict.

How then is one to approach these numerological theories by which Khlebnikov laid such store? The notion that the world's events are governed by a passage of time measured in multiples of twos and threes can certainly be challenged without much difficulty on theoretical grounds, though stranger theories have been known. One approach to Khlebnikov's notions is that we should at least suspend our disbelief. But the answer is more than this. The reader has to enter with Khlebnikov the world which he constructed and see not the minutiae of calculations based on what most would regard as dubious premises, but the grand vision which lies beyond them. A vision of order and harmony which may in Khlebnikov's terms be rationally perceived, but which is nonetheless an aesthetic vision also. To a certain extent the reader must have faith. This might seem paradoxical for a poet who proclaimed that faith had been replaced by measure. But faith is not absent from Khlebnikov's world. On the contrary, it is Khlebnikov's belief or faith in a rational world order, in harmony as opposed to chaos, which is, perhaps, the most fundamental aspect of his world view. Khlebnikov may have proclaimed the arrival of measure, but it is a faith in measure which lies at the very foundation of this proclamation.

Faith and reason combine to make the 'Boards of Fate' as mythopoeic as they are scientific. This is the 'shadow of a theology' which appears behind Khlebnikov's rational and scientific theories and makes the 'Boards of Fate' an alleged successor to the world's religious books. Khlebnikov's numbers may have come to replace the ancient deities, but, since the impulse manifested in the search for harmony and order owes as much to faith as it does to reason, it is not surprising that these gods of old still lurk ominously in the deep waters of Khlebnikov's poetic world:

Gody, lyudi i narody
Ubegayut navsegda,
Kak tekuchaya voda.
V gibkom zerkale prirody
Zvyozdy – nevod, ryby – my,
Bogi – prizraki u t'my.[16] (SP III 7)

(Years, people and nations run away forever like water as it flows. In nature's flexible mirror the stars are a net, the fishes – we, the gods – phantoms in the darkness.)

Notes

1. BIOGRAPHY, DISCOURSE

1 Vladimir Mayakovsky, *Polnoye sobraniye sochineniy v 13-i tomakh*, ed. V. A. Katanyan (Moscow, 1955–61), vol. 12, p. 23 (henceforth PSS followed by volume number and page number). For a translation of Mayakovsky's obituary of Khlebnikov, see *Major Soviet Writers: Essays in Criticism*, ed. Edward J. Brown (Oxford University Press, 1973), pp. 83–8.
2 Ibid.
3 G . . . d (probably A. G. Gornfel'd), 'Nekrolog: V. Khlebnikov', *Literaturnyye zapiski*, 3 (1922), p. 13.
4 Sergey Gorodetsky, 'Velimir Khlebnikov', *Izvestiya*, 5 July 1922.
5 These editions are: *Izbrannyye stikhotvoreniya* (Moscow, 1936); *Stikhotvoreniya* (Leningrad, 1940); and *Stikhotvoreniya i poemy* (Leningrad, 1960).
6 See Boris Yakovlev, 'Poet dlya estetov: (zametki o Velimire Khlebnikove i formalizme v poezii)', *Novyy mir*, 5 (1948), pp. 207–31; and Ye. I. Naumov, *Seminariy po Mayakovskomu* (Moscow–Leningrad, 1953), p. 38.
7 This is the *Neizdannyye proizvedeniya* (Moscow, 1940), edited by Nikolay Khardzhiev and T. Grits. Although excellent, it is not entirely without error. Publication of this volume had been planned earlier than 1940 (note the August 1938 date of the introduction), but the literary and political climate had prevented it from appearing. Doubtless this was the fate of many books, but, since publishers had to bring out something, the Khlebnikov volume was fortunately revived and finally published.
8 Aleksandr Blok, *Sobraniye sochineniy v 8-i tomakh*, ed. V. N. Orlov, A. A. Surkov, K. I. Chukovsky (Moscow–Leningrad, 1960–3), vol. 7, p. 232; Osip Mandelstam, *Sobraniye sochineniy*, 3 vols., ed. G. P. Struve and B. A. Filippov (New York, Inter-Language Literary Associates, 1964–71), vol. 2, p. 390; Mayakovsky, PSS 12, p. 23.
9 Andrey Voznesensky, for example, is quoted as saying that 'without Khlebnikov it is impossible in our time to write verse'; see V. P. Grigor'yev, *Grammatika idiostilya: V. Khlebnikov* (Moscow, 1983), p. 28. A youthful Yevtushenko also devoted a poem to mark his first

acquaintance with a volume of Khlebnikov; see Ye. Yevtushenko, *Izbrannyye proizvedeniya v 2-kh tomakh* (Moscow, 1975), vol. 1, pp. 49–50.

10 Vladimir Markov, *The Longer Poems of Velimir Khlebnikov*, University of California Publications in Modern Philology, vol. 62 (Berkeley and Los Angeles, University of California Press, 1962), p. 18.

11 See Viktor Shklovsky's preface to Dmitry Petrovsky's 'A Tale about Khlebnikov: Memories of Velimir Khlebnikov', in Velimir Khlebnikov, *Snake Train: Poetry and Prose*, ed. Gary Kern (Ann Arbor, Ardis, 1976), pp. 273–313. Petrovsky's memoir (and Shklovsky's preface to it) are translated by Lily Feiler. For the Russian text, see Petrovsky's *Povest' o Velimire Khlebnikove: vospominaniya o Velimire Khlebnikove* (Moscow, 1926). Petrovsky's memoir was first published in *LEF*, 1 (1923), pp. 143–71.

12 For the details surrounding Khlebnikov's birth and early childhood, see Aleksandr Parnis, ' "Konetsarstvo, ved' ottuda ya . . ." ', *Teyegin gerl* (Elista), 1 (1976), pp. 135–51.

13 See Nikolay Khardzhiev, 'Novoye o Velimire Khlebnikove: (k 90-letiyu so dnya rozhdeniya)', in *Den' poezii: 1975* (Moscow, 1975), pp. 203–4 (henceforth Khardzhiev, *Den' poezii*).

14 Khlebnikov had also shown some ability in literature as a schoolboy. In 1899 he had an essay read out as the 'best' in the class. According to the memoir of a schoolfriend, the teacher said that it was 'striking in the originality of its turn of phrase and its very free approach to its theme'. Not long afterwards, however, the memoirist continues, the teacher became disappointed, and said that although Khlebnikov had ability, he was ruining it by striving for 'unusual expressions' (see Khardzhiev, *Den' poezii*, p. 202). Khlebnikov's school reports from Kazan' (*yed. khr.* 154) show, generally, good marks in Russian, though they decline somewhat in 1901–2 (a year when Khlebnikov achieved top marks in algebra and trigonometry).

15 Details of the demonstration and Khlebnikov's refusal to move out of the way of mounted police, even after his father's intervention, are given in IS 10. Khlebnikov appears to be recalling the incident in SP v 139, where he writes of the memory of a 'black cavalry' rushing towards him in a street in Kazan', with the 'crowd of horses' stopping only just before it was upon him. Some time later (probably about 1905) he is reported to have been involved in a revolutionary circle, planning some form of expropriation; see IS 11 and Vera Khlebnikova, 'Vospominaniye Very Khlebnikovoy', in Velemir (sic) Khlebnikov, *Stikhi* (Moscow, 1923), pp. 59–60.

16 The observations from Khlebnikov's lengthy field trip to the Urals, written up, it appears, by his brother Aleksandr, were published (under both their names) as 'Ornitologicheskiye nablyudeniya na Pavdinskom zavode', in *Priroda i okhota* 12 (1911), pp. 1–25. Khlebnikov's earlier article was 'O nakhozhdenii kukushki, blizkoy k *Cuculus intermedius*

Vahl, v kazanskom uyezde Kazanskoy gub.', *Prilozheniye k protokolam zasedaniy obshchestva yestestvoispytateley pri Imperatorskom Kazanskom universitete* 240 (1907), pp. 1–2. A copy of this can be found in Khlebnikov's archive in TsGALI (*yed. khr.* 99). The Khlebnikov archive in TsGALI also includes what seems to be a rough diary of the visit made by his brother Aleksandr (*yed. khr.* 324).

17 See Khardzhiev, *Den' poezii*, p. 204.

18 For reference to Khlebnikov sending his work to Gorky, see Vera Khlebnikova, 'Vospominaniye', p. 60. For the memoir on his youthful literary interests, see Khardzhiev, *Den' poezii*, p. 202.

19 Ivanov dedicated a poem to Khlebnikov in 1909; see Vyacheslav Ivanov, *Stikhotvoreniya i poemy* (Leningrad, 1976), pp. 221–2. Khlebnikov's *Zoo* (*Zverinets*) is almost certainly dedicated to Ivanov, see NP 453; but see also Ivanov, *Stikhotvoreniya i poemy*, p. 481, where the possibility is raised that it was dedicated to someone else.

20 In Vladimir Markov's opinion, for Makovsky 'Khlebnikov's poetry must have seemed not even gibberish, but simply trash'; see his *Russian Futurism: A History* (London, MacGibbon and Kee, 1969), p. 13. It was apparently his 'prose poem' (SP v 287) *Zoo* which Khlebnikov hoped to publish in *Apollon*, see NP 454. This journal was later to become associated with the Acmeist movement.

21 The 'Proclamation of Slav Students', reproduced in SS III 405–6, was published on 16 October 1908. The prose fragment 'Temptation of a Sinner' ('Iskusheniye greshnika') was printed at about the same time in *Vesna* 9 (1908) and is reproduced in SP IV 19–21.

22 Markov, *Russian Futurism*, p. 8.

23 Ibid.

24 The text of the manifesto is given in *Manifesty i programmy russkikh futuristov*, ed. Vladimir Markov (Munich, Wilhelm Fink Verlag, 1967), pp. 50–1. A translation can be found in Markov's *Russian Futurism*, pp. 45–6. There is conflicting evidence as to whether Khlebnikov, although a signatory, actually took part in its writing. Benedikt Livshits, in his *Polutoraglazyy strelets* (Leningrad, 1933), says that Khlebnikov did not take part (p. 129), although Livshits himself was not there to witness the writing. More reliable, perhaps, is the testimony of Kruchonykh, who *was* present when the manifesto was written and who says that Khlebnikov *did* take part in its drafting, along with Kruchonykh himself, Mayakovsky and David Burliuk; see R. V. Duganov, 'Aleksey Kruchonykh 1886–1968: iz vospominaniy', in *Den' poezii: 1983* (Moscow, 1983), p. 159.

25 See Victor Erlich, 'The Place of Russian Futurism within the Russian Poetic Avantgarde: A Reconsideration', *Russian Literature*, 13 (1983), pp. 14–15. In his *Russian Futurism*, p. 384, Markov defined Russian Futurism as 'a post-Symbolist movement in Russian poetry of 1910–1930, which, roughly, put under the same roof all avant-garde forces'. Erlich's argument is that 'the definitions, or the implicit notions of

Russian Futurism ... have been excessively broad' (p. 1). Erlich is (p. 9), unfortunately, slightly misleading about Khlebnikov, whose pan-Slav salute to the 'holy and necessary war' (his 'Proclamation of Slav Students') was, in fact, first published in 1908, as well as being republished in 1914.

26 Khlebnikov uses the word *budetlyanin* consistently throughout his work. This has led to a search for an equivalent neologism in English, such as 'Futurian'. For some critics Khlebnikov's brand of Futurism (*budetlyanstvo*) was an important distinct entity within the Russian Futurist movement as a whole; see, for example, Jean-Claude Lanne, *Velimir Khlebnikov: poète futurien*, 2 vols. (Paris, Institut d'études slaves, 1983). For a discussion of the word *budetlyanin*, see Ronald Vroon, *Velimir Xlebnikov's Shorter Poems: A Key to the Coinages* (Ann Arbor, University of Michigan, 1983), p. 101.

27 For details of the various Futurist groupings and alliances, see Markov, *Russian Futurism*.

28 See the article by Nils Åke Nilsson, 'Futurism, Primitivism and the Russian Avant-Garde', *Russian Literature*, 8–5 (1980), pp. 469–81.

29 Nikolay Khardzhiev has discussed extensively the significant connections between the visual arts and literature in Russia during this period in his 'Poeziya i zhivopis′: (ranniy Mayakovsky)', in *K istorii russkogo avangarda* (*The Russian Avant-Garde*) (Stockholm, Almqvist & Wiksell International, 1976), pp. 7–84. For other versions of this, see *Mayakovsky: materialy i issledovaniya*, ed. V. O. Pertsov and M. Serebryansky (Moscow, 1940), pp. 337–400; and N. Khardzhiev and V. Trenin, *Poeticheskaya kul′tura Mayakovskogo* (Moscow, 1970), pp. 9–49.

30 Markov (ed.), *Manifesty i programmy*, p. 57.

31 See, for example, Markov, *Russian Futurism*, pp. 147–63; Vahan Barooshian, *Russian Cubo-Futurism 1910–1930: A Study in Avant-Gardism* (The Hague–Paris, Mouton, 1974), pp. 145–52; E. J. Brown, *Mayakovsky: A Poet in the Revolution* (Princeton, New Jersey, Princeton University Press, 1973), pp. 49–51; Victor Erlich, 'The Place of Russian Futurism', pp. 4–10; Nikolay Khardzhiev, 'Vesyolyy god Mayakovskogo', in *Vladimir Majakovskij: Memoirs and Essays*, ed. Bengt Jangfeldt and Nils Åke Nilsson (Stockholm, Almqvist & Wiksell International, 1975), pp. 119–41. See also Anna Lawton's book, *Vadim Shershenevich: From Futurism to Imaginism* (Ann Arbor, Ardis, 1981).

32 See, for example, Khardzhiev, 'Vesyolyy god', pp. 120–1; Erlich, 'The Place of Russian Futurism', p. 4.

33 Markov, *Russian Futurism*, p. 382; see also Brown, *Mayakovsky*, p. 50; Erlich, 'The Place of Russian Futurism', pp. 5–9.

34 See Brown, *Mayakovsky*, p. 50; Erlich, 'The Place of Russian Futurism', p. 9.

35 Erlich points convincingly to some of the shared attitudes of the Italian and Russian Futurists ('The Place of Russian Futurism', pp. 9–10).

36 For discussion of the Symbolist influence on Khlebnikov, see Willem Weststeijn, *Velimir Chlebnikov and the Development of Poetical Language in Russian Symbolism and Futurism* (Amsterdam, Rodopi, 1983); and Lanne, *Velimir Khlebnikov*.
37 See Erlich, 'The Place of Russian Futurism', p. 10.
38 Markov (ed.), *Manifesty i programmy*, p. 56. See also Khlebnikov's use of the term 'poisoned arrow' in SP v 66.
39 It is a card-game, among other things, which is depicted in the joint Khlebnikov–Kruchonykh poem *Game in Hell* (SP II 119–35). The poem is discussed in Markov's *The Longer Poems*, pp. 83–6.
40 See Weststeijn, *Velimir Chlebnikov*, p. 7.
41 Yury Tynyanov, 'O Khlebnikove', SP I 26.
42 Four items in issues of the newspaper *Slavyanin* have now been identified as being written by Khlebnikov. They are: 'On Expanding the Frontiers of Russian Literature' ('O rasshirenii predelov russkoy slovesnosti'), 21 March 1913; 'Tempered Heart' ('Zakalyonnoye serdtse'), 24 March 1913; 'Who are the Ugro-Russians?' ('Kto takiye ugrorossy?'), 28 March 1913; 'Western Friend' ('Zapadnyy drug'), 7 July 1913. 'On Expanding . . .' was reproduced in NP 341–2. 'Tempered Heart' has been reproduced in Aleksandr Parnis, 'Neizvestnyy rasskaz V. Khlebnikova', *Russian Literature Triquarterly*, 13 (1975), pp. 468–75 and in Aleksandr Parnis, 'Yuzhnoslavyanskaya tema Velimira Khlebnikova: novyye materialy k tvorcheskoy biografii poeta', in *Zarubezhnyye slavyane i russkaya kul'tura*, ed. M. P. Alekseyev (Leningrad, 1978), pp. 223–51.
43 V. Blyumenfel'd, 'Poeticheskoye naslediye V. Khlebnikova', *Zhizn' iskusstva*, 49 (1928), p. 4.
44 Postcards which Khlebnikov sent to Kruchonykh from Astrakhan' in August 1913 (SP v 299–300) are crammed full with neologisms associated with theatrical terminology. Khlebnikov is to a large extent engaged here in creating Slavonic alternatives for foreign words (for example, *shutynya* to replace *komediya*; *deyuga* or *deyesa* to replace *drama*). Some of the words which he suggests in the postcards were used by him in his prologue for Kruchonykh's opera (SP v 256–7). For details of the production and performances of this Futurist theatre, see Livshits, *Polutoraglazyy strelets*, pp. 183–91; and Mikhail Matyushin 'Russkiye kubo-futuristy (vospominaniya M. V. Matyushina)' in *The Russian Avant-Garde*, pp. 129–58.
45 Nikolay Khardzhiev, 'Novoye o Velimire Khlebnikove', *Russian Literature*, 9 (1975), p. 14 (henceforth Khardzhiev, 'Novoye', *Russian Literature*).
46 For details of the public debates and lectures, see *Polutoraglazyy strelets*, pp. 176–83; and Markov, *Russian Futurism*, pp. 132–9. Khardzhiev (NP 467) says Khlebnikov gave only one public reading in 1913 on 11 November at the Polytechnical Museum in Moscow. Livshits (*Polutoraglazyy strelets*, p. 179) and Markov (*Russian Futur-*

ism, p. 132) indicate that Khlebnikov did, however, appear on stage to take the credits while others read his works or talked of him.

47 See NP 466–7; and Livshits, *Polutoraglazyy strelets*, p. 181.

48 Brown, *Mayakovsky*, p. 61. See also Susan Compton, *The World Backwards: Russian Futurist Books 1912–1916* (London, British Museum Publications, 1978), p. 25; and Markov, *Russian Futurism*, pp. 150–1.

49 Nadezhda Mandelstam, *Hope Abandoned*, trans. Max Hayward (Penguin, 1976), p. 109.

50 Vera Khlebnikova, 'Vospominaniye', p. 58.

51 The incident is described by Livshits, *Polutoraglazyy strelets*, pp. 214–16; by Markov, *Russian Futurism*, pp. 150–1; and by Khardzhiev, 'Vesyolyy god', p. 131, where it is said that Khlebnikov even challenged Kulbin to a duel. Khardzhiev also says that Aleksandr Blok was among those present for the Marinetti lecture.

52 The letter exists in manuscript in a rough copy only. It is not known whether a fair copy version was sent. In NP the letter is given as addressed to Nikolay Burliuk. Khardzhiev changed the addressee of the letter to Marinetti without comment in his 'Vesyolyy god' (p. 131). He confirmed that the letter was indeed addressed to Marinetti when I spoke to him in November 1984.

53 Burliuk's dating of the work in *Tvoreniya* is inaccurate. As Vladimir Markov has written (*Russian Futurism*, p. 194): 'The dates on the cover are ... a part of Burliuk's effort to prove that Russian Futurism antedated its Italian counterpart. Actually, many works in the book are definitely of much later origin.'

54 Stepanov notes that the letter was not published at the time (SP v 354). Markov says it was 'never mailed' (*Russian Futurism*, p. 195). However, David Burliuk does seem to have known of Khlebnikov's discontent. According to Burliuk, on seeing the various collections, Khlebnikov had upbraided him, exclaiming: 'you have ruined me, I never wanted to show anyone my experiments' (IS 475).

55 See Markov, *Russian Futurism*, p. 297.

56 The term 'laws of time' occurs frequently throughout Khlebnikov's work, (for example, SP II 10, SS III 437). For the reference to the founding of the 'state of time', see *yed. khr.* 121, *list* 1. See also SP v 153).

57 For the establishment of the society of the '317', see *yed. khr.* 121, *list* 1. See also Petrovsky, *Snake Train*, pp. 278–80; and Markov, *Russian Futurism*, p. 303. References to the 'chairmen' can be found in SP III 18, SP I 196, SP v 265, and elsewhere. Markov (*Russian Futurism*, p. 303) has described Khlebnikov's notions of world government as a 'Platonic society consisting of the best men living on this earth'.

58 See the brief memoir by Władysław Ziemacki, *yed. khr.* 167, *list* 1.

59 See V. Ya. Anfimov (a psychiatrist who examined Khlebnikov), 'K voprosu o psikhopatologii tvorchestva: V. Khlebnikov v 1919 godu', in

Trudy 3-ey Krasnodarskoy klinicheskoy gorodskoy bol'nitsy, 1 (1935), p. 68.

60 For some details of this, see Petrovsky, *Snake Train*, pp. 307–8. See also SP I 13 and IS 52, where reference is made to another fruitless attempt to 'domesticate' Khlebnikov – also recounted in Sergey Spassky, 'Khlebnikov', *Literaturnyy sovremennik*, 12 (1935), pp. 190–204.

61 See Aleksandr Parnis, 'V. Khlebnikov – sotrudnik *Krasnogo voina*', *Literaturnoye obozreniye*, 2 (1980), pp. 105–12.

62 See V. Katanyan, *Mayakovsky: literaturnaya khronika* (Moscow, 1961), p. 118.

63 See Petrovsky, *Snake Train*, p. 309. Grigory Gel'fandbeyn says he was taken for a spy and arrested by the Whites, see his 'Novyy lad miru', in 'Vechnozelyonyye list'ya: nevydumannyye rasskazy', *Raduga* (Kiev), 1 (1965), p. 118.

64 The psychiatrist Anfimov gave an account of his examinations of Khlebnikov in his article 'K voprosu psikhopatologii tvorchestva'. He found that Khlebnikov diverged from the 'norm', but rather than society needing protection from him, Anfimov recommended a 'special approach to him on the part of the collective in order to obtain from him the maximum benefit' (pp. 70–1). Khlebnikov briefly recounts his Khar'kov experiences in a letter to Osip Brik (NP 384).

65 For details of the Khar'kov performance see A. Mariengof, *Roman bez vran'ya* (Leningrad, 1928), pp. 81–4; and Gordon Mcvay, *Esenin: A Life* (Ann Arbor, Ardis, 1976), pp. 136–7.

66 *Proletkul't*, the Proletarian Cultural and Educational Organization, was set up in 1917 with the aim of fostering a proletarian art. ROSTA, the Russian Telegraph Agency, was the central information organization of the new Soviet state. It was created in 1918 and was particularly involved in agitation and propaganda work, producing wall-newspapers, window-posters, etc.

67 For a memoir of Khlebnikov's 'Persian period', see A. Kosterin, ' "Russkiye dervishi" ', *Moskva*, 9 (1966), pp. 216–21.

68 Khlebnikov's short sojourn in Pyatigorsk is described by D. Kozlov in 'Novoye o Velemire Khlebnikove', *Krasnaya nov'*, 8 (1927), pp. 177–88.

69 Mayakovsky, PSS 12, p. 28.

70 References by Khlebnikov to his works being 'stolen' can be found in *yed. khr.* 125, *list* 50; *yed. khr.* 96, *list* 2. See also Khlebnikov's 'Question into Space' ('Vopros v prostranstvo') about the whereabouts of missing works (SS III 523; and in manuscript form – *yed. khr.* 67, *list* 24 *ob.*); and his accusations against 'publishers' (SP V 274). These issues were taken up after Khlebnikov's death by Pyotr Miturich; see his open letter to Mayakovsky in Khlebnikov's *Vsem. Nochnoy bal* (Moscow, 1927), pp. 17–19. This publication also contains an article by Al'vek airing similar themes, entitled 'Nakhlebniki Khlebnikova' (pp. 6–16). I have

found no evidence to suggest that Mayakovsky (or anyone else) intentionally withheld or plagiarized Khlebnikov's works.

71 Khlebnikov's choice of title for this work was almost certainly influenced by his acquaintance with Buddhist scriptures which had been enclosed in wooden boards with silk wrappings. See, for example, SP v 24, where he talks of 'the books of the Mongols in their silken boards'. The word *doska* (board) can also refer to an icon. Only three sections or extracts (*otryvki*) of Khlebnikov's 'Boards of Fate' have been published (SS III 467–521). They came out in 1922–3, only the first appearing before Khlebnikov's death. One has since been republished in a revised form as V. Khlebnikov, 'Slovo o chisle i naoborot', in Ye. Arenzon, 'K ponimaniyu Khlebnikova: nauka i poeziya', *Voprosy literatury*, 10 (1985), pp. 163–90. There remain several other short articles in manuscript, in varying stages of preparation, which seem to have been intended as further extracts. Khlebnikov's archive in TsGALI lists up to seven extracts in all.

72 Two years later, in 1924, Miturich was to remarry: his second wife was Khlebnikov's sister Vera.

73 Vroon, *Velimir Xlebnikov's Shorter Poems*, p. 4.

74 Weststeijn, *Velimir Chlebnikov*, p. 37; Weststeijn also points out (ibid.) that it is the '*creation* of new meanings which makes Khlebnikov's poetical work so difficult to understand, but at the same time so semantically rich and suggestive'.

75 Vroon, *Velimir Xlebnikov's Shorter Poems*, p. 121.

76 The text of this much-quoted neologistic short poem, as given by Stepanov, is almost certainly distorted. The fault is not particularly Stepanov's, since he was doing no more than basing his text on the first published version of the poem in the 1913 *Prayerbook of the Three* (*Trebnik troikh*). The manuscript of the poem in an early exercise book (*yed. khr.* 60, *list* 102), however, shows that the published version is little more than a brief, imaginative extrapolation based upon a fairly rough text. The text of another Khlebnikov poem in *Prayerbook* has also been shown to have been treated in the same way (compare NP 106 with SP II 275). The extent of the distortion in *Prayerbook* and elsewhere was pointed out by the editors of the NP (p. 14). This, of course, raises questions about the advisability of textual analysis of some Khlebnikov poems.

77 See, for example, Baran's analysis of 'Bekh' and 'O, chervi zemlyanyye': 'Chlebnikov's Poem "Bech" ', *Russian Literature*, 6 (1974), pp. 5–19; 'On Xlebnikov's Love Lyrics: 1. Analysis of "O, červi zemljanye" ', in *Russian Poetics*, UCLA Slavic Studies, vol. 4, ed. Thomas Eekman, Dean S. Worth (University of California, Los Angeles, Slavica, 1983), pp. 29–44.

78 See Baran's 'Xlebnikov and the Mythology of the Oroches', in *Slavic Poetics: Essays in Honour of Kiril Taranovsky*, ed. R. Jakobson, C. H. Van Schooneveld and Dean S. Worth (The Hague–Paris, Mouton, 1973), pp. 33–9.

79 Baran, 'On Xlebnikov's Love Lyrics', pp. 30–1.
80 See Mojmir Grygar, 'Kubizm i poeziya russkogo i cheshkogo avangarda', in *Structure of Texts and Semiotics of Culture*, ed. Jan van der Eng and Mojmir Grygar (The Hague–Paris, Mouton, 1973), pp. 79, 90–3.
81 Baran, 'Chlebnikov's Poem "Bech" ', p. 16; Baran, 'Chlebnikov's "Vesennego Korana": An Analysis', *Russian Literature*, 9 (1981), p. 18 (there is also reference here, p. 12, to 'ciphered layers of meaning in the text'). In his 'O nekotorykh podkhodakh k interpretatsii tekstov Velimira Khlebnikova', in *American Contributions to the Eighth International Congress of Slavists*, vol. 1, *Linguistics and Poetics*, ed. H. Birnbaum (Columbus, Ohio, 1978), p. 111, Baran again talks of Khlebnikov's 'poetic riddles'.
82 Barbara Lönnqvist, *Xlebnikov and Carnival: An Analysis of the Poem 'Poėt'* (Stockholm, Almqvist & Wiksell International, 1979), pp. 55, 108. Lönnqvist also notes the importance of the riddle form for Khlebnikov (p. 55).
83 *Yed. khr.* 72, *list* 1; also cited by Lönnqvist, *Xlebnikov and Carnival*, p. 56, and Grigor'yev, *Grammatika*, p. 104.
84 Lönnqvist, *Xlebnikov and Carnival*, p. 12.
85 Ibid.
86 See Yury Lotman, 'O dvukh modelyakh kommunikatsii v sisteme kul'tury', *Trudy po znakovym sistemam* VI, in *Uchonyye zapiski Tartuskogo gosudarstvennogo universiteta, vypusk* 308 (Tartu, 1973), pp. 227–43 (which Lönnqvist cites).
87 Lönnqvist, *Xlebnikov and Carnival*, p. 12.
88 Ibid., pp. 12–13.
89 Markov (ed.), *Manifesty i programmy*, p. 53.
90 Ibid., p. 68.
91 For an examination of the coding in this poem, see Aleksandr Parnis, 'V. Khlebnikov v revolyutsionnom Gilyane (novyye materialy)', *Narody azii i afriki*, 5 (1967), pp. 162–3.
92 *Yed. khr.* 73, *list* 8.
93 See Roman Jakobson, 'On a Generation that Squandered its Poets', trans. Edward J. Brown, in Brown (ed.), *Major Soviet Writers*, p. 8. See also Nikolay Stepanov's comments in his introduction to Khlebnikov's *Stikhotvoreniya i poemy* (Leningrad, 1960), p. 61, where he says that 'the epos occupies the main place in Khlebnikov's work'.
94 Vladimir Markov's estimate is given in *The Longer Poems*, p. 30. Rudol'f Duganov estimates that there are about 50, but he considers fewer than half of these as being 'epic'. See his 'Problema epicheskogo v estetike i poetike Khlebnikova', *Izvestiya Akademii nauk SSSR, Seriya literatury i yazyka*, vol. 35, 5 (1976), p. 426.
95 Duganov, ibid.
96 Ibid. In spite of the amorphous generic nature of Khlebnikov's work, Duganov maintains that the Khlebnikovian 'word' is 'primordially epic' (p. 439).

97 For these comments of Duganov see ibid. pp. 427–8.
98 Duganov, ibid., p. 429, also comments on 'Ya i Rossiya' in this context.
99 For a discussion of this in Mayakovsky, see Lawrence Leo Stahlberger, *The Symbolic System of Majakovskij* (The Hague–Paris, Mouton, 1964).
100 See, in particular, Ronald Vroon's 'Velimir Khlebnikov's "Razin: Two Trinities": A Reconstruction', *Slavic Review*, vol. 39, 1 (1980), pp. 70–84.
101 Markov, *The Longer Poems*, p. 160.
102 Weststeijn, *Velimir Chlebnikov*, p. 18 (my emphases).

2. THE TOWER OF THE CROWDS

1 Nikolay Nekrasov, *Polnoye sobraniye sochineniy v 15-i tomakh* (Leningrad, 1981–), vol. 2, p. 10. It is generally thought that Nekrasov based these lines on the remark by the Decembrist poet Ryleyev: 'I am not a poet, but a citizen.'
2 Ibid., vol. 3, p. 151.
3 See Nikolay Khardzhiev, 'Mayakovsky i Khlebnikov', in Khardzhiev and Trenin, *Poeticheskaya kul'tura*, p. 98. Ronald Vroon too sees Khlebnikov as discovering a model 'in the linguistic activity of that amorphous entity known as "the people" '. He has, however, some well-argued reservations about the emphasis to be placed on the 'folk impulses' behind Khlebnikov's coinages. Vroon maintains that it is the *principle* of word creation in popular speech which was important for Khlebnikov rather than the imitation of folk poetry. See his *Velimir Xlebnikov's Shorter Poems*, pp. 11–13.
4 Markov, *The Longer Poems*, pp. 174–5.
5 The pamphlet *Teacher and Pupil* was first published in Kherson in 1912. A second version, slightly abridged by Khlebnikov himself, was printed in the third issue of *Union of Youth* in 1913 (SP v 348). The SP text (which I cite in this work) is taken from the second (1913) version.
6 As Markov has pointed out, however, Khlebnikov's 'fierce nationalism and anti-westernism' would have been approved by some of the Symbolists (*Russian Futurism*, p. 13).
7 Khlebnikov outlines this aesthetic programme in his brief article 'On Expanding the Frontiers of Russian Literature' (NP 341–2).
8 For details of and the text of Khlebnikov's Montenegrin tale 'Tempered Heart', see Parnis, 'Neizvestnyy rasskaz' or 'Yuzhnoslavyanskaya tema'.
9 Parnis, 'Yuzhnoslavyanskaya tema', p. 229. It was *Slavyanin* which first carried Khlebnikov's Montenegrin tale 'Tempered Heart' and the article 'On Expanding the Frontiers of Russian Literature'.
10 Quoted in Khardzhiev, *Den' poezii*, p. 204.
11 Barooshian, *Russian Cubo-Futurism*, p. 16; see also the remarks of

Camilla Gray, *The Russian Experiment in Art: 1863–1922* (London, Thames and Hudson, 1971), pp. 115–16; and Krystyna Pomorska, *Russian Formalist Theory and its Poetic Ambience* (The Hague–Paris, Mouton, 1968), pp. 88–90.

12 For comments on Mayakovsky as a 'street poet' whose poems are 'appeals to a crowd', see Korney Chukovsky, 'Akhmatova and Mayakovsky', trans. John Pearson, in Brown (ed.), *Major Soviet Writers*, pp. 49–50. See also Barooshian on Burliuk and Kamensky, *Russian Cubo-Futurism*, pp. 78, 105–7.

13 Mayakovsky laments the plight of the 'voiceless street' in his poem 'A Cloud in Trousers' ('Oblako v shtanakh') (PSS I, p. 181). Vroon, *Velimir Xlebnikov's Shorter Poems*, p. 15, makes the point that, although for Mayakovsky it was the streets which were 'tongue-tied and turn to the poet for aid. For Khlebnikov it is the language itself which needs a voice, and word creation provides the necessary medium.'

14 Aleksandr Parnis gives details of Khlebnikov's work for ROSTA (Russian Telegraph Agency) in Baku in 1920–1, where Khlebnikov was engaged in writing poster captions, in his 'V. Khlebnikov v Bakrosta', *Literaturnyy Azerbaydzhan* (Baku), 7 (1976), pp. 117–19. Khlebnikov's Volga famine verse was written while he was a night watchman for ROSTA in Pyatigorsk in the autumn of 1921. For details see Parnis (ibid.); Kozlov, 'Novoye o Velemire Khlebnikove'; and Stepanov, *Velimir Khlebnikov: zhizn' i tvorchestvo*, pp. 211–12. For examples of Khlebnikov's verse appeals, see SP III 194, 200–1.

15 Khlebnikov had long before the revolution shown some interest in 'humanity' in general. See his 1904 reference to the 'good of the human race' (NP 318); see also the poem 'Crane' ('Zhuravl'') (SP I 76–82), where the monster bird seems to be pitted against the whole of humankind. Other notions which Khlebnikov was developing before the revolution include: the people of the east, in opposition to the people of the west (see, for example, 'Western Friend'); and youth, as opposed to elders (SP III 151–4).

16 Bengt Jangfeldt, 'Russian Futurism 1917–1919', in *Art, Society, Revolution: Russia 1917–1921*, ed. Nils Åke Nilsson (Stockholm, Almqvist & Wiksell International, 1979), p. 115.

17 See, for example, Stepanov's introduction to the 1960 edition of Khlebnikov's verse *Stikhotvoreniya i poemy*, p. 63.

18 Aleksandr Parnis tracked down the original version of this poem (first printed in the newspaper *Krasnyy voin* in 1918) and reproduced it in the journal *Prostor* (Alma Ata), 7 (1966), p. 91. Another version can be found in SP III 150.

19 *Yed. khr.* 112, *list* 1 *ob*. This declaration was dictated by Khlebnikov to the poet Ryurik Ivnyov during a two-day (12–13 September 1918) boat trip on the Volga delta (see Parnis, 'V. Khlebnikov – sotrudnik *Krasnogo voina*', pp. 106–7). The manuscript in TsGALI is in Ivnyov's hand. It is one of two pan-Asian declarations which Khlebnikov

dictated to Ivnyov on that trip. The manuscript of the other ('Azosoyuz') can also be found in TsGALI (*yed. khr.* 112, *listy* 6–9). Both declarations were written in the first person plural.

20 *Yed. khr.* 112, *list* 2.

21 *Zashchityaz'* is a neologism combining a stem meaning 'protect' (*zashchitit'/zashchita*) and what Ronald Vroon has called a 'pseudo-suffix' (-yaz'), meaning 'the spirit or incarnation of that which is designated by the stem' (*Velimir Xlebnikov's Shorter Poems*, pp. 147–8). Khlebnikov may have seen an analogy for this coinage in *vityaz'*, meaning 'champion' or 'hero'.

22 *Yed. khr.* 112, *list* 6. See note 19 above. The name 'Azosoyuz' may also relate to the Russian word *az*, which formed part of the title of another work by Khlebnikov (SP V 24). *Az* is the Church Slavonic for the first person singular pronoun and also designates the first letter in the Cyrillic alphabet; it also stood for Khlebnikov as a symbol of the liberated individual 'I' – see Ronald Vroon's 'Velimir Khlebnikov's "I esli v 'Khar'kovskie ptitsy' . . .": Manuscript Sources and Subtexts', *Russian Review*, 42 (1983), pp. 265–6. The 'Azosoyuz' manifesto describes the aim of the union as the 'rapprochement of the peoples of Asia'. It continues: 'in the majestic sketch of Asia we see the place of Europe as a satellite revolving around the luminary – Asia'. And it puts forward the principle of 'political rayism (*politicheskiy luchizm*) as a basis for the world outlook of the people of Asia'.

23 *Yed. khr.* 112, *list* 6. The youthful Khlebnikov once proposed the 'ideal' of the worker bee, seeing the establishment of such an apian system in human life as being for 'the good of the human race' (NP 318).

24 *Yed. khr.* 89, *list* 3 *ob.* I have increased Khlebnikov's sparse punctuation to facilitate reading, and I have standardized capitalization at the beginning of lines. The poem has also been reproduced by Henryk Baran in his 'Temporal Myths in Xlebnikov: From "Deti vydry" to "Zangezi" ', in *Myth in Literature*, New York University Slavic Papers V, ed. A. Kodjak et al. (Slavica, Columbus, Ohio, 1983), p. 82. Some of the lines were reproduced by Lönnqvist in *Xlebnikov and Carnival*, p. 34.

25 Khlebnikov's 'Proclamation of the Chairmen of the Terrestrial Globe' was written in April 1917 and first published soon afterwards in the second issue of *Chronicle* (*Vremennik*). Stepanov gives two versions in the SP: a rough draft (SP V 162–4); and a fair copy (SP III 17–23), which, Stepanov claims, had been reworked into verse. Khardzhiev is probably right, however, when he says ('Novoye', *Russian Literature*, p. 19) that it is in fact a prose work. (I cite it as such here.)

26 SP III 17–18. The reference here to standing on the 'block' of themselves and their names amid the 'sea' of malicious eyes is clearly an echo of the 'Slap' manifesto, one of whose points was 'to stand on the block of the word "we" amid the sea of whistling and indignation'; see Markov (ed.), *Manifesty i programmy* p. 51.

27 For this definition of *bozhestvar'*, see Vroon, *Velimir Xlebnikov's Shorter Poems*, p. 42.

28 For a poetic exposition of this 'law of the seesaw', see SP II 94. This 'law' is discussed by Lönnqvist in *Xlebnikov and Carnival*, pp. 29–32.

29 The sea is an ubiquitous image in Khlebnikov with diverse metaphoric implications. For a reference to 'people-sea' (*narod-more*), see NP 322.

30 The transformation from 'king' to 'rabbit' is also a linguistic transformation. The relevant lines read:

> Nyne v plenu ya u startsev zlobnykh,
> Khotya ya lish' krolik puglivyy i dikiy,
> A ne korol' gosudarstva vremyon,
> Kak zovut menya lyudi:
> Shag nebol'shoy, tol'ko 'ik',
> I upavsheye O, kol'tso zolotoye,
> Chto katitsya po polu. (SP II 246)

(Now I am a captive of wicked elders, although I am only a wild and frightened rabbit (*krolik*), and not a king (*korol'*) of the state of times, as people call me: a small step, only an 'ik', and a fallen O, a gold ring that rolls along the floor.)

The alternation of poetic hero as 'beggar' and 'tsar' is followed by another juxtaposition:

> Ya zhizn' p'yu iz kubka Motsarta . . .
> Sotnya Sal'yeri
> I ya odin s dushoyu Motsarta. (SP V 116)

(I drink life from the cup of Mozart . . . A hundred Salieris and only I have the soul of Mozart.)

It is an assertion by Khlebnikov of his own poetic genius and an intimation that he saw around him an envious crowd of lesser mortals.

31 The lines are set out here as given by Stepanov in SP. Ronald Vroon informs me, however, that the manuscript reveals they are two distinct pieces. They have been presented as such in Velimir Khlebnikov, *The King of Time: Poems, Fictions, Visions of the Future*, trans. Paul Schmidt, ed. Charlotte Douglas (Cambridge, Massachusetts and London, England, Harvard University Press, 1985), pp. 52–4. Nevertheless, one of the most recent Soviet editions of Khlebnikov, *Stikhotvoreniya, poemy, dramy, proza* (Moscow, 1986), compiled and annotated by R. V. Duganov, gives the lines as a single work, but with a stanza break between lines five and six (p. 127).

32 Duganov, in Khlebnikov's *Stikhotvoreniya, poemy, dramy, proza* (p. 127) dates the poem 1921. It is precisely during this period that we have biographical evidence indicating that Khlebnikov had become lice-infested. *Russian Literature Triquarterly*, 13 (1975) contains the memoir 'Khlebnikov's Bath' by the artist Yuliya Arapova (pp. 465–7), in which, recalling the winter of 1920–1, she describes Khlebnikov as being infested with 'fat, plump lice'. Tired of cleaning up after his visits, but not wanting to deprive the 'homeless, alone and abandoned' Khlebnikov of hospitality, she relates how she and another woman 'deposited Velimir in the state of Adam' into a tub and scrubbed him clean. 'A completely different man emerged,' she writes.

33 According to Stepanov (SP III 373), Petnikov contributed to the final draft. Khardzhiev maintains, however, that, although it bore the signatures of Petnikov and Kamensky (only the names of Petnikov and Khlebnikov appear on the draft in SP V 164), it was Khlebnikov who was the author of the 'proclamation' ('Novoye', *Russian Literature*, pp. 18–19). Khlebnikov was not averse to adopting a 'collective' voice in his declarations even where he was the sole author. Khardzhiev also (p. 18) points, for example, to the *Trumpet of the Martians* manifesto (SP V 151), where we have, among others, the signature of the poet Bozhidar (Bogdan Gordeyev), who had died some two years before the manifesto was published.

34 Khlebnikov signed another edict, published in the first issue of his *Herald of Velimir Khlebnikov* (*Vestnik Velimira Khlebnikova*) in Moscow 1922, as 'Velimir I' (SP V 167). The second *Vestnik* includes the poem 'Rejection' ('Otkaz'), which is also followed by the signature 'Velimir I'.

35 Khlebnikov first mentions his future name Velimir in a letter home (SP V 289) at the end of December 1909. (He also says in this letter that he is being called Lyubek and, moreover, declares himself to be Richard the Lion Heart.) For information on his many pseudonyms and on the etymology of Velimir, see Parnis, 'Yuzhnoslavyanskaya tema', p. 228.

36 See also note 46 to Chapter 1, p. 193.

37 I. Berezark, 'Vstrechi s V. Khlebnikovym', *Zvezda* 12 (1965), p. 175.

38 Tat'yana Vechorka, 'Vospominaniya o Khlebnikove', in *Zapisnaya knizhka Velimira Khlebnikova*, ed. Aleksey Kruchonykh (Moscow, 1925), p. 27.

39 Sergey Spassky, 'Khlebnikov', p. 194.

40 I. I. Abroskina, 'Literaturnyye kafe 20-kh godov: (iz vospominaniy I. V. Gruzinova "Mayakovsky i literaturnaya Moskva")', in *Vstrechi s proshlym, Sbornik materialov Tsentral'nogo gosudarstvennogo arkhiva literatury i iskusstva SSSR, vypusk* 3 (Moscow, 1978), pp. 185–6.

41 Vasily Kamensky, *Zhizn' s Mayakovskim* (Moscow, 1940), p. 60.

42 Ibid., pp. 60–1. Aleksandr Leytes is one of several who also notes Khlebnikov's habit of breaking off a reading with the words 'and so on'; see his 'Vstrechi s Khlebnikovym', *Literaturnaya gazeta*, 4 December 1965.

43 See, for example, Stepanov's introduction to the 1960 edition of Khlebnikov's work, *Stikhotvoreniya i poemy*, p. 6: also Kosterin, ' "Russkiye dervishi" ', p. 221; and Arapova, 'Khlebnikov's Bath', p. 466.

44 Nadezhda Mandelstam, *Hope Abandoned*, p. 110.

45 Ibid., p. 112.

46 Sergey Spassky, *Mayakovsky i ego sputniki* (Leningrad, 1940), p. 76.

47 Aleksandr Leytes, 'Vstrechi'.

48 This poem was first published in Khlebnikov's *Stikhi* in 1923 (p. 43), with two sets of elipses marking indistinct places in the manuscript. In

the SP version Stepanov reproduces the elipses but gives no explanation in the notes as to why they are there. The poetic hero in this poem is associated with a 'star' as well as with the 'Bell of Liberty', hence the transferred epithet 'distant and pale'. One line of the poem makes the association explicit – 'Za to chto napomnil pro zvyozdy' ('Because I reminded you of the stars').

49 Khlebnikov's 'To All' contains distinct echoes of Pushkin's drama 'Boris Godunov', which also dwells in part on the death of the Tsarevich Dmitry and uses the same words as Khlebnikov to describe the murdered boy ('Glyazhu: lezhit zarezannyy tsarevich'). This was a period of Russia's history which held a particular fascination for Khlebnikov. See also his long poem 'Marina Mniszek', published by Aleksandr Parnis in 'Velimir Khlebnikov', *Zvezda*, 11 (1975), pp. 199–205. Khlebnikov's reference in the poem to the Tatar leader Kuchum falling from the lances of the sixteenth-century conqueror of Siberia Yermak appears inaccurate. In fact Kuchum escaped Yermak's lances and returned to ambush him. Yermak drowned while escaping to his boat in the River Irtysh.

50 This poem is a rough version which has, moreover, been reworked, and the manuscript is difficult to read. Stepanov's rendition of the text in the SP leaves much to be desired. Lines have been missed out and some of the readings seem unreliable. I have quoted only those parts of the published text which seem to me to be faithful to the original.

51 Khlebnikov encoded names elsewhere in his work. See, for example, his comments on the code to the hidden name of a friend, Abikh, in 'Isfahan Camel' (SP III 379), commented on by Parnis in 'V. Khlebnikov v revolyutsionnom Gilyane', pp. 162–3. Mayakovsky was, apparently, known by some of his fellow Futurists as 'mayak'. See Kamensky's letter to David Burliuk in *Color and Rhyme* 48 (1961–2).

52 Grigor′yev, *Grammatika*, p. 176.

53 For further evidence of Khlebnikov's preoccupation with the myth of Theseus and the Minotaur, see his 'autobiographical tale' 'Ka^2', where he writes how, in the 'last days of his youth', he was 'vainly seeking Ariadne and Minos, intending to play out in the twentieth century a story of the Greeks' (SP V 128). See also the poster advertising the lecture 'Iron Wings' which Khlebnikov helped to write and which was read by Petrovsky and Tatlin in Tsaritsyn in May 1916. The programme of the lecture included as its final point: 'the future of Futurism as the myth of Theseus and the Minotaur'. For details of the lecture, see Petrovsky, *Snake Train*, pp. 287–9; and for a reproduction of the poster see plate 89 in Larisza Zsadova [Larisa Zhadova] (ed.), *Vlagyimir Jevgrafovics Tatlin* ([Budapest], Corvina Kiado, [1985]).

54 A manuscript of the poem in the ledger known as the *Grossbuch* shows that Khlebnikov regarded his Minotaur in terms of a personification of war. In this version *krovavo* ('bloodily') is an insertion, taking the place of *voynoyu* ('like war') which has been crossed out (*yed. khr.* 64, *list* 57).

55 Earth also features prominently in the Khlebnikovian portrayal of rebirth. In 'Before the War' ('Pered voynoy'), for example, with the committal of the body to the ground at death, man is transformed into all that grows or feeds upon the earth and attains a 'second soul' (SP IV 140–1).

56 This recalls the regeneration of Khlebnikov after the bath by Arapova ('a completely different man emerged' – see note 32 to this chapter). This poem and the 'lice' poem are placed on the same page by Stepanov (SP V 72), indicating also a proximity in date. The importance of water imagery in Khlebnikov was noted by Kruchonykh, who wrote: 'to trace his attitude towards water – this means to research the history of his creative work'. See *Neizdannyy Khlebnikov*, 19 (1930), p. 15.

57 This poem makes use of another major Khlebnikovian image, that of 'hair'. See, for example, SP V 25 and IS 239–40, where hair is associated not with fire, but with the flow of rivers. Curiously, with regard to the image of a blazing Khlebnikov, at the end of 1921, during a journey on a hospital train, Khlebnikov seems to have been set upon by some epileptics, who doused his beard with kerosene and tried to set him alight. It seems, however, likely that this incident occurred after the poem was written. For a reference to the incident, see Kruchonykh's 'Iz zhizni Velimira Khlebnikova' in Khlebnikov's *Zverinets* (Moscow, 1930), p. 17.

58 *Yed. khr.* 75, *list* 4 *ob*.

59 On an autobiographical level, the poem probably reflects Khlebnikov's experiences in Iran. See, for example, the letter to his sister Vera dated 14 April 1921, which tells how upon arrival in Enzeli he went swimming until the chatter of his teeth reminded him that 'it was time to get dressed and to put on the human casing – that dungeon which shuts man away from the sun and the wind and the sea' (SP V 320). For a discussion of metaphor in this poem, see Weststeijn, *Velimir Chlebnikov*, pp. 186–94.

3. THE TOWER OF THE WORD

1 Weststeijn, *Velimir Chlebnikov*, p. 18.

2 See also Grigor′yev's comments in *Grammatika*, p. 75.

3 Markov (ed.), *Manifesty i programmy*, p. 65.

4 This is a point also made by Ronald Vroon in his *Velimir Xlebnikov's Shorter Poems*, p. 7. In writing this chapter I am happy to acknowledge a great debt to Vroon's excellent study of Khlebnikov's coinages, and particularly to his fine exposition of Khlebnikov's 'verbal universe' (pp. 3–24).

5 Grigor′yev also views Khlebnikov's 'self-sufficient' word as a word which is not so much divorced from everyday life as supplementary to it ('svyazannoye s "bytom" otnosheniyem dopolnitel′nosti'), see his *Grammatika*, p. 64.

6 *Yed. khr.* 73, *list* 8; also quoted in Grigor'yev, *Grammatika*, p. 73.
7 Markov, *Russian Futurism*, p. 7.
8 Vladimir Markov's translation is in *Russian Futurism*, pp. 7–8. Other translators of the poem include: Gary Kern in Khlebnikov's *Snake Train*, p. 63; Alexander Kaun in *Soviet Poets and Poetry* (Berkeley and Los Angeles, University of California Press, 1943), p. 24; and Paul Schmidt in Velimir Khlebnikov, *The King of Time*, p. 20. For comments on translating this poem and examples of translations into various languages, see Nils Åke Nilsson, 'How to Translate Avant-garde Poetry. Some Attempts with Xlebnikov's "Incantation by Laughter"', in *Velimir Chlebnikov: A Stockholm Symposium*, ed. Nils Åke Nilsson (Stockholm, Almqvist and Wiksell International, 1985), pp. 133–50.
9 These are all listed in Vroon's *Velimir Xlebnikov's Shorter Poems*.
10 Ibid., pp. 29, 101.
11 Ibid., pp. 30, 148–9.
12 Benedikt Livshits and David Burliuk gathered together some of the critical responses to the Russian Futurists and republished them in *First Journal of the Russian Futurists* (*Pervyy zhurnal russkikh futuristov*) (Moscow, 1914); see Markov, *Russian Futurism*, p. 177.
13 Livshits, *Polutoraglazyy strelets*, pp. 46–7.
14 See Parnis, 'Yuzhnoslavyanskaya tema', pp. 232–51. As Parnis points out (p. 232) the 'Montenegrin language' as such does not exist. The people speak a dialect of Serbo-Croat, which does, however, have distinctive 'Montenegrin words'.
15 Grigor'yev discusses this and other borrowings from Slavonic languages in *Grammatika*, pp. 67–8.
16 This is also discussed by Vroon, *Velimir Xlebnikov's Shorter Poems*, pp. 18–19.
17 Ibid., p. 10.
18 For a discussion of the relationship between sound and meaning in Khlebnikov, see Weststeijn, *Velimir Chlebnikov*, pp. 1–37.
19 And a brief reference to another notion which preoccupied Khlebnikov around this time – that 'the simplest words in our language were preserved in prepositions' (SP v 172). This was discussed in more detail elsewhere by Khlebnikov (SP v 255); see also Vroon, *Velimir Xlebnikov's Shorter Poems*, p. 18.
20 Grigor'yev (*Grammatika*, p. 113) sees traces of Khlebnikov's consonantal theories as early as 1908.
21 It is important to note that Khlebnikov was by no means unique in attributing semantic qualities to individual letters or sounds. Contemporaries such as Bal'mont, in his *Poeziya kak volshebstvo* (Moscow, 1915), and Andrey Bely, in his *Glossolaliya: poema o zvuke* (Berlin, 1922), developed similar notions extensively, and, moreover, applied them poetically. For some interesting remarks on their respective ideas, see the chapter 'Zvuk i smysl' in Yefim Etkind's

Materiya stikha (Paris, Institut d'études slaves, 1978). Notably, some years earlier, outside Russia, the French poet (and teacher of English) Mallarmé was engaged in assigning semantic qualities to the initial letters of words. Mallarmé's ideas and their relevance to Khlebnikov's notions are discussed in Lanne, *Velimir Khlebnikov*, pp. 61–6.

22 *Yed. khr.* 88, *list* 5.

23 For these terms, see SP v 203, 207, 217.

24 Vroon, *Velimir Xlebnikov's Shorter Poems*, p. 169.

25 Discussing the Old Russian consonantal system, W. K. Matthews describes *f* as a 'foreign phoneme, figuring in loan-words mainly from Byzantine Greek'. See his *Russian Historical Grammar* (University of London, The Athlone Press, 1967), p. 97.

26 Take, for example, the recent study published in the USSR by A. P. Zhuravlyov, *Zvuk i smysl* (Moscow, 1981). Ronald Vroon (*Velimir Xlebnikov's Shorter Poems*, p. 195) points to the conclusion of another Soviet researcher in this field, M. V. Panov: 'The sounds of language are associatively bound to concepts having nothing to do with sound. These associations are more or less identical for the majority of speakers of a given language . . .'

27 A further 'triumvirate' can be seen in another division by Khlebnikov of the word into the following categories: 'the word is tambour; the word is flax; the word is fabric' ('slovo-pyal'tsy; slovo-lyon; slovo-tkan'') (SS III 383). Ronald Vroon (whose translation I use) suggests the following interpretation in his *Velimir Xlebnikov's Shorter Poems* (p. 15): 'the word is a construct whose components include: 1) meaning (the ready cloth or fabric), 2) sound (the material from which the fabric is woven), and 3) the rules governing the combination of threads of sound into fabrics of meaning (the tambour or frame)'. Grigor'yev arrives at a similar interpretation in his *Grammatika* (p. 16): 'the word is not only a ready product of historical development or something produced by someone and intended for use ("fabric"), not only the material for poetic and other transformations ("flax"), but also the instrument for these transformations ("tambour")'. One has little difficulty matching up this threesome with the other threesome of the word 'for the ear, for the intellect and a pathway for fate'. This is particularly so if we note that in the same article Khlebnikov contends that 'besides the language of words there is the mute language of concepts from units of the intellect (*a fabric of concepts ruling the former*)' (SP v 188) (my emphasis). The 'word-fabric' is associated, therefore, with meaning, with concepts and the intellect; the 'word-flax' is associated with the 'language of words', with sound and the 'ear' (*slukh*); and the 'word-tambour' with the guiding framework for sound and meaning, with a deeper level of meaning which bears within it the natural wisdom of language and provides a 'pathway for fate'.

28 Both represented considerable shifts in geometrical and mathematical perception. Euclid features in the 'birthright' poem cited earlier. The

figure of Lobachevsky acquires the trappings almost of an alter ego in Khlebnikov's poetic world. The 'revolution' which Lobachevsky caused with his non-Euclidian geometry is perceived by Khlebnikov in similar terms to the social and political revolution of 1917. The scientific 'rebel' Lobachevsky even becomes associated in Khlebnikov's mind with the warrior rebel Razin. As with Razin, biographical factors also play a part. In the first half of the nineteenth century Lobachevsky was for almost 20 years rector of Kazan′ University where Khlebnikov himself studied mathematics. One of Khlebnikov's most notable references to Lobachevsky occurs in *Goodworld* (SP I 184) where Russia's revolutionary cities are adorned with 'Lobachevsky's curves'.

29 Note, for example, SP V 198, where the 'teacher' explains his definition of the initial consonant *l* by sketching pictures of the objects in question. Khlebnikov's formulas also strongly reflect the concept of motion, of points moving through space. A. G. Kostetsky, who compiled a brief glossary of Khlebnikov's 'alphabet of the intellect', concluded that Khlebnikov's definitions covered three main semantic areas: space, motion and mathematical concepts; see his 'Lingvisticheskaya teoriya V. Khlebnikova', in *Strukturnaya i matematicheskaya lingvistika*, 3 (1975), pp. 34–9.

30 Vroon, *Velimir Xlebnikov's Shorter Poems*, p. 19, uses this term.

31 'Artists of the World' was supposed to have been published in the collection *Internatsional iskusstva* in 1919, but the collection never appeared. The typescript of the article remains extant. It was finally first published in 1928; see SP V 352, and Vroon, *Velimir Xlebnikov's Shorter Poems*, p. 195.

32 Vroon, ibid., reproduces them.

33 This is not strictly true, though Japan adopted Chinese characters for its written language early in the Christian era and apparently used classical written Chinese for several centuries as its formal written language.

34 See V. P. Grigor′yev (*Grammatika*, p. 89), who cites Khlebnikov's archive (*yed. khr.* 14, *list* 5). Grigor′yev sees Khlebnikov's 'algebraical language' as an 'absolute synonym' of the 'language of the stars' (p. 112). In *Zangezi* Khlebnikov refers to an 'algebra of words' (SP III 332). One reference by Khlebnikov seems to equate the symbols of algebra with Arabic characters. He writes (*yed. khr.* 73, *list* 5): 'like the writing of Islam, it is not for nothing that the laws of time remind us of an algebra text book'. Khlebnikov is probably referring here to the Koran.

35 Markov (*Russian Futurism*, p. 303) suggests that this passage is from Caesar's *De bello Gallico*. It cannot be Caesar, however, since the event described is the defeat of the Huns by Flavius Aetius in the fifth century.

36 See Grigor′yev, *Grammatika*, pp. 79–80; and see also his 'Iz istorii interlingvistiki: Leti sozvezd′ye chelovech′ye (V. Khlebnikov – interlingvist)', in *Uchonyye zapiski Tartuskogo universiteta, vypusk* 613

(1982), pp. 153–66. Grigor′yev also comments on Khlebnikov's attitude towards Esperanto, which Khlebnikov said he found 'very well-structured, light and beautiful, but poor in sounds and not varied', and with an 'excess of homonyms and a poverty of synonyms' (*Grammatika*, p. 80).

37 See Kruchonykh's 'Novyye puti slova', in Markov (ed.), *Manifesty i programmy*, p. 66.

38 Markov, *Russian Futurism*, p. 44. 'Dyr bul shchyl' was first published in Kruchonykh's collection *Pomada* in early 1913. The poem was subsequently republished in other collections.

39 See the plate of the page containing the poem (when reproduced in *Te li le*) in Compton's *Russian Futurist Books* (illustration 13).

40 Markov (ed.), *Manifesty i programmy*, pp. 61–2, 66.

41 Markov (*Russian Futurism*, p. 347) writes that 'for Kruchonykh . . . the emotional essence of *zaum′* was obviously in the centre'. This is evident from Kruchonykh's 1913 and 1921 declarations which say: 'Thought and speech cannot catch up with the emotional experience of someone inspired; therefore, the artist is free to express himself not only in a common language (concepts), but also in a private one (a creator is individual), as well as in a language that does not have a definite meaning (is not frozen), that is *transrational*. A common language is binding; a free one allows more complete expression.' (I quote this from Markov's *Russian Futurism*, p. 345.) Kruchonykh's notion of *zaum′* was not static and developed as a very broad concept to include 'the invented names of characters', 'interjections', 'nicknames', etc. (Markov, ibid., pp. 345–6). Other notable exponents and developers of 'transrational' poetry were Igor′ Terent′yev and, in particular, Il′ya Zdanevich. For more information on these writers, see Markov's *Russian Futurism*, and Gerald Janecek, *The Look of Russian Literature: Avant-Garde Visual Experiments, 1900–1930* (Princeton, New Jersey, Princeton University Press, 1984).

42 Commentators rightly point to a distinction between Khlebnikov's views on 'transrational language' (orientated strongly towards meaning) and Kruchonykh's (free from definite meaning); see, for example, Vroon, *Velimir Xlebnikov's Shorter Poems*, p. 6; Pomorska, *Russian Formalist Theory*, pp. 94–5, 108. Kruchonykh did not, however, by any means have a total disregard for meaning or content in the development of his 'transrational language'. Indeed, it was one of his contentions that a 'new verbal form creates a new content'; see Markov (ed.), *Manifesty i programmy*, p. 64. Khlebnikov's view of the cognitive function of language is matched by Kruchonykh's idea that the artist would pass 'through the word to direct understanding' ('cherez slovo k neposredstvennomu postizheniyu'); see ibid., p. 66. This is close to Khlebnikov's contention of 'transrational' words being able to penetrate directly to the feelings (SP v 225). For Kruchonykh, the word was not so much without sense, as 'broader than sense' (ibid.).

43 My emphasis. 'Correspondences' were, of course, a key element of Symbolist theory and the word forms the title of a celebrated poem by Baudelaire. Rimbaud's renowned poem 'Voyelles', equating vowels and colours, was well known to the Hylaean Futurists. Indeed, it is cited in Nikolay Burliuk's theoretical article 'Poeticheskiye nachala'; see Markov (ed.), *Manifesty i programmy*, p. 79. Synaesthetic ideas were also taken up and developed by the Russian Symbolists, in particular Bal'mont and Bely. Commenting on 'Bobeobi', Krystyna Pomorska rightly notes that the picture Khlebnikov paints here in sound is not so much a Symbolist as a Cubist canvas (see her *Russian Formalist Theory*, pp. 98–9). See also Vroon, *Velimir Xlebnikov's Shorter Poems*, pp. 181–3.

44 See Vroon, *Velimir Xlebnikov's Shorter Poems*, pp. 181–2. Vroon points out that *ch*, which does not figure in Khlebnikov's glossary, seems to signify here a silvery colour, *puch' i chapi* referring to the 'silver black sheen of the rook's wings'.

45 Khlebnikov possibly had in mind here Kruchonykh's vowel poem, contained in his 1913 'Declaration of the Word as Such' ('Deklaratsiya slova kak takovogo'), reproduced in Markov (ed.), *Manifesty i programmy*, pp. 63–4. Commenting on this declaration, Khlebnikov told Kruchonykh that his vowel combinations had 'a certain meaning and content' and could 'become the basis for a universal (vselenskiy) language' (NP 367).

46 *Au* is, according to the dictionary of Dal', a folk term for the month of June. For an analysis of this poem in terms of its 'chromataic and spatial configurations', see Vroon, *Velimir Xlebnikov's Shorter Poems*, pp. 185–6.

47 See Vroon, *Velimir Xlebnikov's Shorter Poems*, pp. 20–1, 186–7.

48 Khlebnikov made the jotting: 'the gods in *zaum'*'. See Grigor'yev, *Grammatika*, p. 87.

49 Ronald Vroon, 'Four Analogues to Xlebnikov's "Language of the Gods"', in *The Structure of the Literary Process: Essays in Memory of Felix Vodička*, ed. M. Cervenka, P. Steiner and R. Vroon (Amsterdam, John Benjamins, 1982), p. 581.

50 Vroon, *Velimir Xlebnikov's Shorter Poems*, p. 188.

51 See Grigor'yev, *Grammatika*, p. 63.

52 For reference to Jakobson introducing Khlebnikov to Sakharov's book, see Khardzhiev, 'Novoye', *Russian Literature*, p. 16. At about the same time that he pointed Khlebnikov towards the Sakharov book, Jakobson was himself preoccupied with 'transrational language' and poetic experiments. An example of Jakobson's 'transrational' verse, under the pseudonym R. Alyagrov, was published by Kruchonykh in his *Zaumnaya gniga* (Moscow, 1915). See Markov, *Russian Futurism*, p. 334; and Janecek, *The Look of Russian Literature*, pp. 180–2.

53 For magical language as an analogue for Khlebnikov's 'language of the gods', see Vroon's 'Four Analogues', p. 590. It is to this type of

'transrational language' that Vroon assigns the words of the dying Amenhotep in 'Ka' ('manch! manch!'); *Velimir Xlebnikov's Shorter Poems*, p. 188.

54 See, for example, Bal'mont's *Poeziya kak volshebstvo*; Bely's 'Magiya slov', in his *Simvolizm* (Moscow, 1910), pp. 429–48; and Blok's 'Poeziya zagovorov i zaklinaniy', *Sobraniye sochineniy*, vol. 5, pp. 36–65.

55 See Markov, *Russian Futurism*, p. 13.

56 In April 1913 Khlebnikov inscribed a copy of *Trap for Judges* II to Gorodetsky, noting that he had carried Gorodetsky's *Yar'* close to his breast 'for a whole summer'. See SP I 46; and Khardzhiev, 'Novoye', *Russian Literature*, pp. 19–20.

57 David Burliuk, for example, called Khlebnikov a 'silent magician and sorcerer' in his 'Ot laboratorii k ulitse: (evolyutsiya futurizma)', *Tvorchestvo* (Vladivostock), 2 (1920), p. 24. More recently George Ivask has described him as 'a magician in the mysterious realm of verbal revelations, a prehistorical wizard inspired by amazing intuition'; see his 'Russian Modernist Poets and the Mystic Sectarians', in *Russian Modernism: Culture and the Avant-Garde 1900–1930*, ed. George Gibian and H. W. Tjalsma (Ithaca and London, Cornell University Press, 1976), p. 101.

58 See V. Shklovsky, 'Predposylki futurizma', *Golos zhizni*, 18 (1915), pp. 6–9; see also his 'O poezii i zaumnom yazyke', *Sborniki po teorii poeticheskogo yazyka* I (Petrograd, 1916), pp. 1–15.

59 Markov (ed.), *Manifesty i programmy*, p. 67.

60 Ibid.

61 Ibid.; see also p. 62.

62 Vroon, *Velimir Xlebnikov's Shorter Poems*, p. 189.

63 Vroon, 'Four Analogues', p. 587.

64 Izanagi is one of a pair of Japanese deities, male and female, the other being Izanami. Khlebnikov seems to have muddled up their sexes. *Monogatori* (*monogatari*) means 'tales' in Japanese (as in *Genji monogatari – Tales of Genji*, or *Ise monogatari – Tales of Ise*). Khlebnikov viewed *monogatori* in terms of a Japanese 'tale of chivalry' (*rytsarskiy roman*); see Kruchonykh (ed.), *Zapisnaya knizhka*, p. 13. Shang Ti (Lord on High) is an early, at one point the highest, Chinese deity, one of the prime dispensers of change and fate, inaccessible to persons of lower rank. Like T'ien (heaven), this god could be worshipped only by the emperor as man's representative on earth. Indra, in Hindu belief, is the foremost god of the Vedic pantheon, the god of war and rain. According to the translator of *Goodworld*, Gale Weber, Maa-Emae (Maan-Emo) is the earth mother in Finnish mythology; see *Russian Literature Triquarterly*, 12 (1975), p. 160. Stepanov, however, (IS 490) sees it as a Polynesian deity. Gale Weber sees (*Russian Literature Triquarterly*. p. 160) Tsintekuatl' as Cinteotl, the Toltec Indian maize god, though with the ending *-kuatl* (probably related to *-coatl* – 'snake'

in the names of Aztec mythology) Khlebnikov may well have had in mind another god such as Quetzalcoatl (Feathered Snake) or Cihuacoatl (Snake Woman). Either way Khlebnikov was certainly interested in the language of the Aztecs. Ziemacki's memoir (*yed. khr.* 167, *list* 1 *ob.*) quotes Khlebnikov as saying that he saw an 'affinity between the Russian and Aztec languages, for example, the morpheme (*chastitsa*) – *tel'* as in the Russian words, *sozdatel'* (creator) and *vayatel'* (sculptor) corresponds to the Aztec *-tl'*, for example, Jenochti*tl*an, nahua*tl*, peyo*tl*'. According to Khlebnikov's note in the *Zapisnaya knizhka* (p. 13), Unkulunkulu is an African equivalent of the Slav god Perun, a god of thunder.

65 Markov, *The Longer Poems*, p. 149; see also Khardzhiev and Trenin, *Poeticheskaya kul'tura*, pp. 292–3.

66 Khlebnikov is thought to have had the Belgian painter Felicien Rops in mind with the word *roops'*; see Kern (ed.) *Snake Train*, p. 249. Khlebnikov's poem is distinctly reminiscent of Baudelaire's 'Les Phares', which also uses the names of artists and their work as 'correspondences' in the evocation of a poetic landscape.

67 The translation is in Kern (ed.) *Snake Train*, p. 67. The references to this poem and magic can be found in Duganov, 'Kratkoye "iskusstvo poezii" Khlebnikova', *Izvestiya Akademii nauk SSSR, Seriya literatury i yazyka*, vol. 33, 5 (1974) pp. 418, 422. Duganov sees (p. 419) a model for the neologism *dostoyevskiymo* in the word *pis'mo* (letter/writing); see also Vroon, *Velimir Xlebnikov's Shorter Poems*, p. 124.

68 In translating *mene* as 'for me' I follow Grigor'yev's suggestion (*Grammatika*, pp. 96–7) that it is the dative case of the first person singular pronoun *ya*. The word *mana* can be found in the dictionary of Dal' as a noun formed from the verb *manit'* (to attract, entice).

69 *Nizar'* is, of course, the palindrome of Razin. See Vroon, *Velimir Xlebnikov's Shorter Poems*, p. 42. See also the definitions given in Dal' for *niz*, which can relate specifically to the lower reaches of a river.

70 Mayakovsky was somewhat off target when he wrote of some of Khlebnikov's palindromic verse that it was 'just deliberate trickery'. Though Mayakovsky immediately contradicts himself when he writes that 'trickery was of little interest to Khlebnikov'. See his PSS, 12, p. 25. Notably, the potential of the palindrome was remarked upon by Kruchonykh in his 'Novyye puti slova', when he wrote that the Hylaean poets had noted that it was possible to read the word backwards which gave it 'a deeper sense'; see Markov (ed.), *Manifesty i programmy*, p. 71.

71 For illuminating comments on these and other details about the poem, see Vroon, *Velimir Xlebnikov's Shorter Poems*, pp. 178–9. For further comments on anagrams in Khlebnikov's work, see Lönnqvist, *Xlebnikov and Carnival.*

72 This reference to the 'truths' contained in his 'language of the stars'

recalls the image of the poetic hero as a 'warrior of the truth' in 'Lone Performer'.

73 For a further analysis of this poem, see Vroon, *Velimir Xlebnikov's Shorter Poems*, pp. 169–71; a different version of this combination of the languages is used by Khlebnikov in *Zangezi* (SP III 330–2).

74 See Vroon, *Velimir Xlebnikov's Shorter Poems*, p. 175.

75 For a discussion of such 'transrational' compounds, see Grigor'yev, *Grammatika*, p. 82; and Vroon, *Velimir Xlebnikov's Shorter Poems*, pp. 175–6. Khlebnikov brings *Ve* and *El'* together in a poem in SP III 139. He uses the phrase *viel' kryla*. Vroon sees the meaning of this as the 'wing's spiral movement downward (*v* = rotation, *l* = descent)'. This interpretation is backed up by Kruchonykh's 'Materials for a Glossary of Neologisms (Coinages) of V. Khlebnikov' (TsGALI, *fond* 1334, *opis'* 1, *yed. khr.* 979) where he defines *viel'* in terms of 'to twist' (*vit'sya*), 'spindle' (*vereteno*), and even a 'spiral' (*spiral'*) (*list* 8). This glossary was probably being compiled in 1922, and at one point Khlebnikov himself contributes to it.

76 For references to Khlebnikov's 'duel of words' and Grigor'yev's comments, see *Grammatika*, p. 87.

77 Initial mutation in Khlebnikov's work is discussed in Vroon, *Velimir Xlebnikov's Shorter Poems*, pp. 165–8.

78 Ibid., p. 176.

79 Vroon comments on the meanings of *k* in ibid., pp. 168–9.

80 See Grigor'yev, 'Iz istorii interlingvistiki', pp. 158–9.

81 For a diagrammatic geometrical analysis of this passage, see Vroon, *Velimir Xlebnikov's Shorter Poems*, pp. 171–4.

82 See Grigor'yev, *Grammatika*, pp. 93–4.

83 See ibid.

84 See, for example, the passage quoted above at the end of section *III*, Chapter One. A similar word/number combination can be seen in Khlebnikov's interpretation of the saying 'tri da tri budet dyrka' (where *tri* is the imperative from the verb meaning 'to rub') in terms of *tri* as the number three; see Grigor'yev, *Grammatika*, p. 125.

85 Jakobson's letter is quoted in Khardzhiev, 'Poeziya i zhivopis'', pp. 56–7.

86 Khardzhiev says (ibid., p. 57) that Kruchonykh's poem was written in 1915 but has not been preserved.

87 See, for example, the poem 'Numbers' ('Chisla') in SP II 98. See also his 'Beast + Number' ('Zver' + chislo') in Parnis, 'Velimir Khlebnikov', *Zvezda*, p. 199. One number which figures prominently in Khlebnikov's work, but which is not specifically related to the calculations on the 'laws of time' is $\sqrt{-1}$. For a discussion of this mathematical expression and other elements of Khlebnikov's fascination with the number, see Grigor'yev, *Grammatika*, pp. 119–30; see also Lönnqvist, *Xlebnikov and Carnival*.

88 Khlebnikov seems to have had a particular interest in Scriabin, an

interest which was apparently reciprocated. See Grigor'yev, *Grammatika*, pp. 131–42.

89 *Yed. khr.* 86, *list* 46 *ob*.

90 *Yed. khr.* 75, *list* 2.

91 *Yed. khr.* 118, *list* 1.

92 *Yed. khr.* 74, *list* 24. When Khlebnikov referred to his 'tower of the multitudes' (SP IV 82), it is possible that he had in mind not only his 'tower of the crowds' but also another 'multitude', the sets of numbers which he builds up in towers to make mathematical expressions. See also SP IV 300–2.

4. FROM WARRIOR TO PROPHET

1 Grigor'yev also rightly links these early and late writings in his *Grammatika*, p. 92.

2 *Yed. khr.* 73, *list* 5.

3 Osip Mandelstam, *Sobraniye sochineniy*, vol. 2, p. 390. Mandelstam goes on to say (ibid.) that Khlebnikov's poetry was 'idiotic in the genuine, inoffensive, Greek meaning of the word'. The *Lay of Igor's Campaign* is considered to be one of the greatest early Russian works of literature. It is believed to date from the twelfth century.

4 See NP 342. Przhevalsky was a famous nineteenth-century explorer and traveller. The era of the battle of Kulikovo was, of course, not entirely unknown to Russian literature at this time. Blok's cycle of poems, for example, entitled 'Na pole Kulikovom' was written in 1908.

5 I incorporate the correction given in NP 15–16.

6 For some interesting comments on the nature of Khlebnikov's nationalist and pan-Slav sympathies, see Ronald Vroon's 'Velimir Chlebnikov's "Chadži-Tarchan" and the Lomonosovian Tradition', *Russian Literature*, 9 (1981), pp. 107–31.

7 Khlebnikov denotes the German people by the coinage *nem'*; see Vroon, *Velimir Xlebnikov's Shorter Poems*, p. 71. *Nem'* is, of course, associated both with Germans (*nemtsy*) and with muteness (*nemoy*). With this Khlebnikov juxtaposes *slav'*, which he associates with the Slav nation, with glory (*slava*) and even with the word *slovo* (see Vroon, ibid., p. 72).

8 'Western Friend' (*Slavyanin*, 7 July 1913) also reveals the increasing 'Asiatic' proportions of Khlebnikov's anti-westernism and the broadening positions of his nationalism and pan-Slavism. Khlebnikov writes at one point that 'it is possible to answer the circle of European alliances with a circle of Asiatic alliances – the friendship of Moslems, the Chinese and the Russians . . .'.

9 Copies of two poems by this girl ('Militsa') are still extant in Khlebnikov's archive (*yed. khr.* 135). The strength of his desire to see her poems published can be judged from his letter to Matyushin (SP V 294–5).

10 See Parnis, 'Yuzhnoslavyanskaya tema', p. 223.
11 Khardzhiev, 'Novoye', *Russian Literature*, p. 12.
12 This manifesto, entitled '!budetlyanskiy' (the adjective from Khlebnikov's neologism for Futurist – *budetlyanin*), was, according to Stepanov (SP v 349), intended for the Futurist collection *Roaring Parnassus* (*Rykayushchiy Parnas*), but was not published in Khlebnikov's lifetime. Khlebnikov noted on the manuscript that he was writing it not on behalf of himself, 'but for Lunev, he is responsible for the unity of views expressed'; and he also wrote 'Lunev or [everyone] Kruchonykh' (SP v 349). Parnis, perhaps on this basis, sees Lunev as being a pseudonym which Khlebnikov used 'jointly with A. Kruchonykh' ('Yuzhnoslavyanskaya tema', p. 228). It was, however, a pseudonym which Khlebnikov also used for his 'We and Houses' ('My i doma') (SP IV 339). Khlebnikov also wrote on the manuscript of the '!budetlyanskiy' declaration that it was 'anonymously for the Futurist Concord' ('bez imeni v Poladu Budetlyanskuyu') (SP v 349); it seems, therefore, to have been written by Khlebnikov as a type of group declaration. In the notes to the SP (v 349) Stepanov suggests that Khlebnikov 'made a distinction between his "programmatic" articles and his own personal poetic principles'.
13 This statement occurs in the letter which was published as addressed to Nikolay Burliuk, but which was in fact addressed to Marinetti.
14 It is somewhat puzzling that Khlebnikov should place himself in Yaroslavl' region in mid-May 1905 when the battle of Tsushima occurred (14–15 May), since Khlebnikov seems at this time already to have embarked upon the extensive natural history field trip in the Urals with his brother Aleksandr. It is possible that Khlebnikov was visiting the Yaroslavl' region before arriving in the Urals, but one entry in the published account of the trip bearing the date 11 May would appear to rule this out ('Ornitologicheskiye nablyudeniya', p. 7). There is evidence that Khlebnikov visited Yaroslavl' region in early 1904 after his release from prison in Kazan' (IS 10–11), and this may account for the confusion. Khlebnikov again refers to being in Yaroslavl' region at the time of the battle of Tsushima in SP II 10.
15 Khlebnikov was interested in Japanese literature too. The aesthetic programme which he set out in a letter to Kruchonykh includes as one of its points 'Japanese versification' (SP v 298). There is little doubt that some of Khlebnikov's short verse owes a debt to Japanese literary forms (see, for example, SP II, 93–5, 97). See also Khlebnikov's reference to Japanese poems in a letter to his mother dating from 1917 (SP v 313), and the reference by one memoirist (in Khardzhiev, *Den' poezii*, p. 202) to the youthful Khlebnikov learning Japanese. Vroon, 'Four Analogues', pp. 588–9, sees Japanese as one of the analogues for Khlebnikov's 'language of the gods'. Khlebnikov's attitude to Japan is discussed in Salomon Mirsky's *Der Orient im Werk Velimir Chlebnikovs* (Munich, Verlag Otto Sagner, 1975), pp. 36–48.

16 'Smorodina' means currant (as in redcurrant or blackcurrant). It is possible that this is a reference to the brand name of a pre-revolutionary perfume.
17 See also Mirsky, *Der Orient*, p. 40.
18 Khlebnikov writes: 'That is why in the Iliad rivers leave their banks to give aid and interfere in the battle and proceed within the ranks of the enemy forces . . . Rivers are hostile to the people of the continent, and peninsulas to the people of the sea' (SS III 426).
19 The monument which gives the poem its title is the famous sculpture of Tsar Aleksandr III by Prince Trubetskoy. The poem relates in part how this monument leaves its pedestal and appears at the scene of the conflict.
20 Lönnqvist, *Xlebnikov and Carnival*, pp. 105–6.
21 Incorporating the insertion of *Khrista*, as suggested in NP 17.
22 See Baran, 'Chlebnikov's Poem "Bech" '.
23 I quote the poem from ibid., p. 7.
24 Ibid., p. 18.
25 Ibid.
26 Roman Jakobson dates it as early as before 1911; see his 'Iz melkikh veshchei Velimira Khlebnikova: Veter – penie', *Selected Writings* III, ed. Stephen Rudy (The Hague–Paris–New York, Mouton, 1981), p. 573. In Khlebnikov's *Stikhotvoreniya, poemy, dramy, proza*, published in 1986, it is dated tentatively 1912–13 (p. 58). The poem was first published in the collection *Four Birds* (*Chetyre ptitsy*). This collection includes a number of titles for the poems of Khlebnikov which were evidently invented by the editors of the volume: see SP II 318; and Markov, *Russian Futurism*, p. 297. The title 'The Pecheneg Cup' comes from a manuscript of the poem discovered by Aleksandr Parnis; see Stepanov, *Velimir Khlebnikov: zhizn' i tvorchestvo*, p. 65.
27 See the notes to the translation of the poem in Kern (ed.), *Snake Train*, p. 246, which suggest that the poem refers to the thirteenth-century battle at the Kalka River, when Russian forces were defeated by some of the troops of Genghis Khan. 'If one sees here a Tatar victory, then the howl of the bones sounds as a warning', the notes in *Snake Train* say. The Kalka battle certainly enjoys some prominence in Khlebnikov's work (SP II 245, III 78, SS III 419, NP 175). An account of the shaping of Svyatoslav's skull into a cup by the Pechenegs can be found in one of the early Russian chronicles. It is also referred to in the writings of Herodotus, with which Khlebnikov was acquainted; see, for example, Henryk Baran, 'Xlebnikov and the *History* of Herodotus', *Slavic and East European Journal*, vol. 22, 1 (1978), pp. 30–4.
28 Lönnqvist, *Xlebnikov and Carnival*, p. 36.
29 Mayakovsky, PSS I, p. 319. Mayakovsky's articles of this period make frequent reference to Khlebnikov's militancy, talking, for example, of his 'battle cries' (*boyevyye klichi*) (PSS I, p. 322). Many of Russia's writers responded patriotically to the outbreak of war. For a discussion

of some responses, see Orest Tsekhnovitser, *Literatura i mirovaya voyna 1914–1918* (Moscow, 1938).

30 I. Postupal'sky, 'V. Khlebnikov i futurizm', *Novyy mir*, 5 (1930), p. 192.

31 Stepanov, *Velimir Khlebnikov: zhizn' i tvorchestvo*, p. 161.

32 Many of the early battles between the Russians and the Germans in the First World War took place among the Masurian Lakes in East Prussia. It is possible that Khlebnikov had these battles in mind. The lake, however, is a key element in Khlebnikov's work, making frequent appearances, and the lack of specificity in this poem gives the battle a certain timeless quality. It may be of some note that Khlebnikov also referred to the battlefield of Kulikovo, where Russia fought the Tatars, as 'full of blue lakes' (SP III 77). The battlefield in the poem 'Funeral' is also referred to in terms of 'a hundred lakes' (SP II 229).

33 For the eagle owl as a bird of evil portent, see the dictionary of Dal', which cites the saying: 'pugach (filin) ne k dobru krichit (khokhochet)' – 'the eagle-owl is no harbinger of good'.

34 As in 'Death in a Lake', in 'Funeral' there seems to be a deliberate blurring of the time scales. Although 'pilots' (*lyotchiki*) are mentioned, the Russians are denoted by the old term *russy*. Moreover, as well as sharing with 'Death in a Lake' references to 'lakes', both poems also mention rivers. It is also worth pointing out that the title of the poem, 'Trizna', contains an anagram of the name Razin.

35 This recalls the lines of 'Children of the Otter': 'Do sey pory ne znayem, kto my:/Svyatoye ya, ruka il' veshch'?' (Up till now we do not know who we are: a sacred I, a hand or thing?) (SP II 164). 'Children of the Otter', however, like 'Things were too blue', still holds out the prospect of Russian vengeance: 'Boytesya russkikh presledovat',/My snova podymem nozhi' (Fear to pursue the Russians, we shall again take up our knives) (SP II 161).

36 The Monmouth and Otranto were British ships engaged in action against the Germans off the coast of Chile on 1 November 1914. The Monmouth was sunk with all hands.

37 Compare an earlier (pre-1914) portrayal by Khlebnikov of a 'world-youth', the 'Youth I-World' (SP IV 35), who refers to himself with pride as a 'cell of the hair or the mind of the great person who bears the name of Russia' (presaging the later man-state portrayals).

38 Khardzhiev dates the poem October–November 1915 in his *Den' poezii* publication (p. 209), where he publishes a different, longer version of the poem.

39 The wolf takes its place alongside the other monsters of war and fate in Khlebnikov's work. In the variant of the poem which Khardzhiev publishes in *Den' poezii*, the wolf is simply a 'beast' (*zver'*). The female reaper portrayed here is another Khlebnikovian personification of death.

40 The poem at one point refers to the rise and fall of stocks and shares

which the war was causing ('Padayut Bryanskiye, rastut u Mantashova'), with the implications that money was being made by the 'elders' out of the deaths of Russia's young men.

41 This poem, beginning 'Young men and women, remember' ('Devy i yunoshi, vspomnite'), was first published in *Peta* (Moscow, 1916). A version of the poem was also published in Khlebnikov's 1923 *Stikhi* (p. 41), where it is dated 1915.

42 Markov, *Russian Futurism*, p. 299.

43 The bowstring (*tetiva*) occurs elsewhere in Khlebnikov's work. It is possibly the 'bowstring of war' (as in SP IV 73) which Khlebnikov has in mind here.

44 See, for example, Tsekhnovitser, *Literatura i mirovaya voyna*, p. 300.

45 Markov, *Russian Futurism*, p. 298.

46 John Milner in his book *Vladimir Tatlin and the Russian Avant-Garde* (New Haven and London, Yale University Press, 1984), p. 124, refers to Kamensky hoping to exhibit a live mouse in a mousetrap at The Year 1915 exhibition, which opened in Moscow in April 1915.

47 The full title of this piece is 'Conversation. V. Khlebnikov Looking at the States. From the Book of Successes. Folio 1 of 317' ('Razgovor. Vzirayushchiy na gosudarstva V. Khlebnikov. Iz knigi udach. List 1-y iz 317'). It was published in 1917 in *Chronicle* 2. For another reference to the 'mousetrap' of war and fate, see SP IV 144–5.

48 As usual, Khlebnikov is consistent in this brief prose work in his use of the word *budetlyanin* for Futurist.

49 The changing of clothes is an image of regeneration on a par with those involving fire and water which Khlebnikov also used. Some archetypal images of regeneration are discussed with reference to Khlebnikov and others by A.M. Panchenko and I.P. Smirnov in 'Metaforicheskiye arkhetipy v russkoy srednevekovoy slovesnosti i v poezii nachala XX v.', in *Drevnerusskaya literatura i russkaya kul'tura XVIII–XX vv., Trudy otdela drevnerusskoy literatury, Institut russkoy literatury, Akademiya nauk SSSR* XXVI (Leningrad, 1971), pp. 33–49.

50 Henryk Baran, 'The Problem of Composition in Velimir Chlebnikov's Texts', *Russian Literature*, 9 (1981), p. 93. 'Wind – singing' ('Veter – peniye') is the main subject of analysis in Roman Jakobson's 'Iz melkikh veshchei'.

51 Khardzhiev, 'Novoye', *Russian Literature*, p. 19.

52 'October on the Neva' was published in SP IV 105–13, but for a more reliable text, see Parnis, 'V. Khlebnikov – sotrudnik *Krasnogo voina*', pp. 110–11. The reference in this text to plunging a sharpened stake into the single eye of the monster war and of hiding in the fleece of sheep is, of course, an echo of the confrontation with the Cyclops recounted in Homer's Odyssey.

53 Parnis, 'V. Khlebnikov – sotrudnik *Krasnogo voina*', p. 110.

54 See Petrovsky, *Snake Train*, pp. 300–4.

55 The poem calls on the 'serf of the rich' to 'grab the constellation of

Aquarius by the moustache' and to 'beat' the constellations of the Dogs (SP I 184).

56 Quoted from Parnis, *Prostor*, p. 91.

57 Parnis, 'V. Khlebnikov – sotrudnik *Krasnogo voina*', p. 106. Sentiments which were echoed by some of the propaganda workers in Iran, see Kosterin, ' "Russkiye dervishi" ', p. 218.

58 This was the 'anti-NEP' poem 'Stop Fooling' ('Ne shalit'') (SP III 301), which was published in *Izvestiya* in early March 1922, apparently with the assistance of Mayakovsky whose 'Prozasedavshiyesya' was published in the same issue. See Stepanov, *Velimir Khlebnikov: zhizn' i tvorchestvo*, p. 228.

59 Parnis, *Literaturnyy Azerbaydzhan*, p. 118.

60 See, for example, Kosterin, ' "Russkiye dervishi" '.

61 *Yed. khr.* 64, *list* 39. For more details about this poem, see Vroon, 'Velimir Khlebnikov's "I esli v 'Khar'kovskie ptitsy' . . ." '.

62 See Petrovsky, *Snake Train*, p. 309.

63 *Yed. khr.* 64, *list* 31 *ob.* The poem has been reworked by Khlebnikov and the manuscript contains insertions and deletions.

64 Ibid.

65 On the Chairman of the *Cheka*'s reluctance to play the role of executioner and the poem's relationship with Khlebnikov's 'Rejection', see Vroon, 'Velimir Khlebnikov's "I esli v 'Khar'kovskie ptitsy' . . ." ', pp. 263–4.

66 In 'Night Search' (SP I 252–73) Red sailors are locked in a burning flat behind an iron door with its 'grid' (SP I 325). The grid (*reshotka*) serves as an image for Khlebnikov's 'laws' of fate (see, for example, SS III 425). Other external forces are also at work in this poem: sentence is pronounced on the sailors by a God/Christ figure, and the whole of the poem is governed by a mathematical epigraph relating to Khlebnikov's 'laws'. For a discussion of the epigraph to the poem, see R. D. B. Thomson, 'Khlebnikov and 3^6+3^{6}'', in *Russian and Slavic Literature*, ed. R. Freeborn, R. R. Milner-Gulland and C. A. Ward (Slavica Publishers Inc., 1976), pp. 297–312. For another study of the poem, see also my 'Image and Symbol in Khlebnikov's "Night Search" ', *Russian Literature Triquarterly*, 12 (1975), pp. 279–94.

67 Kornely Zelinsky, 'Na velikom rubezhe', *Znamya*, 12 (1957), pp. 147–8.

68 I borrow Ronald Vroon's term; see his 'Velimir Khlebnikov's "Razin: Two Trinities" ', p. 84. See also elsewhere in this work for an informed discussion on the relevance of the Razin figure for Khlebnikov.

69 I again cite Vroon. See his ' "Sea Shore" ("Morskoi bereg") and the Razin Constellation', *Russian Literature Triquarterly*, 12 (1975), pp. 295–326.

70 Khlebnikov, *Stikhi*, p. 32.

71 For details of this and its relevance to Khlebnikov's own biography, see Vroon, 'Velimir Khlebnikov's "Razin: Two Trinities" '.

72 See Parnis, 'V. Khlebnikov v revolyutsionnom Gilyane', p. 163.
73 Stepanov, *Velimir Khlebnikov: zhizn' i tvorchestvo*, p. 165.
74 Khlebnikov, *Stikhi*, p. 32.
75 It also recalls the image of the number taking on the labours of the helmsman in 'Children of the Otter' (SP II 163). The passage in *Goodworld* which contains the hybrid Khlebnikov/Razin presentation is commented on by Mirsky in the section on Razin in his *Der Orient*, pp. 90–105. See also Lönnqvist, *Xlebnikov and Carnival*, pp. 39–41.
76 According to Ronald Vroon, Khlebnikov became enamoured of a young girl he was tutoring during his brief trip to Iran and came to regard her as his own 'Persian princess'. This inverted reflection of Razin's experience has, therefore, a basis in Khlebnikov's autobiography. See Vroon, 'Velimir Khlebnikov's "Razin: Two Trinities" ', pp. 77–84.
77 Khlebnikov discusses his 'mistake' in predicting First World War battles in his letter to Matyushin (NP 375–7).
78 *Yed. khr.* 72, *list* 2.
79 See *yed. khr.* 73, *list* 11; *yed. khr.* 77, *list* 15; SP III 354; SS III 476; see also Grigor'yev, *Grammatika*, p. 146.
80 Sergey Spassky, 'O Khlebnikove', *Literaturnyy Leningrad*, 14 November 1935.
81 Qurrat al-Ain was a Persian poetess, opponent of polygamy and follower of the Babi (later Bahai) movement, which was suppressed by the Persian shah Naser ad-Din. She was executed in 1852.
82 Markov, *Russian Futurism*, p. 301. V. Pertsov has remarked that the 'poet in Khlebnikov quarrelled with the scientist (uchonyy)'; see his *Poety i prozaiki velikikh let* (Moscow, 1969), p. 210. See also Lönnqvist's discussion of the 'conflict in Khlebnikov's own attitude toward writing poetry and making calculations for "Doski sud'by" ' (*Xlebnikov and Carnival*, p. 123).
83 Some of these 'oppositions' are discussed in Grigor'yev, *Grammatika*, pp. 142–54; and also in Lönnqvist, *Xlebnikov and Carnival.*
84 In *The Longer Poems* (pp. 25–6) Markov argued that the three aspects of Khlebnikov's creative personality (responsible for artistic work, experimental work and 'numerous pieces of a wayward character', including mathematical analyses) should be 'whenever possible, kept separate'. He does, however, note here that 'the boundaries separating these three aspects of Khlebnikov's intellectual activity are sometimes blurred'. Moreover, he talks elsewhere of 'the inextricable merger of his poetry with his projects and research' (*Russian Futurism*, p. 300).
85 The memoirist is N. Baryutin (otherwise known as Amfian Reshetov), who worked on the journal *Makovets* and was allowed by Khlebnikov at the beginning of 1922 to have a 'lucky dip' in his sack of manuscripts (NP 416). I quote here from his memoir on Khlebnikov in TsGALI, *fond* 2283, *opis'* 1, *yed. khr.* 6, *list* 13 *ob.*
86 On poetry and prophecy, see, for example, George Thomson's essay

Marxism and Poetry (London, Lawrence & Wishart, 1975) (first published 1945), where he points out (p. 28) that 'in primitive thought there is no clear line between prophecy and poetry'.

87 Tzvetan Todorov, 'Number, Letter, Word', in *The Poetics of Prose*, trans. Richard Howard (Oxford, Basil Blackwell, 1977), p. 203.

88 In the sixteenth century Isker was the chief town of Siberia. It was taken from the Tatar leader Kuchum by the 'conqueror of Siberia', Yermak.

89 This notion that the future was somehow enshrined in his poetic works is also evident in the late, incomplete poem 'What are you to do' ('Chto delat' vam') (SP V 111–18), which mentions the titles of various of his works and refers, for example, to 'instructions given in time'. Stepanov's reproduction of the work in the SP is not without its faults. Omissions include some passages which are harmless enough, but which might by the time of publication have been considered sensitive. For example, clearly alluding to the prophetic nature of his 'Madame Lenine' ('Gospozha Lenin'), published in 1913, Khlebnikov makes a reference to 'Lenin in women's clothing' (*yed. khr.* 98, *list* 36).

90 While Khlebnikov the decoder was deciphering the allusions of past tales, Khlebnikov the encoder was busy creating similar codes of his own. 'Allusions' (*namyoki*) is a term which Khlebnikov applied to his own work (SP II 11, V 195). His view of the folk tale as prophetic is almost certainly the key to the following lines in 'Iranian Song' ('Iranskaya pesnya'):

Veryu skazkam naperyod:
Prezhde skazki – stanut byl'yu . . . (SP III 130)

(I believe in folk tales in advance, folk tales in the past – in the future fact . . .)

91 Todorov, *Poetics of Prose*, p. 193.

92 This is discussed in Lönnqvist, *Xlebnikov and Carnival*, pp. 122–4.

93 'Liberty' here is the Russian word *volya*, which can also mean 'will'.

94 I quote from Grigor'yev, *Grammatika*, p. 129.

95 *Yed. khr.* 73, *list* 5.

96 *Yed. khr.* 72, *list* 3.

97 Aseyev, 'V. V. Khlebnikov', *Tvorchestvo* (Vladivostok), 2 (1920), p. 28; Markov, *Russian Futurism*, p. 302.

98 It is also a vision of unity between scientist and crowd, which echoes the unity of the poetic I and crowd in the man-state of 'I and Russia'.

99 *Yed. khr.* 75, *list* 2.

100 One should also note the image of the traveller or navigator.

101 In SP V 315 the date and origin of the letter are given incorrectly as Khar'kov, 2 January 1920. This was rightly corrected in SS III, p. x, to Baku, 2 January 1921. In fact the letter in manuscript *is* dated 2 January 1920 (see *yed. khr.* 141, *list* 8), but Khlebnikov has made the error common at the turn of a year of absentmindedly writing the old year's date.

102 *Yed. khr.* 73, *list* 5.

103 Note also the following passage from 'Scratch Across the Sky':

> Cherez 317 (π + e) volny tatar
> Bitva pri Kalke – gibel' Rossii.
> Deti tak yasno, tak prosto!
> Zachem-zhe vam glupyy uchebnik?
> Skoreye uchites' igrat' na ladakh
> Voyny bez dikogo vizga smerti –
> My zvukolyudi! (SP III 78)

(In 317 (π + e) the waves of the Tatars, the battle at Kalka – the ruin of Russia. Children, it is so clear, so simple! What need have you then of the stupid textbook? Better to learn how to play on the frets of war without the wild wail of death – we are soundpeople!)

104 *Yed. khr.* 72, *list* 11.

5. THE SINGLE BOOK

1 See Tsezar' Vol'pe, 'Stikhotvoreniya Velimira Khlebnikova', a review of Khlebnikov's *Stikhotvoreniya* (Leningrad, 1940), in *Literaturnoye obozreniye*, 17 (1940), p. 35.

2 Mayakovsky, PSS 12, p. 23.

3 V. Trenin and N. Khardzhiev, 'Retushirovannyy Khlebnikov', *Literaturnyy kritik*, 6 (1933), p. 146.

4 Livshits, *Polutoraglazyy strelets*, p. 45.

5 For the manuscript of this letter see the David Burliuk archive at the Gorky Institute of World Literature (*Institut mirovoy literatury imeni Gor'kogo*), abbreviated to IMLI, *fond* 92, *opis'* 1, *yed. khr.* 25, *list* 2-*list* 2 *ob*. This quote is from *list* 2. Extracts from the letter were published in NP 12, 14. Zheverzheyev is described by Markov (*Russian Futurism*, p. 56) as a 'wealthy patron of the arts'. Burliuk's letter is dated 4 April 1913.

6 Mayakovsky, PSS 12, p. 27.

7 Aseyev, 'V. V. Khlebnikov', p. 29.

8 David and Mariya Burliuk, 'Kanva znakomstva s Khlebnikovym: (1909–1918)', *Color and Rhyme*, 55 (1964–5), p. 36.

9 Burliuk, IMLI, *fond* 92, *opis'* 1, *yed. khr.* 25, *list* 2-*list* 2 *ob*.

10 Kruchonykh (ed.), *Zapisnaya knizhka*, p. 11.

11 Barooshian, *Russian Cubo-Futurism*, p. 36; though Barooshian's suggestion that Khlebnikov also allied himself with the Futurists 'for financial reasons' (ibid.) is highly dubious.

12 Kruchonykh's memoirs (TsGALI, *fond* 1334, *opis'* 1, *yed. khr.* 36, *list* 80) relate how Khlebnikov:

> ... was desperate to get to the capital to publish his works, mainly his calculations on future wars.
>
> In 1921, already in Moscow, he told me about his discoveries, confiding in me: —The English would pay dearly to stop these calculations from being published!
>
> I laughed and assured Khlebnikov that the English would not give a farthing,

despite the fact that the 'boards of fate' threatened them with ruin, unsuccessful wars, the loss of their fleet etc.

Khlebnikov was offended, but still, evidently convinced, he gave me his calculations for publication.

Kruchonykh did not publish the numerological work with which Khlebnikov entrusted him. It was the artist Pyotr Miturich who finally helped Khlebnikov to publish his calculations on time.

13 Parnis, '"Konetsarstvo, ved' ottuda ya . . ."', p. 136.
14 Anfimov, 'K voprosu o psikhopatologii tvorchestva', p. 68.
15 Ibid.
16 For more details of this 'declaration', see Petrovsky, *Snake Train*, p. 308; see also Sergey Spassky, 'Khlebnikov', pp. 196–7.
17 See Petrovsky, *Snake Train*, p. 308.
18 See, for example, Stepanov's comments in SP III 371, and IS 477; Trenin and Khardzhiev, 'Retushirovannyy Khlebnikov', p. 142.
19 Petrovsky, *Snake Train*, p. 289; Mayakovsky, PSS 12, p. 23; Burliuk, IMLI, *fond* 92, *opis'* 1, *yed. khr.* 25, *list* 2 *ob*. (also carried in NP 12).
20 Mayakovsky, PSS 12, p. 23.
21 On the opening page of his preface to Khlebnikov's *Tvoreniya* collection, Burliuk writes: 'Khlebnikov is not like the poets who write on a typewriter; whose manuscripts are enclosed in folders with a gold border, every line known to their author.' One wonders, however, how much at variance with his times Khlebnikov was with his 'bardic' methods of creation. As Clarence Brown notes in his *Mandelstam* (Cambridge University Press, 1973), pp. 1–2: 'the means by which the later poems of Mandelstam "came down" to us recall the age anterior to Gutenburg, not to mention that of the typewriter and the photostatic copier. Many readers will find it difficult to realize that we live in a time when poetry has had to survive in the most ancient of its repositories, the human memory.' The reason for this, of course, was Stalin's terror. Note also how Mandelstam 'kept his poems in his head, and believed so strongly in their objective existence that once he finished them he had no fear of losing them' (ibid., p. 2).
22 Many of Khlebnikov's works exist in more than one variant. See, for example, Ronald Vroon's discussion of the 'at least five variants' of 'And if in "Khar'kov Birds"' ('I yesli v "Khar'kovskiye ptitsy"') in his 'Velimir Khlebnikov's "I esli v 'Khar'kovskie ptitsy' . . ."', pp. 250–3; Khardzhiev's reference to four variants of 'Of the Last Supper's eyes the Neva knows much' ('Taynoy vecheri glaz znayet mnogo Neva') in NP 416; Stepanov's reference to the 'equivalent' variants of 'Three Sisters' ('Tri sestry') and 'Iranian Song' in IS 477. Khlebnikov's archive in TsGALI contains many examples of such multiple variants.
23 Markov (ed.), *Manifesty i programmy*, p. 57.
24 For an interesting account of the composition of this joint manifesto, see Gerald Janecek, 'Kručenykh and Chlebnikov Co-Authoring a Manifesto', *Russian Literature*, 8 (1980), pp. 483–98.

25 Mayakovsky, PSS 12, p. 23.

26 Khlebnikov makes a similar statement in another letter to Kruchonykh (in fact he 'insists' here that others have a right to alter his text); see B. N. Kapelyush, 'Arkhivy M. V. Matyushina i Ye. G. Guro', in *Yezhegodnik rukopisnogo otdela Pushkinskogo doma na 1974 god*, ed. K. D. Muratova (Leningrad, 1976), p. 17. The problem is in determining the parameters of such an attitude. Where does unwelcome distortion end and creative partnership begin?

27 Kornely Zelinsky, 'Na velikom rubezhe', p. 150.

28 A. Urban, 'Filosofskaya utopiya: (poeticheskiy mir V. Khlebnikova)', *Voprosy literatury*, 3 (1979), p. 160.

29 See Chapter One, pp. 22–3.

30 Vroon, 'Velimir Khlebnikov's "I esli v 'Khar'kovskie ptitsy' . . ."', p. 270.

31 There was a proliferation of cyclic compositions in Russian poetry at the beginning of this century. Khlebnikov's own tendency towards cycles should be seen in this context.

32 The general consensus has been that Khlebnikov's concept of genre was fluid. Stepanov pointed out (SP II 299), for example, that 'Khlebnikov's works violate the normal concept of genre to such an extent that it is often impossible to separate verse from prose, a lyric poem (*stikhotvoreniye*) from a long poem (*poema*), and a long poem from a play . . .'. Khlebnikov did, however, use accepted terms to describe his work (*stikhotvoreniye, rasskaz*, etc., though only rarely, if at all, *poema*), but his favourite term seems to be simply *veshch'* (thing). For Khlebnikov's penchant for rare genres such as the dialogue, see Henryk Baran's 'The Problem of Composition', pp. 95–100.

33 Khlebnikov introduced new formal concepts within the 'supertale'. *Zangezi* is divided into *ploskosti* (planes or levels), a term used in art and geometry. 'Children of the Otter' is divided into *parusa* (sails). For some remarks on the latter, see Baran, 'The Problem of Composition', pp. 101–2.

34 Osiris was probably chosen by Khlebnikov as the hero of this prospective work because of the 'fragmentary' connotations of this Egyptian deity. After his death he was cut into pieces in order to prevent Isis from finding his body.

35 See, for example, Markov's remarks in *The Longer Poems*, pp. 170–1, where he talks of the possibility of 'Washerwoman' being a 'supertale' and also refers to a draft plan for the work. This plan (SP III 384–5) and others (*yed. khr.* 16, *list* 5) bear a marked resemblance to those which Khlebnikov drew up for the 'supertale' *Zangezi* (SP III 387). Interestingly, *The Present Time* and 'Washerwoman' seem at one point to have been planned with regard to vocal work. A manuscript relating to these works includes reference to 'chorus of the rich', 'chorus of the poor', 'liturgy of uprising', with such directions as 'together and solo' (*yed. khr.* 125, *list* 28).

36 See, for example, the poem beginning 'Wind – singing' (SP II 258). The first four lines of this work recur as the beginning of another poem in SP III 26; and the remaining five lines as the ending of a different poem in SP II 96. For further comments on the *zagotovka*, see Markov, *The Longer Poems*, pp. 87–8.
37 The texts which make up 'War in a Mousetrap' began their lives as independent works before being brought together. Moreover, as Ronald Vroon notes (*Velimir Xlebnikov's Shorter Poems*, p. 34), many of the texts in 'War in a Mousetrap' were again granted their independence by Khlebnikov just before his death. 'And if in "Khar'kov Birds"' exists both as an independent poem (in several versions) and as part of the 'supertale' 'A's Unbound' (see Vroon, 'Velimir Khlebnikov's "I esli v 'Khar'kovskie ptitsy' . . ."', pp. 250–3).
38 Compton, *The World Backwards*, p. 69.
39 Ibid.
40 Markov (ed.), *Manifesty i programmy* p. 57.
41 David and Mariya Burliuk, 'Kanva znakomstva', p. 37.
42 Viktor Shklovsky, 'Voskresheniye slova', in *Texte der Russischen Formalisten*, vol. 2 (Munich, Wilhelm Fink Verlag, 1972), p. 14.
43 Boris Yakovlev, 'Poet dlya estetov', p. 215.
44 Ibid.
45 See Markov, *The Longer Poems*, p. 214.
46 Ibid., p. 57.
47 Khlebnikov dates the incident precisely (26 January 1918), and describes elsewhere in the same short prose sketch the clashes he witnessed at this time in Astrakhan' between revolutionary and counter-revolutionary forces (see Parnis, 'V. Khlebnikov – sotrudnik *Krasnogo voina*', p. 108).
48 Baran, 'Chlebnikov's "Vesennego Korana"', p. 3.
49 Ibid.
50 Khlebnikov is doubtless drawn towards this analogy by the similarity of the Russian words *stikh* (a line of verse) and *stikhiya* (element). He would have seen this as the 'wisdom of language' linking concepts which were apparently distant, but related at a deeper level. One might think initially that Khlebnikov would be engaged in false etymology here, since these two Russian words derive from different Greek words. However, I am grateful to Dr Peter Mackridge of St Cross College, Oxford, for pointing out to me that the two Greek words from which the Russian words *stikh* and *stikhiya* derive are, in fact, themselves etymologically related.
51 Rudol'f Duganov once used the expression 'living organism' (*zhivoy organizm*) to describe Khlebnikov's short poem 'O dostoyevskiymo begushchey tuchi!'; see his 'Kratkoye "iskusstvo poezii" Khlebnikova', p. 424.
52 See also 'Pussy Willow Twig' ('Vetka verby') (SP V 146), where Khlebnikov lists his writing implements as comprising a twig of pussy

willow, a porcupine needle and some Zheleznovodsk blackthorn. These were no doubt not metaphoric but 'real' pens which the shortages of the times forced upon him.

53 Lönnqvist, *Xlebnikov and Carnival*, p. 112.

54 *Yed. khr.* 74, *listy* 25, 40. Khlebnikov follows this statement with a brief 'column' giving the names of his 'proto-people', the years of their births, and mathematical formulas, showing how the births succeed each other according to a specific determinable pattern.

55 Vroon, *Velimir Xlebnikov's Shorter Poems*, p. 9.

56 Tzvetan Todorov, *The Poetics of Prose*, p. 195.

57 In the Bible there is particular use of the concept of the 'book of life', ranging from Exodus 32.32 to the last chapter of Revelations (22.19); and also of the notion of 'people' or 'names' written in the 'book of life' (Daniel 12.1, Philippians 4.3). Such elements are also present in the Koran, where there is frequent reference to the notion that all of life's varied phenomena are 'recorded' in Allah's 'book' (22.69, 10.62, 27.77). Perhaps one of the most striking presentations of this 'book of life' in the Koran is the following (6.59):

> But Allah best knows the evil-doers. He has the keys of all that is hidden: none knows them but He. He has knowledge of all that land and sea contain: every leaf that falls is known to Him. There is no grain of soil in the darkest bowels of the earth, nor anything green or sear, but is recorded in His glorious Book.

(I quote from N. J. Dawood's translation in the Penguin Classics 1984 edition, pp. 430–1).

58 The letter containing these lines included the first version of Khlebnikov's prose poem *Zoo* (see also NP 285–8).

59 See Baran, 'Chlebnikov's "Vesennego Korana"'.

60 See *yed. khr.* 83.

61 *Yed. khr.* 82, *list* 17.

62 *Yed. khr.* 73, *list* 3; see also Grigor'yev, *Grammatika*, p. 130.

63 In addition to the Vedas, the Koran and the Gospels, we also have here 'the books of the Mongols in their silken boards'. These are almost certainly the Buddhist texts of the Mongol Kalmyks. Note in this connection the use by Khlebnikov of the word 'boards' for his own 'book' – the 'Boards of Fate' ('Doski sud'by').

64 Formally, the religious books contain many of the qualities towards which Khlebnikov was striving in his 'supertale'. They are, generally speaking, composite texts, made up from 'independent fragments', which can, moreover, be of varying genre. Religious texts also freely use 'coded' 'difficult' writings, which the reader has to try to interpret. With his belief in the power of the word Khlebnikov was, of course, well aware of the strange efficacy of coded discourse. He once, for example, wrote:

> The speech of the highest reason, even if unintelligible, falls like seeds upon the black soil of the spirit and later in its enigmatic way pushes forth its shoots. Does the earth really understand the writing of the grain which the sower casts upon it? No. But the autumn corn still grows in response to these seeds. (SP v 226)

POSTSCRIPT

1 Markov, *Russian Futurism*, p. 307.

2 Konstantin Kedrov, '"Zvyozdnaya azbuka" Velimira Khlebnikova: literaturovedcheskaya gipoteza', *Literaturnaya uchoba*, 3 (1982), p. 84. See also L. Zhadova, '"Tolpa prozrachno-chistykh sot"', *Nauka i zhizn'*, 8 (1976), p. 105.

3 These have been reproduced in several publications now, including Zhadova, '"Tolpa prozrachno-chistykh sot"', p. 107.

4 For references to these terms, see SP III 23, 317, 340; SS III 508.

5 See, for example, John Milner's *Vladimir Tatlin*. On hearing of Khlebnikov's death, tatlin wrote in a letter to Miturich that Khlebnikov had been 'the main thing that had happened to us over all time' ('glavnoye chto sluchilos' za vsyo vremya s nami'); see *yed. khr.* 338, *list* 1.

6 Though Mayakovsky continued to maintain that Khlebnikov was a poet for 'the few', for 'producers', for other poets, who would then process his poetic work and make it accessible to the masses. See Mayakovsky, PSS 12, p. 165.

7 See Nadezhda Mandelstam, *Hope Abandoned*, p. 615; and also her *Hope Against Hope*, trans. Max Hayward (Penguin, 1975), p. 429.

8 See R. R. Milner-Gulland, 'Zabolotsky: Philosopher-Poet', *Soviet Studies*, vol. 22, 4 (1971), p. 605.

9 Olesha's comments are contained in the Moscow 1930 edition of Khlebnikov's *Zoo*, pp. 3–4.

10 See Yakovlev, 'Poet dlya estetov'. This attack on Khlebnikov was published at the height (1948) of the Party's post-war assault on intellectual life, which became known as the *Zhdanovshchina*, named after the Party official (Andrey Zhdanov) with whom it was most closely associated.

11 Osip Mandelstam, *Sobraniye sochineniy*, vol. 2, p. 391.

12 See Stepanov's comments in SP I 45; see also Markov, *The Longer Poems*, p. 110; and Vroon, 'Velimir Chlebnikov's "Chadži Tarchan" and the Lomonosovian Tradition'.

13 See his preface to Petrovsky's 'A Tale about Khlebnikov', in *Snake Train*, p. 275.

14 I quote here from R. H. Robins, *A Short History of Linguistics* (London, Longmans, 1967), p. 113.

15 See Grigor'yev, *Grammatika*, p. 134.

16 This poem is distinctly reminiscent of Derzhavin's famous last poem, 'Reka vremyon v svoyom stremlen'i'.

Selected Bibliography

I. Primary sources: works by Khlebnikov

Khlebnikov's works have appeared in numerous periodicals, miscellanies, journals and newspapers, both during his life and after his death. Apart from the 1928–33 *Sobraniye proizvedeniy*, there has also been a confusing array of single-volume editions, containing selected works. The several volumes published in 1985 and 1986 to mark the centenary of Khlebnikov's birth have added to this confusion. His works (both published and previously unpublished) are continuing to appear in a disorganized manner. They are in considerable need of a new comprehensive, coherently annotated, collected edition. The aim of this brief bibliography is not to list all Khlebnikov's diverse publications. Rather I shall restrict myself to listing his main collected and individual editions. I am including in the list those centenary volumes which have appeared while this book was in preparation. Where other published works by Khlebnikov have been consulted for this study, references have been given in the notes.

One problem in compiling any bibliography of Khlebnikov is his occasional joint authorship with Kruchonykh. Below I list only the two editions of *Igra v adu*. One should also note *Slovo kak takovoye*, which bears both names, but which is, I suspect, more Kruchonykh than Khlebnikov, as well as such 'joint' collections as *Mirskontsa* (Moscow, 1912), *Pomada* (Moscow, 1913), *Bukh lesinnyy* (St Petersburg, 1913), *Starinnaya lyubov'. Bukh lesinnyy* (St Petersburg, 1914), and *Te li le* (St Petersburg, 1914). These collections include not only individual poems by each author, but also individual works which seem to bear the hand of both Kruchonykh and Khlebnikov (see, for example, NP 405–6).

Details about Khlebnikov's appearances in Futurist publications can be found in abundance in Markov's *Russian Futurism*, and in the bibliography of the same author's *The Longer Poems*. Of use, too, is the early 'Bibliografiya Velemira Khlebnikova 1908–1925' by V. Sillov in Khlebnikov's *Nastoyashcheye* (Moscow, 1926).

I have not attempted to list the many translations into various languages of Khlebnikov's work. The English-speaking reader should, however, note: *Snake Train: Poetry and Prose*, ed. G. Kern (Ann Arbor, Ardis, 1976); and the excellent *The King of Time: Poems, Fictions, Visions of the Future*, trans. Paul Schmidt (Cambridge, Massachusetts and London, England, Harvard University Press, 1985). Details of some translations are given by Markov in the extremely useful bibliographical pages which preface the third volume of the *Sobraniye sochineniy*.

One of the most interesting of the Khlebnikov publications listed below is the *Neizdannyy Khlebnikov* series, published at about the same time as (and in some ways as a rival to) the five-volume *Sobraniye proizvedeniy*. This publication – a reproduction of hand-written copies of Khlebnikov's manuscripts – was issued by the self-styled 'Group of Friends of Khlebnikov'. There were, apparently, 30 issues. I have seen the majority of these, but not all. Because of the limited circulation, they are now quite rare. The 'Chlebnikov Association', founded in 1985 after an international conference at the University of Amsterdam, has reproduced some of the issues.

The archives of Khlebnikov which were consulted for this work are the large holdings in the Central State Archive for Literature and Art (*Tsentral'nyy gosudarstvennyy arkhiv literatury i iskusstva*) (TsGALI), *fond* 527, *opis'* 1; and the small collection of manuscripts held in the Gor'ky Institute of World Literature (*Institut mirovoy literatury imeni Gor'kogo*) (IMLI), *fond* 139, *opis'* 1. Two other Khlebnikov archives, to which I was not able to gain access, can be found in the Leningrad Saltykov-Shchedrin State Public Library (*Gosudarstvennaya publichnaya biblioteka imeni Saltykova-Shchedrina*), *fond* 1087; and the State Literary Museum (*Gosudarstvennyy literaturnyy muzey*), fond 203.

The following works are listed chronologically:

Uchitel' i uchenik (Kherson, 1912)
Igra v adu (Moscow, 1912)
Igra v adu, 2nd edition (Moscow, 1913)
Ryav! Perchatki: 1908–1914 (St Petersburg, 1913)
Izbornik stikhov: 1907–1914 (St Petersburg, 1914)
Tvoreniya: 1906–1908 (Moscow, 1914)
Bitvy 1915–1917: novoye ucheniye o voyne (Petrograd, 1914)
Vremya mera mira (Petrograd, 1916)
Truba marsian (Khar'kov, 1916)
Oshibka smerti (Moscow, 1917)
Ladomir (Khar'kov, 1920)
Noch' v okope (Moscow, 1921)
Vestnik Velimira Khlebnikova, 1–2 (Moscow, 1922)
Zangezi (Moscow, 1922)
Otryvok iz dosok sud'by, 1–3 (Moscow, 1922–3)
Stikhi (Moscow, 1923)
Zapisnaya knizhka Velimira Khlebnikova, ed. A. Ye. Kruchonykh (Moscow, 1925)
Nastoyashcheye (Moscow, 1926)
Vsem. Nochnoy bal (Moscow, 1927)
Sobraniye proizvedeniy, 5 vols., ed. N. Stepanov (Leningrad, 1928–33)
Neizdannyy Khlebnikov, 1–30, ed. A. Ye. Kruchonykh (Moscow, 1928–[1934])

Zverinets (Moscow, 1930)
Izbrannyye stikhotvoreniya, ed. N. Stepanov (Moscow, 1936)
Stikhotvoreniya, ed. N. Stepanov (Leningrad, 1940)
Neizdannyye proizvedeniya, ed. N. Khardzhiev and T. Grits (Moscow, 1940)
Stikhotvoreniya i poemy, ed. N. Stepanov (Leningrad, 1960)
Sobraniye sochineniy, 4 vols., ed. V. Markov (Munich, Wilhelm Fink Verlag, 1968–72) [A reprint of the *Sobraniye proizvedeniy*, the *Neizdannyye proizvedeniya*, and also including previously uncollated and unpublished work.]
Ladomir: poemy (Moscow, 1985)
Stikhotvoreniya, poemy, dramy, proza, ed. R. V. Duganov (Moscow, 1986)

II. Secondary sources: works devoted to Khlebnikov

This bibliography is not exhaustive. For other bibliographies of works on Khlebnikov, see Markov, *The Longer Poems* and SS III; see also Ronald Vroon's *Velimir Xlebnikov's Shorter Poems* and Viktor Grigor'yev's *Grammatika idiostilya*.

Al'vek, 'Nakhlebniki Khlebnikova', in V. Khlebnikov *Vsem. Nochnoy bal* (Moscow, 1927), pp. 6–16
Anfimov, V. Ya. 'K voprosu o psikhopatologii tvorchestva: V. Khlebnikov v 1919 godu', in *Trudy 3-ey Krasnodarskoy klinicheskoy gorodskoy bol'nitsy*, I (1935), pp. 66–73
Arapova, Yu. 'Khlebnikov's Bath', *Russian Literature Triquarterly*, 13 (1975), pp. 465–7
Arenzon, Ye. 'K ponimaniyu Khlebnikova: nauka i poeziya', *Voprosy literatury*, 10 (1985), pp. 163–90
Aseyev, N. 'V. V. Khlebnikov', *Tvorchestvo* (Vladivostok), 2 (1920), pp. 26–9
Aseyev, N. and Kruchonykh, A. 'Velemir Khlebnikov: k desyatiletiyu so dnya smerti (1922–28 iyunya–1932)', *Literaturnaya gazeta*, 29 June 1932
Baran, H. 'Chlebnikov's Poem "Bech"', *Russian Literature*, 6 (1974), pp. 5–19
'Chlebnikov's "Vesennego Korana": An Analysis', *Russian Literature*, 9 (1981), pp. 1–22
'O nekotorykh podkhodakh k interpretatsii tekstov Velimira Khlebnikova', in *American Contributions to the Eighth International Congress of Slavists*, vol. I, *Linguistics and Poetics*, ed. H. Birnbaum (Columbus, Ohio, 1978), pp. 104–25
'On the Poetics of a Xlebnikov Tale: Problems and Patterns in "Ka"', in *Structural Analysis of Narrative Texts*, New York University Slavic Papers II, ed. A. Kodjak, M. Connolly, K. Pomorska (Columbus, Ohio, 1980), pp. 112–31
'On Xlebnikov's Love Lyrics: I. Analysis of "O, červi zemljanye"', in

Russian Poetics, UCLA Slavic Studies, vol. 4, ed. Thomas Eekman, Dean S. Worth (University of California, Los Angeles, Slavica, 1983), pp. 29–44.

'Temporal Myths in Xlebnikov: From "Deti vydry" to "Zangezi"', in *Myth in Literature*, New York University Slavic Papers v, ed. A. Kodjak et al. (Columbus, Ohio, Slavica, 1983), pp. 63–88

'The Problem of Composition in Velimir Chlebnikov's Texts', *Russian Literature*, 9 (1981), pp. 87–106

'Xlebnikov and the *History* of Herodotus', *Slavic and East European Journal*, vol. 22, 1 (1978), pp. 30–4

'Xlebnikov and the Mythology of the Oroches', in *Slavic Poetics: Essays in Honour of Kiril Taranovsky*, ed. R. Jakobson, C. H. Van Schooneveld and D. S. Worth (The Hague–Paris, Mouton, 1973), pp. 33–9

'Xlebnikov's Poetic Logic and Poetic Illogic', in *Velimir Chlebnikov: A Stockholm Symposium*, ed. Nils Åke Nilsson (Stockholm, Almqvist & Wiksell International, 1985), pp. 7–25

Berezark, I. 'Vstrechi s V. Khlebnikovym', *Zvezda*, 12 (1965), pp. 173–6

Blyumenfel'd, V. 'Poeticheskoye naslediye V. Khlebnikova', *Zhizn' iskusstva*, 49 (1928), pp. 4–5

Bowlt, J. E. 'Introduction to Yuliya Arapova's Description of Khlebnikov's Bath', *Russian Literature Triquarterly*, 13 (1975), pp. 463–4

Burliuk, D. 'Viktor Vladimirovich Khlebnikov', in V. V. Khlebnikov, *Tvoreniya: 1906–1908* (Moscow, 1914), [no page numbers]

Burliuk, D. and Burliuk, M. 'Kanva znakomstva s Khlebnikovym: (1909–1918)', *Color and Rhyme*, 55 (1964–5), pp. 35–9

Cooke, R. F. 'Image and Symbol in Khlebnikov's "Night Search"', *Russian Literature Triquarterly*, 12 (1975), pp. 279–94

'Magic in the Poetry of Velimir Khlebnikov', *Essays in Poetics*, vol. 5, 2 (1980), pp. 15–42

'The Poetic World of Velimir Khlebnikov: An Interpretation' (unpublished D. Phil. thesis, University of Sussex, 1983)

Duganov, R. V. 'Kratkoye "iskusstvo poezii" Khlebnikova', *Izvestiya Akademii nauk SSSR, Seriya literatury i yazyka*, vol. 33, 5 (1974), pp. 418–27

'K rekonstruktsii poemy Khlebnikova "Noch' v okope"', *Izvestiya Akademii nauk SSSR, Seriya literatury i yazyka*, vol. 38, 5 (1979), pp. 458–70

'Poet, istoriya, priroda', *Voprosy literatury*, 10 (1985), pp. 130–62

'Problema epicheskogo v estetike i poetike Khlebnikova', *Izvestiya Akademii nauk SSSR, Seriya literatury i yazyka*, vol. 35, 5 (1976), pp. 426–39

'Velimir Khlebnikov 1885–1922', in *Den' poezii: 1982* (Moscow, 1982), pp. 164–7

Gel'fandbeyn, G. 'Novyy lad miru', in 'Vechnozelyonyye list'ya: nevydumannyye rasskazy', *Raduga* (Kiev), 1 (1965), pp. 118–19

Gofman, V. A. 'Yazykovoye novatorstvo Khlebnikova', in his *Yazyk literatury* (Leningrad, 1936), pp. 185–240
Goncharov, B. P. 'Mayakovsky i Khlebnikov: (k probleme kontseptsii slova)', *Filologicheskiye nauki*, 3 (93) (1976), pp. 8–18
G . . . d (probably A. G. Gornfel'd) 'Nekrolog: V. Khlebnikov', *Literaturnyye zapiski*, 3 (1922), p. 13
Gorodetsky, S. 'Velimir Khlebnikov', *Izvestiya*, 5 July 1922
Grigor'yev, V. P. *Grammatika idiostilya: V. Khlebnikov* (Moscow, 1983)
'Iz istorii interlingvistiki: Leti, sozvezd'ye chelovech'ye (V. Khlebnikov – interlingvist)', in *Uchonyye zapiski Tartuskogo universiteta, vypusk* 613 (1982), pp. 153–66
'"Lobachevsky slova"', *Russkaya rech'*, 5 (1985), pp. 22–8
'Onomastika Velimira Khlebnikova: (individual'naya poeticheskaya norma)', in *Onomastika i norma*, ed. L. Kalakutskaya (Moscow, 1976), pp. 181–200
'Skorneniye', in *Aktual'nyye problemy russkogo slovoobrazovaniya, Sbornik nauchnykh statey* (Tashkent, Ukituvchi, 1982)
'Sobstvennyye imena i svyazannyye s nimi apellyativy v slovotvorchestve Khlebnikova', in *Onomastika i grammatika*, ed. L. Kalakutskaya (Moscow, 1981), pp. 196–222
Grits, T. and Khardzhiev, N. 'Novoye o Khlebnikove', *30 dney*, 7 (1935), pp. 65–8
Grygar, M. 'Stikhi i kontekst: zametki o poezii V. Khlebnikova', in *Voz'mi na radost': To Honour Jeanne van der Eng-Leidmeier* (Amsterdam, 1980), pp. 111–24
Ivanov, Vyach. Vs. 'Struktura stikhotvoreniya Khlebnikova "Menya pronosyat na slonovykh"', in *Trudy po znakovym sistemam 3, Uchonyye zapiski Tartuskogo universiteta, vypusk* 198, (Tartu, 1967), pp. 156–71
Jakobson, R. 'Iz melkikh veshchei V. Khlebnikova: Veter – penie', in his *Selected Writings* III (The Hague–Paris–New York, Mouton, 1981), pp. 568–76
Noveyshaya russkaya poeziya: nabrosok pervyy: Viktor Khlebnikov (Prague, 1921)
Janecek, G. 'Kručenych and Chlebnikov Co-Authoring a Manifesto', *Russian Literature*, 8 (1980), pp. 483–98
Kamensky, V. 'O Khlebnikove: slavozhd'', in V. V. Khlebnikov, *Tvoreniya: 1906–1908* (Moscow, 1914), [no page numbers]
Kedrov, K. '"Zvyozdnaya azbuka" Velimira Khlebnikova: literaturovedcheskaya gipoteza', *Literaturnaya uchoba*, 3 (1982), pp. 78–89
Khardzhiev, N. 'Novoye o Velimire Khlebnikove: (k 90-letiyu so dnya rozhdeniya)', in *Den' poezii: 1975* (Moscow, 1975), pp. 201–11
'Novoye o Velimire Khlebnikove', *Russian Literature*, 9 (1975), pp. 5–24
Khlebnikova, V. 'Vospominaniye Very Khlebnikovoy', in Velimir Khlebnikov, *Stikhi* (Moscow, 1923), pp. 57–62
Knight, C. D. 'Past, Future, and the Problem of Communication in the

Work of V. V. Khlebnikov', (unpublished M. Phil. dissertation, University of Sussex, 1975)
Kosterin, A. '"Russkiye dervishi"', *Moskva*, 9 (1966), pp. 216–21
Kostetsky, A. G. 'Lingvisticheskaya teoriya V. Khlebnikova', in *Strukturnaya i matematicheskaya lingvistika*, 3 (1975), pp. 34–9
Kozlov, D. 'Novoye o Velemire Khlebnikove', *Krasnaya nov'*, 8 (1927) pp. 177–88
Kruchonykh, A. Ye. 'Azef-Iuda-Khlebnikov', in *Milliork* (Tbilisi, 1919), pp. 19–32
'Iz zhizni Velimira Khlebnikova', in V. V. Khlebnikov, *Zverinets* (Moscow, 1930), pp. 14–17
'O Khlebnikove i drugikh', in V. V. Khlebnikov, *Zverinets* (Moscow, 1930), pp. 13–14
'Predisloviye', in V. Khlebnikov, *Bitvy 1915–1917: novoye ucheniye o voyne* (Petrograd, 1914), p. 1
Lanne, J.-C. *Velimir Khlebnikov: poète futurien*, 2 vols., (Paris, Institut d'études slaves, 1983)
Levitina, A. 'O prirode neologizmov V. Khlebnikova', in *Materialy XXVI nauchnoy studencheskoy konferentsii* (Tartu, 1971), pp. 124–6
Leytes, A. 'Khlebnikov, kakim on byl', *Novyy mir*, 1 (1973), pp. 224–37
'Vstrechi s Khlebnikovym', *Literaturnaya gazeta*, 4 December 1965
Lönnqvist, B. 'Chlebnikov's "Imaginist" Poem', *Russian Literature*, 9 (1981), pp. 47–58
Xlebnikov and Carnival: An Analysis of the Poem 'Poèt' (Stockholm, Almqvist & Wiksell International, 1979)
'Xlebnikov's Plays and the Folk-Theater Tradition', in *Velimir Chlebnikov: A Stockholm Symposium*, ed. Nils Åke Nilsson (Stockholm, Almqvist & Wiksell International, 1985), pp. 89–121
Loshchits, Yu. M. and Turbin, V. N. 'Tema vostoka v tvorchestve Khlebnikova', *Narody azii i afriki*, 4 (1966), pp. 147–60
Marinchak, V. A. '"Samovitoye slovo" V. Khlebnikova', *Russkaya rech'*, 2 (1978), pp. 58–62
Markov, V. *The Longer Poems of Velimir Khlebnikov*, University of California Publications in Modern Philology, vol. 62 (Berkeley and Los Angeles, University of California Press, 1962)
Mayakovsky, V. V. 'V. V. Khlebnikov', in his *Polnoye sobraniye sochineniy v 13-i tomakh*, ed. V. A. Katanyan (Moscow, 1955–61), vol. 12, pp. 23–8
Mirsky, S. *Der Orient im Werk Velimir Chlebnikovs* (Munich, Verlag Otto Sagner, 1975)
Miturich, P. V. 'Otkrytoye pis'mo khudozhnika P. V. Mituricha Mayakovskomu', in Velemir Khlebnikov, *Vsem. Nochnoy bal* (Moscow, 1927), pp. 17–19
Neymayer, Ye. 'O Velemire Khlebnikove', *Raduga* (Kiev), 11 (1965), pp. 135–8

Nilsson, N. Å. 'Futurism, Primitivism and the Russian Avant-Garde', *Russian Literature*, 8–5 (1980), pp. 469–81

'How to Translate Avant-Garde Poetry. Some Attempts with Xlebnikov's "Incantation by Laughter"', in *Velimir Chlebnikov: A Stockholm Symposium*, ed. Nils Åke Nilsson (Stockholm, Almqvist & Wiksell International, 1985), pp. 133–50

Olesha, Yu. Preface to V. V. Khlebnikov, *Zverinets* (Moscow, 1930), pp. 3–4

Panov, M. V. 'O chlenimosti slov na morfemy', in *Pamyati akademika V. V. Vinogradova* (Moscow, 1971), pp. 170–9

Parnis, A. Ye. 'K 90-letiyu so dnya rozhdeniya Velimira Khlebnikova: "I voysko pesen povedu..."', *Literaturnaya gazeta*, 12 November 1975

'"Konetsarstvo, ved' ottuda ya ... "', *Teyegin gerl* (Elista), 1 (1976), pp. 135–51

'Neizvestnyy rasskaz V. Khlebnikova', *Russian Literature Triquarterly*, 13 (1975), pp. 468–75

'"Ulozhitsya li v strochku slovo?"', *Literaturnaya gazeta*, 13 November 1985

'Velemir Khlebnikov', *Prostor* (Alma-Ata), 7 (1966), p. 91

'Velimir Khlebnikov', *Zvezda*, 11 (1975), pp. 199–205

'V. Khlebnikov – sotrudnik *Krasnogo voina*', *Literaturnoye obozreniye*, 2 (1980), pp. 105–12

'V. Khlebnikov v Bakrosta', *Literaturnyy Azerbaydzhan* (Baku), 7 (1976), pp. 117–19

'V. Khlebnikov v revolyutsionnom Gilyane (novyye materialy)', *Narody azii i afriki*, 5 (1967), pp. 156–64

'Yuzhnoslavyanskaya tema Velimira Khlebnikova: novyye materialy k tvorcheskoy biografii poeta', in *Zarubezhnyye slavyane i russkaya kul'tura*, ed. M. P. Alekseyev (Leningrad, 1978), pp. 223–51

Petrovsky, D. 'A Tale about Khlebnikov: Memories of Velimir Khlebnikov', trans. Lily Feiler, in V. Khlebnikov, *Snake Train: Poetry and Prose*, ed. G. Kern (Ann Arbor, Ardis, 1976), pp. 273–313

Polukhina, V. 'For the Centenary of Velimir Khlebnikov: (A review of some recent publications)', *Essays in Poetics*, vol. 10, 1 (1985), pp. 66–80

Postupal'sky, I. 'O pervom tome Khlebnikova', *Novyy mir*, 12 (1929), pp. 237–42

'V. Khlebnikov i futurizm', *Novyy mir*, 5 (1930), pp. 187–96

Punin, N. 'Zangezi', *Zhizn' iskusstva* (Leningrad), 20 (1923), pp. 10–12

Radzishevsky, V. '"Prinadlezhu k mestu vstrechi Volgi i Kaspiya morya ...": Tam, gde zhil Velimir Khlebnikov', *Literaturnaya gazeta*, 17 August 1983

Rayt, R. 'Vse luchshiye vospominaniya ... (otryvki iz knigi)', in *Uchonyye zapiski Tartuskogo universiteta, vypusk* 184, (1966), pp. 266–70

Ritter, A. C. 'Velimir Khlebnikov: Poetry and Prose 1917–1922' (unpublished D. Phil. thesis, University of Oxford, 1977)

Samorodova, O. 'Poet na Kavkaze: vospominaniya', *Zvezda*, 6 (1972), pp. 186–94

Sedakova, O. 'Obraz fonemy v "Slove o El'" Velimira Khlebnikova', in *Razvitiye fonetiki sovremennogo russkogo yazyka* (Moscow, 1971), pp. 273–7

'Velimir Khlebnikov – poet skorosti', *Russkaya rech'*, 5 (1985), pp. 29–35

Slinina, E. V. 'Tema prirody v poezii V. Khlebnikova i N. Zabolotskogo', in *Voprosy metodiki istorii literatury, Uchonyye zapiski Leningradskogo gosudarstvennogo pedagogicheskogo instituta*, vol. 465 (Pskov, 1970), pp. 42–57

'V. Khlebnikov o Pushkine', in *Pushkin i yego sovremenniki, Uchonyye zapiski Leningradskogo gosudarstvennogo pedagogicheskogo instituta*, vol. 434 (Pskov, 1970), pp. 111–24

Spassky, S. 'Khlebnikov', *Literaturnyy sovremennik*, 12 (1935), pp. 190–204

'O Khlebnikove', *Literaturnyy Leningrad*, 14 November 1935

Stepanov, N. 'Naslediye Velemira Khlebnikova', *Na literaturnom postu*, 22–3 (1927), pp. 84–90

'O Velimire Khlebnikove: (k pyatidesyatiletiyu so dnya smerti)', *Zvezda*, 6 (1972), pp. 183–6

'Poet-utopist', *Literaturnyy Leningrad*, 14 November 1935

'Tvorchestvo Velimira Khlebnikova', in Velimir Khlebnikov, *Sobraniye proizvedeniy*, 5 vols., ed. N. Stepanov (Leningrad, 1928–33), vol. 1, pp. 31–64

'Velimir Khlebnikov', in *Istituto universitario orientale: Annali: Sezione slava*, 10 (Naples, 1967), pp. 171–99

'Velimir Khlebnikov', in V. V. Khlebnikov, *Stikhotvoreniya* (Leningrad, 1940), pp. iii–xl

'Velimir Khlebnikov', in V. V. Khlebnikov, *Stikhotvoreniya i poemy* (Leningrad, 1960), pp. 5–68

Velimir Khlebnikov: zhizn' i tvorchestvo (Moscow, 1975)

'V. V. Khlebnikov: biograficheskiy ocherk', in V. V. Khlebnikov, *Izbrannyye stikhotvoreniya* (Leningrad, 1936), pp. 5–77

Stobbe, P. *Utopisches Denken bei V. Chlebnikov* (Munich, Verlag Otto Sagner, 1982)

Strunin, V. I. '"Chtob v dvukh slovakh byl vodopad..." (V. Khlebnikov o poezii)', in *Sovetskaya poeziya 20–30-kh godov, Chelyabinskiy gosudarstvennyy pedagogicheskiy institut, vypusk* 5 (Chelyabinsk, 1977), pp. 61–77

'Na puti k istorizmu (poemy V. Khlebnikova o narodnoy bor'be)', in *Stanovleniye sotsialisticheskogo realizma*, ed. V. P. Rakov (Moscow, 1981), pp. 49–57

'Osmysleniye sobytiy revolyutsii v poemakh Velimira Khlebnikova', in *Problemy sovetskoy poezii*, 2 (Chelyabinsk, 1974), pp. 72–82

Tal'nikov, D. 'Poet nesovershennykh vozmozhnostey', in *Gul vremeni* (Moscow, 1929), pp. 290–309

Tartakovsky, P. 'Poet; revolyutsiya; vostok: (tvorchestvo Velimira Khlebnikova i irano-tadzhikskoye khudozhestvennoye naslediye)', *Pamir* (Dushanbe), 7 (1977), pp. 84–96

Tatlin, V. 'O Zangezi', *Zhizn' iskusstva* (Leningrad), 18 (1923), p. 15

Thomson, R. D. B. 'Khlebnikov and 3^6+3^{6}', in *Russian and Slavic Literature*, ed. R. Freeborn, R. R. Milner-Gulland and C. A. Ward (Slavica Publishers Inc., 1976), pp. 297–312

Todorov, T. 'Number, Letter, Word', in *The Poetics of Prose*, trans. Richard Howard (Oxford, Basil Blackwell, 1977), pp. 190–204

Trenin, V. and Khardzhiev, N. 'Retushirovannyy Khlebnikov', *Literaturnyy kritik*, 6 (1933), pp. 142–50

Tynyanov, Yu. 'O Khlebnikove', in Velimir Khlebnikov, *Sobraniye proizvedeniy*, 5 vols., ed. N. Stepanov (Leningrad, 1928–1933), vol. 1, pp. 17–30

Urban, A. 'Filosofskaya utopiya: (poeticheskiy mir V. Khlebnikova)', *Voprosy literatury*, 3 (1979), pp. 153–83

Uspensky, B. A. 'K poetike Khlebnikova: problemy kompozitsii', in *Sbornik statey po vtorichnym modeliruyushchim sistemam*, ed. Yu. Lotman (Tartu, 1973), pp. 122–7

Vanshenkin, K. 'K 100-letiyu so dnya rozhdeniya Velimira Khlebnikova', *Literaturnaya gazeta*, 13 November 1985

Vechorka, T. 'Vospominaniya o Khlebnikove', in *Zapisnaya knizhka Velimira Khlebnikova*, ed. A. Ye. Kruchonykh (Moscow, 1925), pp. 21–30

Vinokur, G. 'Khlebnikov', *Russkiy sovremennik*, 4 (1924), pp. 222–6

Vol'pe, Ts. 'Stikhotvoreniya Velimira Khlebnikova', *Literaturnoye obozreniye*, 17 (1940), pp. 33–7

Vroon, R. 'Four Analogues to Xlebnikov's "Language of the Gods"', in *The Structure of the Literary Process: Essays in Memory of Felix Vodička*, ed. M. Cervenka, P. Steiner and R. Vroon (Amsterdam, John Benjamins, 1982), pp. 581–97

'"Sea Shore" ("Morskoi bereg") and the Razin Constellation', *Russian Literature Triquarterly*, 12 (1975), pp. 295–326

'Velimir Chlebnikov's "Chadži-Tarchan" and the Lomonosovian Tradition', *Russian Literature*, 9 (1981), pp. 107–31

'Velimir Khlebnikov's "I esli v 'Khar'kovskie ptitsy' . . .": Manuscript Sources and Subtexts', *Russian Review*, 42 (1983), pp. 249–70

'Velimir Khlebnikov's "Razin: Two Trinities": A Reconstruction', *Slavic Review*, vol. 39, 1 (1980), pp. 70–84.

Velimir Xlebnikov's Shorter Poems: A Key to the Coinages (Ann Arbor, University of Michigan, 1983)

Weststeijn, W. G. *Velimir Chlebnikov and the Development of Poetical Language in Russian Symbolism and Futurism* (Amsterdam, Rodopi, 1983)

Yakovlev, B. 'Poet dlya estetov: (zametki o Velimire Khlebnikove i formalizme v poezii)', *Novyy mir*, 5 (1948), pp. 207–31

Zhadova, L. ' "Tolpa prozrachno-chistykh sot" ', *Nauka i zhizn'*, 8 (1976), pp. 102–7

III. Other works

Abroskina, I. I. 'Literaturnyye kafe 20-kh godov: (iz vospominaniy I. V. Gruzinova "Mayakovsky i literaturnaya Moskva")', in *Vstrechi s proshlym, Sbornik materialov Tsentral'nogo gosudarstvennogo arkhiva literatury i iskusstva SSSR, vypusk* 3 (Moscow, 1978), pp. 174–92.

Bal'mont, K. *Poeziya kak volshebstvo* (Moscow, 1915)

Barooshian, V. D. *Russian Cubo-Futurism 1910–1930: A Study in Avant-Gardism* (The Hague–Paris, Mouton, 1974)

Baryutin N. M. 'Moi vstrechi s Khlebnikovym', 'Vospominaniye o vstrechakh s Khlebnikovym', unpublished memoirs in *Tsentral'nyy gosudarstvennyy arkhiv literatury i iskusstva, fond* 2283, *opis'* 1, *yed. khr.* 6

Bely, A. *Glossolaliya: poema o zvuke* (Berlin, 1922)

'Magiya slov', in his *Simvolizm* (Moscow, 1910), pp. 429–48

Blok, A. *Sobraniye sochineniy v 8-i tomakh*, ed. V. N. Orlov, A. A. Surkov, K. I. Chukovsky (Moscow–Leningrad, 1960–3)

Brik, L. 'Iz vospominaniy', in *Al'manakh: s Mayakovskim* (Moscow, 1934), pp. 59–79

Brown, C. *Mandelstam* (Cambridge University Press, 1973)

Brown, E. J. (ed.) *Major Soviet Writers: Essays in Criticism* (Oxford University Press, 1973)

Mayakovsky: A Poet in the Revolution (Princeton, New Jersey, Princeton University Press, 1973)

Burliuk, D. Archive in *Rukopisnyy otdel, Institut mirovoy literatury imeni Gor'kogo, fond* 92, *opis'* 1

'Ot laboratorii k ulitse: (evolyutsiya futurizma)', *Tvorchestvo* (Vladivostok), 2 (1920), pp. 22–5

Chukovsky, K. 'Akhmatova and Mayakovsky', trans. J. Pearson, in *Major Soviet Writers: Essays in Criticism*, ed. E. J. Brown (Oxford University Press, 1973), pp. 33–53

Litsa i maski (St Petersburg, 1914)

Compton, S. P. *The World Backwards: Russian Futurist Books 1912–1916* (London, British Museum Publications, 1978)

Duganov, R. V. 'Aleksey Kruchonykh 1886–1968: iz vospominaniy', in *Den' poezii: 1983* (Moscow, 1983), pp. 157–62

Erlich, V. 'The Place of Russian Futurism within the Russian Poetic Avantgarde: A Reconsideration', *Russian Literature*, 13 (1983), pp. 1–18

Etkind, Ye. *Materiya stikha* (Paris, Institut d'études slaves, 1978)

Gorky, M. 'O futurizme', *Zhurnal zhurnalov*, 1 (1915), pp. 3–4

Gray, C. *The Russian Experiment in Art: 1863–1922* (London, Thames and Hudson, 1971)

Grygar, M. 'Kubizm i poeziya russkogo i cheshkogo avangarda', in *Structure of Texts and Semiotics of Culture*, ed. Jan van der Eng and Mojmir Grygar (The Hague–Paris, Mouton, 1973), pp. 59–101

Ivask, G. 'Russian Modernist Poets and the Mystic Sectarians', in *Russian Modernism: Culture and the Avant-Garde 1900–1930*, ed. George Gibian and H. W. Tjalsma (Ithaca and London, Cornell University Press, 1976), pp. 85–106

Jakobson, R. 'From Alyagrov's Letters', in *Russian Formalism: A Retrospective Glance. A Festschrift in Honor of Victor Erlich*, ed. Robert Louis Jackson and Stephen Rudy (Yale Center for International and Area Studies, New Haven, 1985), pp. 1–5

'On a Generation that Squandered its Poets', trans. E. J. Brown, in *Major Soviet Writers: Essays in Criticism*, ed. E. J. Brown (Oxford University Press, 1973), pp. 7–32

'Subliminal Verbal Patterning in Poetry', in *Selected Writings* III (The Hague–Paris–New York, Mouton, 1981), pp. 136–47

Janecek, G. *The Look of Russian Literature: Avant-Garde Visual Experiments, 1900–1930* (Princeton, New Jersey, Princeton University Press, 1984)

Jangfeldt, B. *Majakovskij and Futurism 1917–1921* (Almqvist & Wiksell International, Stockholm, 1977)

'Russian Futurism 1917–1919', in *Art, Society, Revolution: Russia 1917–1921*, ed. Nils Åke Nilsson (Stockholm, Almqvist & Wiksell International, 1979), pp. 106–37

Kamensky, V. *Zhizn' s Mayakovskim* (Moscow, 1940)

Kapelyush, B. N. 'Arkhivy M. V. Matyushina i Ye. G. Guro', in *Yezhegodnik rukopisnogo otdela Pushkinskogo doma na 1974 god*, ed. K. D. Muratova (Leningrad, 1976), pp. 3–23

Katanyan, V. *Mayakovsky: literaturnaya khronika* (Moscow, 1961)

'Ne tol'ko vospominaniya', *Russian Literature Triquarterly*, 13 (1975), pp. 477–86

Khardzhiev, N. 'Poeziya i zhivopis': (ranniy Mayakovsky)', in *K istorii russkogo avangarda (The Russian Avant-Garde)* (Stockholm, Almqvist & Wiksell International, 1976), pp. 7–84

'Vesyolyy god Mayakovskogo', in *Vladimir Majakovskij: Memoirs and Essays*, ed. Bengt Jangfeldt and Nils Åke Nilsson (Stockholm, Almqvist & Wiksell International, 1975), pp. 108–51

Khardzhiev, N. and Trenin, V. *Poeticheskaya kul'tura Mayakovskogo* (Moscow, 1970)

Kruchonykh, A. Ye. Archive in *Rukopisnyy otdel*, *Institut mirovoy literatury imeni Gor'kogo*, *fond* 411, *opis'* 1

Archive in *Tsentral'nyy gosudarstvenny arkhiv literatury i iskusstva*, *fond* 1334, *opis'* 1

Zaumniki (Moscow, 1922)

Zaumnyy yazyk u Seyfullinoy, Vs. Ivanova, Leonova, Babelya, I. Sel'vinskogo, A. Vesyologo i dr. (Moscow, 1925)

Lawton, A. *Vadim Shershenevich: From Futurism to Imaginism* (Ann Arbor, Ardis, 1981)
Livshits, B. *Polutoraglazyy strelets* (Leningrad, 1933)
Lodder, C. *Russian Constructivism* (New Haven and London, Yale University Press, 1983)
McVay, G. 'Alexei Kruchenykh: The Bogeyman of Russian Literature', *Russian Literature Triquarterly*, 13 (1975), pp. 571–90
Esenin: A Life (Ann Arbor, Ardis, 1976)
Mandelstam, N. *Hope Abandoned*, trans. Max Hayward (Penguin, 1976)
Hope Against Hope, trans. Max Hayward (Penguin, 1975)
Mandelstam, O. *Sobraniye sochineniy*, 3 vols., ed. G. P. Struve and B. A. Filippov (New York, Inter-Language Literary Associates, 1964–71)
Mariengof, A. *Roman bez vran'ya* (Leningrad, 1928)
Markov, V. (ed.) *Manifesty i programmy russkikh futuristov* (Munich, Wilhelm Fink Verlag, 1967)
Russian Futurism: A History (London, Macgibbon and Kee, 1969)
Matyushin, M. 'Russkiye kubo-futuristy (vospominaniya M. V. Matyushina)', in *K istorii russkogo avangarda (The Russian Avant-Garde)* (Stockholm, Almqvist & Wiksell International, 1976), pp. 129–58
Mayakovsky, V. *Polnoye sobraniye sochineniy v 13–i tomakh*, ed. V. A. Katanyan (Moscow, 1955–61)
Mercier, A. *Les sources ésotériques et occultes de la poésie symboliste (1870–1914)*, vol. 2, *Le symbolisme européen* (Editions A.-G. Nizet, 1974)
Milner, J. *Vladimir Tatlin and the Russian Avant-Garde* (New Haven and London, Yale University Press, 1984)
Milner-Gulland, R. 'Zabolotsky: Philosopher-Poet', *Soviet Studies*, vol. 22, 4 (1971), pp. 595–608
Naumov, Ye. I. *Seminariy po Mayakovskomu* (Moscow–Leningrad, 1953)
Panchenko, A. M. and Smirnov, I. P. 'Metaforicheskiye arkhetipy v russkoy srednevekovoy slovesnosti i v poezii nachala XX v.', in *Drevnerusskaya literatura i russkaya kul'tura XVIII–XX vv.*, *Trudy otdela drevnerusskoy literatury, Institut russkoy literatury, Akademiya nauk SSSR* XXVI (Leningrad, 1971), pp. 33–49
Pertsov, V. *Poety i prozaiki velikikh let* (Moscow, 1969)
Pertsov, V. and Serebryansky, M. (ed.) *Mayakovsky: materialy i issledovaniya* (Moscow, 1940)
Pomorska, K. *Russian Formalist Theory and its Poetic Ambience* (The Hague–Paris, Mouton, 1968)
Proffer, E. and Proffer, C. R. (ed.) *The Ardis Anthology of Russian Futurism* (Ann Arbor, Ardis, 1980)
Robins, R. H. *A Short History of Linguistics* (London, Longmans, 1967)
Shklovsky, V. *Mayakovsky and his Circle*, trans. and ed. Lily Feiler (Pluto Press, 1974)

'O poezii i zaumnom yazyke', *Sborniki po teorii poeticheskogo yazyka* 1 (Petrograd, 1916), pp. 1–15
'Predposylki futurizma', *Golos zhizni*, 18 (1915), pp. 6–9
'Voskresheniye slova', in *Texte der Russischen Formalisten*, vol. 2 (Munich, Wilhelm Fink Verlag, 1972), pp. 2–17
Zoo or Letters Not About Love, trans. Richard Sheldon (Ithaca and London, Cornell University Press, 1971)
Slonim, M. *From Chekhov to the Revolution: Russian Literature 1900–1917* (Oxford University Press, 1962)
Soviet Russian Literature: Writers and Problems 1917–1967 (Oxford University Press, 1967)
Spassky, S. *Mayakovsky i yego sputniki* (Leningrad, 1940)
Stahlberger, L. L. *The Symbolic System of Majakovskij* (The Hague–Paris, Mouton, 1964)
Stepanov, N. *Poety i prozaiki* (Moscow, 1968)
Trenin, V. and Khardzhiev, N. 'Mayakovsky o kachestve stikha', in *Al'manakh s Mayakovskim* (Moscow, 1934), pp. 257–302
Tsekhnovitser, O. *Literatura i mirovaya voyna 1914–1918* (Moscow, 1938)
Vroon, R. '*Puti tvorchestva*: The Journal as a Metapoetic Statement', in *Russian Literature and American Critics*, ed. Kenneth Brostrom (Ann Arbor, Michigan Slavic Publications, 1984), pp. 219–39
Zelinsky, K. 'Na velikom rubezhe', *Znamya*, 12 (1957), pp. 147–89
Zhuravlyov, A. P. *Zvuk i smysl* (Moscow, 1981)
Zsadova, L. [Zhadova, L] *Vlagyimir Jevgrafovics Tatlin* ([Budapest], Corvina Kiado, [1985])

Author's Note

To mark the centenary of Khlebnikov's birth, in late 1985 and 1986 four single-volume editions of his works were produced in the USSR. Two of these, *Ladomir: poemy* and *Stikhotvoreniya, poemy, dramy, proza*, are included in the bibliography. Two others, *Stikhotvoreniya i poemy*, ed. R. Duganov (Volgograd, Nizhne-Volzhskoye knizhnoye izdatel'stvo, 1985) and *Tvoreniya*, ed. V. P. Grigor'yev and A. Ye. Parnis (Moscow, Sovetskiy pisatel', 1986), appeared while this book was already at proof stage. Of the centenary volumes *Tvoreniya* is a major advance in Khlebnikov studies. Although only a single volume, it is a substantial collection, some 700 pages long, which contains authoritative texts of Khlebnikov's works and notes on their provenance. Moreover, unlike the other volumes, it contains many of Khlebnikov's theoretical articles and republishes (for the first time in the USSR since 1928) the long poem 'Night Search'. It does not, however, contain material from the 'Boards of Fate'.

Index to works by Khlebnikov discussed or noted in the text
Titles in Russian

Index to works by Khlebnikov discussed or noted in the text
Titles in English translation

General Index